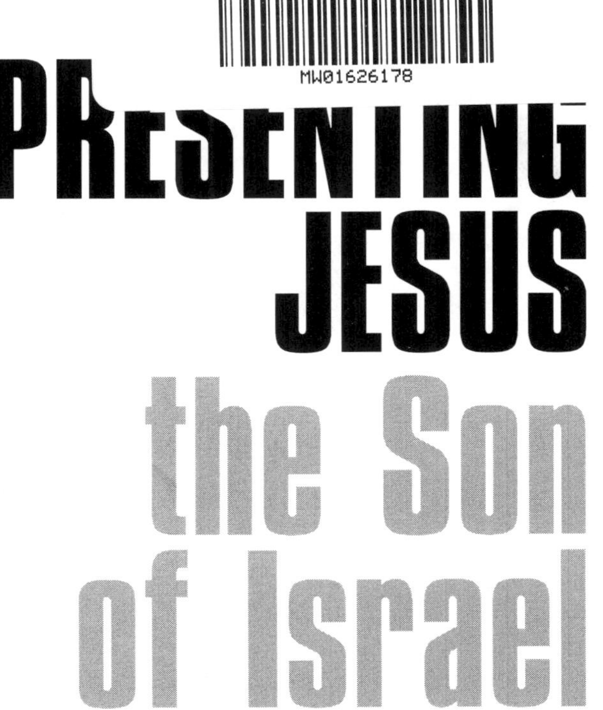

PRESENTING JESUS the Son of Israel

A JEWISH COMMENTARY ON THE GOSPELS

VOLUME I

RIVI LITVIN

MILESTONES
INTERNATIONAL PUBLISHERS

PRESENTING JESUS, THE SON OF ISRAEL
A Jewish Commentary on the Gospels—Volume I

Rivi Litvin

Cover and Interior Page design by MileStones International Publishers

ISBN: 978-1-943852-80-2 (paperback)
ISBN: 978-1-943852-81-9 (ebook)
Library of Congress Control Number: 2017957050

MileStones International Publishers
PO Box 904, Travelers Rest, SC 29690
www.truepotentialmedia.com

Printed in the United States of America.

This book is dedicated with great love to Dr. Annamalai and Dr. Tony Jimenez who saved my life and with the help of God healed me from terminal cancer. I forever will be indebted to you. Without your role in my life, this book would have never seen the light of day. I cannot thank you enough.

CONTENTS

PREFACE

"We Jews know him in a way—in the impulses and emotions of his essential—that remains inaccessible to the Gentiles subject to him."

MARTIN BUBER SAID THESE WORDS ABOUT JESUS IN 1963. Unfortunately, the situation remains the same today.

Many worthy commentaries of the Gospels exist, but most do not seek out to present Jesus as he appeared on Earth—in his culture and among his Jewish people. Context is essential to truly understand a topic, and this is one of the main reasons for my deep and driving desire to write this commentary. *Presenting Jesus, the Son of Israel—A Jewish Commentary on the Gospels* gives people a fuller understanding of the true historical Jesus.

I was raised in an Orthodox Jewish community. As an adult, I was armed with a new view of the world and a deep curiosity for various religions. In my mid-20s, around a campfire in Switzerland, I found myself with an assortment of other seekers from various faiths. During the course of our conversations around the fire, one of my Christian friends casually dropped into conversation two points. One, many inside Christian circles believe that the church is the true Israel. Two, God rejected the historical people of Israel. I stared at him across the fire, completely dumbfounded that anyone—let alone someone who claims to be a follower of the Jewish Messiah—could state this so simply. It was a painful and life-changing moment for me, and one that impacted the rest of my journey greatly. That night I understood how deep the roots of anti-Semitic rhetoric can go, and how so much of it stems out of a lack of knowledge and understanding regarding the Jewish life of Jesus.

The way we live our lives is the true testament to who we are, and Jesus lived his life on Earth as a Jew. It is both devastating and dangerous to overlook this.

I spent the next couple of decades researching, teaching and writing, striving to shed some light on the truth. My studies led me to the greatest work of my life—this book. My hope is to open a small window into the vast Jewish world of Jesus and to impart this valuable and life-changing knowledge to his current followers.

It is also my hope this commentary stand as a voice for truth. Sadly, I have come across many commentators who exhibit anti-Semitic attitudes that have caused them to present the rabbis and Jewish sages in a negative light. This is devastating because it continues to further the cause of Replacement Theology, which presents Jesus as a Christian rather than an observant Jew, or as a son of Greece rather than a son of Israel.

It is the campfire all over again.

Jesus was a Jew. He was a Chassid (pious person) who taught the Tanach (Hebrew Scriptures) and who was immersed in Israel's tradition and customs. This was a man who did all he could to enlighten his followers and to bring them closer to God almighty, the Creator of the Universe.

I am here to present to you a look at the Gospels within its accurate historical settings when its momentous events took place. It was imperative to approach this using both the Torah and rabbinic literature as sources because they bring great illumination to the words of Jesus. They are for support, not detraction. Indeed, the messages of Jesus testify that he was immersed in the Judaism of his day since all his messages reflect the Jewish thought and teaching at that time. It is truly a shame that for two thousand years, the history of Jesus and his teachings have been cut off from Israel.

Although this is an academic work, I wrote this commentary in populace language, so it is accessible to everyone who wants to learn. I find it is better to simplify in order to give the reader a sharper look. Some material may be new for you, but many of the topics discussed here are not new since others before me have worked hard to pave the way to present the Gospels from a Jewish perspective. As such, I am indebted to Professor David Flusser, Rabbi Pinchas Lapide, Rabbi Samuel Tobias Lachs, Rev. John Lightfoot, Alfred Edersheim, Dr. Geza Vermes, Professor Brad Young, Klaussner, and Dr. Robert Lindsey.

It was my privilege to work on this book and to bring to you a comprehensive presentation of the entirety of Jesus' life and his teachings from a Jewish and Israeli perspective—all accumulated in one place for the first time.

Many thanks to my family for enduring all the hours I spent on this project! And thank you to everyone who has stood by me and supported my efforts during the last thirty years as I researched the Gospels and created this work.

Rivi

ACKNOWLEDGMENTS

THANK YOU:

To my good friend Paula Hart for your monumental contribution in making this book happen. Your daily help in my life means the world to me, and your financial support enabled me to complete this volume and publish it. I am so grateful for your friendship.

Thank you to my wonderful friends Andrew and Cecilia Hernandez for encouraging me, providing your financial support, and for constantly reminding me how important this book is. Thank you to my sister-in-law, Wilma McRae, for your time and help in editing this book.

You have all been instrumental in making this book happen, and I am deeply grateful!

JUDAH & ISRAEL
BOOKS OF KINGS & CHRONICLES
CAPTIVITIES
DATES OF CAPTIVITIES

PART 1

CHAPTER 1

BEFORE HIS BIRTH—AN OVERVIEW OF THE GOSPELS

A STUDY OF THE LIFE OF JESUS IS ALSO A STUDY OF THE Gospels since this is the body of literature from which we get most of the information about him. Primarily, this work is concerned with the Synoptic Gospels, which are Matthew, Mark and Luke. However, I have also considered information recorded in John's Gospel.

The first three Gospels are called "Synoptic," from the Greek word SYNOPSETHAI, meaning "to view together." They are called synoptic because each one records the same event, namely, the life of Jesus. However, their records are not the same and according to scholars, each one appears to emphasize different aspects of his life and teachings.

The Gospels date back to the end of the first century CE. However, the earliest Greek manuscript that exists today originated about three centuries later[1].

Regardless, the Gospels' vocabulary, their syntax and their idioms suggest that some of them initially were written in Hebrew, definitely written by a person whose mother tongue was Hebrew.

None of the Synoptic Gospels provide us with the name of its author. It was the Church Fathers of the late second and third centuries who attributed the authorship of the Gospels to Matthew, Mark and Luke. Traditionally, it was believed that Matthew wrote first, probably because the Church Fathers were aware of the existence of the Gospel of Matthew in Hebrew. One of the fathers even claimed he had a copy in his possession and had translated it from Hebrew to Greek and Latin[2]. According to church tradition, it was Matthew the disciple who wrote his Hebrew Gospel to the Jews[3].

The first three Gospels are called "Synoptic," from the Greek word SYNOPSETHAI, meaning "to view together."

Initially, the understanding by biblical scholars was that Matthew wrote his gospel first, then Luke, and lastly Mark, copying from both of them. In the beginning of the 1900s, another theory developed that gave priority to the Gospel of Mark. It claimed that both Matthew and Luke used Mark as a source in writing their Gospels. This idea is still held today by many in the church, despite historical testimony that suggests otherwise.

According to the *International Standard Bible Encyclopedia*:

> "Mark was probably written by John-Mark the disciple and interpreter of Peter. He handed down to us in writings that which had been preached by Peter. Evidence for this claim can be found among the Fathers of the Church, for instance, Clement of Alexandria wrote towards the end of the second century: 'Mark wrote his Gospel from matter preached by Peter.'"

In the writings of Eusebius (he iii 39), we find another patristic testimony saying:

> "Mark who had been Peter's interpreter, wrote down carefully as much as he remembered, recording both sayings and doings of the Messiah, not however in order; for he was not a hearer of the lord, nor a follower, but later a follower of Peter, as I said. And he adapted his teachings to the needs of his hearers as one who is engaged in making a compendium of the lord's precepts."

The first mention of this Gospel is found around 170 CE. It was quoted very seldom by the Church Fathers, and up to the 5th century, it was barely mentioned.

Although it was accepted as part of the canon, its location within it was unsettled. It was never entered in first place, and in some listings it was put in last place (e.g., the Old Latin, and the Greek MSS D and W).

The first commentary on Mark was written in the 5th century by Victor of Antioch. Augustine claimed that Matthew was written first and that Mark followed. It was understood in this way until modern criticism came along.

Initially, the understanding by biblical scholars was that Matthew wrote his gospel first, then Luke, and lastly Mark.

Between the two theories about the writer of Mark, it is claimed often that he added and compiled many loose stories to which he added his own comments and connected them.

There is general agreement that the Gospel of Mark was written between 65 to 67 CE in Rome[4].

In 1922 a third theory gave priority to the Gospel of Luke, then to Mark, and lastly to Matthew. In the 1960s, the late Dr. Robert Lindsey also proposed a theory that gave priority to the Gospel of Luke. His theory did not go very far because Christian scholars did not adopt it, although some Jewish scholars did.

I also give priority to Luke; therefore, in this study, we are going to follow Luke's order for the most part.

Luke made the following claim in Luke 1:3:

> "It seems fitting for me as well, having investigated everything carefully from the beginning, to write it out for you in consecutive order, most excellent Theophilus."

Luke claimed that he wrote his Gospel in a chronological order, that he researched it carefully and that he used eye-witness accounts in his investigation—all appear to be good reasons to give priority to his order. No other Gospel writer made such a claim.

Since Luke had the character and the personality of a teacher, he must have been skilled in research and been concerned with presenting his findings in a systematic order. Luke was also a detail-oriented person as is evident from his writings. His Gospel has many details that are missing from the other Gospels and is the longest of them all. By profession Luke was a physician, and that is also reflected in his writings. In the account of the death of Jesus, it was Luke who recorded that both water and blood came out of Him; the other two recorded blood only.

The Gospel of John is different from the others. John wrote at a later time, and it appears that his main purpose was to write information about the life of Jesus, which the other writers did not provide.

Luke may have been a proselyte. In other words, he probably was a convert to Judaism. According to scholars Luke wrote to Greeks and in his Gospel appears to emphasize Jesus' humanity.

Matthew wrote his Gospel to the Jews of his day. He emphasized and presented Jesus as a Messiah; he called Jesus "The king of the Jews." He also appeared to have a concern to provide in his Gospel an answer to the question of "why the physical Kingdom of God was not established right then and there." Since the Jewish people at that time and throughout history have always expected a conqueror Messiah to come and establish the physical Kingdom of God in Israel, and since Jesus did not get rid of the Roman regime nor established the Kingdom of God on earth in his lifetime, Mathew must have felt that there was a need to provide an explanation concerning it.

Mark wrote his Gospel to the Romans. He presented Jesus as God's servant. Mark's text is relatively Semitic, although he used non-Semitic phrases, such as the often repeated terms "and immediately" or "forthwith" more than 40 times in his Gospel. The Greek term is KAI EUTHUS, and it is a term that has no equivalent in ancient Hebrew[5].

The Gospel of John is different from the others. John wrote at a later time, and it appears that his main purpose was to write information about the life of Jesus, which the other writers did not provide. He was more interested in what Jesus said rather than his actions, with the exception of his miracles.

Most of Jesus' teachings and discourses are found in the Gospel of John. John highlighted the theme of Jesus the son and presented him as "The son of God." John also had a strong emphasis on the contrast between light and darkness, a theme that runs throughout his Gospel, which brought people to the conclusion that he belonged with the Qumran community, although this is not the case. John also emphasized in his Gospel the number "seven," which he used frequently. John recorded seven signs, seven discourses and seven I Am statements.

CHAPTER 1 ENDNOTES

1. Bart D. Eharman, *Misquoting Jesus*, pp. 75-83.
2. Jerome, *Lives of Illustrious Men*, chapter 3.
3. Eusebius, *Ecclesiastical History*, III 39, 16.
4. *The International Standard Bible Encyclopedia*, Vol. III, p. 249.
5. Lindsey, Robert Lisle, *Jesus Rabbi & Lord*, Oak Greek, WI. (Cornerstone Publishing), 1990, p. 19.

CHAPTER 2

THE GENEALOGIES OF JESUS

MATTHEW CHAPTER 1 AND LUKE CHAPTER 3

In the Tanach (The Hebrew Bible) genealogical records can be found quite often. Two types exist:

Lists that record an historical event. These often claim to list "the generations of...." or "The account of..." A classic example is found in Genesis 2:4: "This is the account of the heavens and the earth when they were created, in the day that The Lord God made Earth and Heaven." Another example can be found in Genesis 5:1.

Lists that record people's lineage. These include, for example, the generations of Noah in Genesis 6:9, the generations of his sons in Genesis 10:1, the generations of the sons of Israel in I Chronicles 2, and the generations of David in I Chronicles 3. There are many other examples.

The word genealogy in Hebrew is the word TOLDOT, and it can be spelled in full or missing formats. Full format includes two of the letter Vav[1] and is written as "**תולדות**". The missing format includes only one Vav, and it is spelled as "**תֹּדוְלת**".

The full spelling occurs only in two places in the Bible, in the verse we just read from Genesis 2:4 that talks about the generations of the Heavens and the earth. According to the rabbis, this is because the angel of death was not yet in the world. After the sin of Adam and Eve, everything changed, and so the word Toldot appeared in its missing format. This is—and with the exception of the generations of Peretz, where the word Toldot appears again in its full spelling, according to the rabbis—"because from him The Messiah will rise and will swallow death" (Isaiah 25:8).

We do not know when the tradition of recording genealogies developed and became established in Israel, but we do know that it is indeed an ancient tradition. In Israel, only by establishing a connection with a family or a tribe, could one establish his status as a citizen. In the past, lists were composed for official use, such as a national census, military service and for levying taxes. Genealogical lists in Israel are also found from the time of Ezra. Ezra 2:62 mentions a list of priestly families who had returned from exile. Nehemiah 7:5 mentions "The book of the genealogy" of those who returned first.

Matthew began his Gospel with the genealogy of Jesus. His purpose must have been to show that Jesus' lineage was according to the biblical requirements of the lineage for the Messiah.

The genealogies of individual families used to be passed down, according to oral tradition, by the families themselves. The lineage of the priests and the Levites were very important because without proving their background, they could not qualify for temple service.

For instance, in the historical accounts of the Books of Esther, Judith and Tovit, the genealogies of the main characters are given in detail. In Esther we have the lineage of Mordechai (Esther 2:5), in Tovit we have the lineage of Tovit (Tovit 1:1), and we also have the lineage of Judith (Judith 8:1).

With regards to the lineage of priests, a general genealogical list that recorded the genealogy of all the priestly families was kept and maintained at the temple. We know that even the priests in the Diaspora (Jewish communities outside of Israel) used to provide the office that maintained it with full details concerning their marriages[2].

A special priestly tribunal was responsible for the upkeep of the lists and the verification of oaths. The priests functioned according to established rules, and they based their decisions on the evidence they collected from eyewitnesses and from documents.

Genealogical tables used to be considered very important by Israel, particularly after the exile to Babylon. Israel used to rely heavily upon these tables in order to ensure family purity. This concern was even greater when it came to the priesthood families.

Matthew began his Gospel with the genealogy of Jesus. His purpose must have been to show that Jesus' lineage was according to the biblical requirements of the lineage for the Messiah.

Only Matthew and Luke recorded the early life of Jesus. Both of them wrote about his birth from Joseph's point of view, probably due to the fact that the people around them considered Joseph to be Jesus' father (Luke 4:22).

It was natural for Matthew to give the legal genealogy through Joseph, although he went to great extents to show that Joseph was not actually Jesus' father.

Matthew and Luke's genealogies have 19 names in common. Luke mentions 19 names before Matthew begins his genealogy.

According to the genealogies, both Joseph and Mary were descendants from the royal line of David. Mary, in addition, was also related to the priesthood on her mother's side. This is interesting because—according to Jewish tradition, in the Messiah, there is going to be a union between Judah and Levi—he will be both a King and a priest[3]. Accordingly, the rabbis claimed that rabbi Hillel was a descendant of these two tribes; they emphasized in particular his Davidic descent[4].

Both of the genealogies claim that Jesus had no human father and was, therefore, born of the Holy Spirit. Matthew traced Jesus' genealogy to David and to Abraham. He said Jesus was a descendant of Abraham, that he was Jewish, and according to the promise given by God to Abraham, through Him all the nations of the world will be blessed.

It was not so important for Matthew to communicate that Jesus was the son of Noah, for instance. Since he was writing to Jews, he figured it was much more important for them to know that Jesus was a son of the covenant that God made with Israel, that he was a Jew, and that he was a descendant of David. In other words, Jesus had a genealogy that was fitting for a Messiah.

Luke traced Jesus' genealogy all the way back to Adam. One of the differences between these two genealogies is that Matthew's list begins with Abraham and descends to Jesus. Luke's list begins with Jesus and ascends to Adam. Matthew traced Jesus' genealogy from King Solomon, who was the son of David (II Samuel 12:24). Meanwhile, Luke traced it back from Nathan, who was also the son of David (I Chronicles 3:5).

Luke, in addition, attempted to refute a slander against Jesus of an illegitimate birth that must have circulated in Israel at that time. This slander is reflected in John 8:41. In the discussion between Jesus and the Pharisees, Jesus said, "You are doing the deeds of your father," they said to him, "we were not born of fornications, we have one father, even God." Circulating in the first century was a slanderous claim that Jesus was the son of a Roman soldier named Pantheras and of Mary. Origen, a Church Father, was familiar with this claim and mentioned it in his writings[5].

Matthew listed the genealogies of Joseph. In doing so, he broke Jewish law several times. Matthew skipped names in his genealogy, but that was common practice in biblical genealogies. However, he also mentioned women, which went against the rules of Jewish genealogies. Four women are mentioned: Tamar, Rachav, Ruth and Bat-Sheva. All four women were Gentile by birth, which is also not allowed in a Jewish genealogy. However, all four had become part of the Davidic line.

Tamar played the harlot for Judah, her father-in-law, and bore him twins (Genesis 38:1). Rachav was a prostitute by profession and became the mother of Boaz, according to the New Testament (Hebrews 4; James 2:45). According to Jewish sources, Rachav became Joshua's wife[6].

Ruth was a Moabite and, as such, she probably should have been disqualified from membership in Israel. Deuteronomy 23:3 states, "no Ammonite or Moabite will enter the assembly of the Lord, none of their descendants, even to the tenth generation, shall ever enter the assembly of The Lord."

Nevertheless, Ruth became part of the Messianic line (Ruth 4). According to the rabbis, this was possible because the Hebrew text recorded the words

"Ammonite" and "Moabite" in the male singular form; therefore, they said this prohibition was concerning Moabite men and not women.

Bat-Sheva committed adultery with David (II Samuel 11) and bore him a legitimate heir to the throne—King Solomon. She is also considered to be a Gentile, and according to rabbinic tradition, she was the granddaughter of Achitofel, who was not an Israelite[7]. Matthew refers to her as the wife of Uriya in order to emphasize her adulterous behavior.

It is quite possible that in mentioning these four women, who were guilty of sexual sins, Matthew attempted in his own way to refute the slander that was circulating at the time. Perhaps, Matthew was saying, even if you believe the rumor and think that Jesus was conceived improperly, it does not really change anything because in the line of King David, the Messianic line, we have four women who were definitely, and not maybe, guilty of sexual sins. And yet, God is greater than these. In spite of their sins, God used them.

Matthew listed the genealogies of Joseph. He skipped names in his genealogy, but that was common practice in biblical genealogies. However, he also mentioned women, which went against the rules of Jewish genealogies.

Matthew divided his genealogy into three sections, each containing 14 generations:

From Abraham to David—14 generations,

From Solomon to Jeconiah—14 generations,

From Shealtiel to Jesus—should also be 14, but it is missing one name.

The name David in Hebrew has the numerical value of 14 (דָוִד), and this is probably one of the reasons why Matthew divided his genealogy in this way.

The number 14 must have had some importance to Matthew since he omitted some names in order to maintain numerical consistency.

But this is not a problem since we also find in the Tanach genealogies omitted names as well. You can find an example in Ezra 7:1–6.

It is possible that Matthew was attempting to communicate to the religious authorities at the time his understanding of the status and importance of Jesus. The rabbis claimed that 14 generations had passed from Moses to the time of the rabbinical period[8]. Matthew, perhaps, was saying how much more we should take Jesus' position seriously since 14 generations, three times, had passed between Him and Abraham.

Matthew, in his genealogy, recorded that Joseph's father was Jacob (Matthew 1:16). Luke, on the other hand, recorded Joseph to be the son of Eli (Luke 3:23). That leaves us with the task of finding out who was really Jesus' grandfather.

Matthew's first two sections seem dependent on the genealogical information found in I Chronicles 1:34–3:19. Matthew recorded only three names for the period of the Egyptian exile: Esron, Aram and Aminadav. This is in spite of the fact that this period lasted 430 years. However, his record agrees with God's promise in Genesis 15:16 to lead Israel back in the fourth generation. But it does not agree with Genesis 15:13, which states that Israel will be in Egypt for 400 years.

Problems in the genealogies

The first problem we encounter was mentioned earlier. Matthew and Luke refer to different numbers of generations. Matthew lists 26 generations between David and Jesus. Luke lists forty generations. However, it is a problem easily solved.

Two things to note here: Firstly, it is important to realize that it is common for generations in one branch to increase more rapidly than in another.

Secondly, some lists are more detailed than others. It all depends on the author and his intentions.

Matthew omitted names in his genealogy[9]. Again this can be easily solved since omission of generations in a genealogy is common practice in the

Tanach; therefore, it is not unique to this case. The purpose of the genealogy is not to account for every generation that existed, but rather to establish the existence of continuous succession; therefore, genealogies have always included the most prominent ancestors.

Matthew, in his genealogy, recorded that Joseph's father was Jacob (Matthew 1:16). Luke, on the other hand, recorded Joseph to be the son of Eli (Luke 3:23). That leaves us with the task of finding out who was really Jesus' grandfather. Here are several possible explanations:

A person named Julius Africanus, who lived in the third century CE, suggested that Matthew provided Joseph's genealogy through Joseph's actual father, Jacob. He claimed that Luke provided Joseph's genealogy through Joseph's legal father.

Eli, according to Julius' understanding, died childless. Therefore, his half brother Jacob, who had the same mother but a different father, was obligated by the law of Levirate marriage[10], to marry his brother's widow. And he did so, and together they had Joseph. As a result, Joseph was the physical son of Jacob, but the legal son of Eli.

Jacob was David's descendant through Solomon, and Eli was David's descendant through Nathan. Therefore, through both of them, Joseph was a descendant of David and so was his legal son Jesus. According to this view, Matthew provided Joseph's physical lineage, and Luke provided Joseph's legal lineage.

Others have suggested that the differences between the two genealogies were due to the fact that Matthew and Luke wrote the genealogies of two different individuals. In actuality, the claim is that Matthew provided Joseph's genealogy, whereas Luke provided Mary's genealogy. This notion is incorrect.

However, those who believe it have explained that since it was improper to provide the genealogy of the mother, Luke mentioned Joseph's name instead of Mary's. This was appropriate, they say, since Joseph was married to her. As a result of his marriage, he also became the son of Eli and definitely his heir.

This idea involves a built-in assumption that Eli never had a son and, therefore, Mary became his heiress. In the Torah in Numbers 27:7–8, we are told that a daughter of a man who died without sons shall inherit him. If Eli indeed died without sons, then Mary was his rightful heiress.

The same situation is also discussed in Numbers 36:1–12, except here the text states, in addition, that a daughter of a man who died without sons should be married within her tribe in order for his share to remain within the tribe. This indeed was the situation in the case of Joseph and Mary since both were of the tribe of Judah. As we can see, Mary complied with this stipulation as well.

In the Bible and in Jewish practices, the term "son of" does not necessarily refer to the actual son of that person, although it could be the case. The term "son of" denotes a reference to a "direct descendant" of a person. For instance, my grandson Daniel is a direct descendant of my late father, Mordechai.

Therefore, in a genealogy list, Daniel may appear as the son of Mordechai, even though, in reality, Mordechai did not beget him. Usually, in a Jewish genealogy, the person of whom the genealogy is taken is described as "the son of" all the names mentioned. This is also the case in Jesus' genealogies.

So in Luke's genealogy, it is Jesus then who is the direct descendant of Eli, of Matat, of Levi—and so on—of Abraham and of Adam. In order to understand it better, let us take a look at Genesis 36:2. In the King James translation, it says:

> "Esau took his wives of the daughters of Canaan; Adah the daughter of Elon the Hittite and Aholibamah the daughter of Anah the daughter of Zibeon."

The New American Standard translation is practically the same, except the end: "And Aholibamah the daughter of Anah the granddaughter of Zibeon the Hivite."

Here, the King James translation is the accurate one, although the way it appears in English, this translation is not very clear. Let me explain. Aholibamah was a woman and one of Esau's wives. We are told that she was the daughter of Anah, the daughter of Zibeon.

It is important to realize that both references are made to Aholibamah. She was the daughter of Anah, but she also was the daughter of Zibeon. Anah was not a woman; Anah was a man. However, the American Standard translation, not understanding the nature of biblical genealogies, turned him into a woman. We get this impression even from the King James translation if we are not familiar with this issue.

Going back to the text of Luke 3:23, the phrase "being as was supposed the son of Joseph" probably should have been put in parenthesis here in order to fit the biblical understanding of the term "son of," which we just discussed and which, in this case, refers to Jesus and not to Joseph.

The Greek text is definitely in line here with the Hebraic concept. The Greek text states "Jesus…being son, as was supposed of Joseph, of Eli." The Greek text does not connect the word "son" with Joseph as the English text does. This appears to be the best solution for this dilemma.

It is also interesting to note that Matthew was writing to Jews, and thus he appropriately provided the parental genealogy, whereas Luke was writing to Gentiles, and Gentiles were not so concerned with it. Nevertheless, he too provided a parental genealogy.

Matthew's genealogy made mention of Jeconiah. Matthew 1:12 says, "And after the deportation to Babylon, to Jeconiah was born Shealtiel; and to Shealtiel, Zerubabel."

In the Bible and in Jewish practices, the term "son of" does not necessarily refer to the actual son of that person, although it could be the case. The term "son of" denotes a reference to a "direct descendant" of a person.

Jeconiah was the King of Judah, and in his time, Jeremiah the prophet sent a scroll that was dictated by himself and written by Baruch Ben Neriyahu to the king, stating that the King of Babylon will come and destroy the land.

Needless to say, Jeconiah did not like this message at all. In spite of the advice he received from many, he burned the scroll. As a result, God commanded Jeremiah to write another scroll that would include the entire message of the first one, and to add:

> "And concerning Jehoiakim king of Judah you shall say, thus say The Lord, you have burned this scroll, saying, why have you written on it that the king of Babylon shall certainly come and destroy this land, and shall make man and beast to cease from it? Therefore, thus says The Lord concerning Jehoiakim king of Judah, he shall have no one to sit on the throne of David, and his dead body shall be cast out to the heat of the day and the frost of the night." (Jeremiah 36:29–30)[11]

From this text, we learn that God put a curse on Jeconiah. As a result, no descendant of Jeconiah was ever supposed to sit on David's throne. Yet Matthew, who provided Joseph's genealogy, included Jeconiah in the list. Therefore, Joseph's line was condemned. And since Joseph was Jesus' legal father, Jesus' line was condemned as well.

The common solution offered to solve this problem involves the understanding that Matthew intended in his genealogy to show the Jewish population of his day that Jesus was not the physical son of Joseph. If he was, then he could not possibly be the Messiah because of the curse of Jeconiah.

This is also the reason, it is said, that Matthew focused on the virgin birth immediately following the genealogies. Matthew is understood to be saying that Jeconiah's curse does not apply to Jesus because he was not born of Joseph's loins; however, since he was Joseph's legal son, he had, by virtue of adoption, the legal right to the Davidic line.

Matthew is understood to be saying that Jeconiah's curse does not apply to Jesus because he was not born of Joseph's loins.

This view assumes incorrectly that Luke provided us with Mary's genealogy, and her genealogy is in the line of Nathan and not Solomon's.

It goes on to assume that Nathan's line was not affected by the Jeconiah curse; therefore, it provided Jesus with a physical right to the Davidic line as well.

However, being a descendant of Nathan proved that Jesus was a physical descendant of David, but it did not really fulfill God's promise to David in II Samuel 7:12–17, which clearly states that "When your days are complete and you lie down with your fathers, I will raise up your descendant after you, who will come forth from you, and I will establish his kingdom. He shall build a house for my name, and I will establish the throne of his kingdom forever." The right to the throne then runs through Solomon's line, not through Nathan's.

This assumption, of course, is incorrect. Although Jeconiah's name was not included in Luke's genealogy, his son and grandson's names were included. Luke 3:27: "The son of Joanan, the son of Rhesa, the son of Zerubabel, the son of Shealtiel, and the son of Neri." As we saw earlier from Matthew 1:12, we learn that Shealtiel was the son of Jeconiah, and Zerubabel was his great-grandson. Both genealogies then are affected by the curse of Jeconiah.

Christian scholars who discovered this fact came up with different explanations in an attempt to solve the dilemma. Here are two of their interpretations:

Some claim that both genealogies are referring to four different individuals who lived in the same period of time. They say that the Shealtiel and Zerubabel of Matthew's must have been very respectable and, therefore, the people who were mentioned by Luke must have been named after them. This is despite the fact that these two names are rare.

Another explanation claims that Shealtiel could not have been the son of Jeconiah because God put a curse on Jeconiah, saying he will be childless.

This idea is also based on Luke 3:27, which states that Shealtiel was the son of Neri. Therefore, a theory of another levirate marriage was developed. The claim is that Jeconiah and Neri were brothers. Jeconiah died childless because of the curse, and so Neri, his brother, was under obligation to marry Jeconiah's widow. So he did, and they begot Shealtiel, who was then the physical son of Neri, but the legal son of Jeconiah.

All these mental exercises are done in order to solve what appear to be contradictions in the text. In the process, scholars developed theories that truly stand in direct contradiction to the Scriptures since I Chronicles 3:17–18 states clearly that Shealtiel was Jeconiah's son.

According to Matthew's genealogy, Shealtiel was indeed Jeconiah's son. Matthew, in accordance with I Chronicles 3:17, recorded that Shealtiel "was born" to Jeconiah. Luke, on the other hand, used the term "the son of." And as we have seen before, this term implies that he was a descendant of Neri, just like he was a descendant of David. But it does not imply that Shealtiel was actually born to him.

Let us examine for a moment the idea of Jeconiah dying childless. Take a look at Jeremiah 22:30:

> "Thus says The Lord, write this man down childless, a man who will not prosper in his days; for no man of his descendants will prosper sitting on the throne of David or ruling again in Judah."

The term "childless" in Hebrew, according to the Hebraic dictionary, is the word ARIRI. This word has three possible meanings: A) someone who never had children and never will. B) Someone who had children, but after they died had no others. C) Loneliness, sadness[12].

Did Jeconiah die childless? No! He did not! Not according to I Chronicles 3:17–18:

> "And the sons of Jeconiah, the prisoner, were Shealtiel his son, and Malchiram, Pedsiah, Aniazzar, Jekamayiah, Hoshama and Nedabiah."

From this text, it is obvious that Jeconiah had at least seven sons.

What are we to understand from the fact that both of the genealogies of Jesus are affected by the Jeconiah curse? How could God put an end to Solomon's line by cursing Jeconiah and seemingly as a result of it, put an end to anyone ever sitting on David's throne?

In this text, we also have a translation mistake. The term translated as "the prisoner"— ASIR—does mean "prisoner." But the way it is located in the structure of the sentence in Hebrew, it should have been understood as a reference to Shealtiel.

Some rabbis claimed that Shealtiel must have been born in prison, and that is why he is described in the text as Shealtiel the prisoner.

The rabbis said Jeconiah's kingdom meant nothing since it lasted only three months and ten days, and therefore amounted to nothing, and was considered as if it never took place.[13].

So, in light of all of this information, what is the solution to the problem of Jeconiah? And what are we to understand from the fact that both of the genealogies of Jesus are affected by the Jeconiah curse? How could God put an end to Solomon's line by cursing Jeconiah and seemingly as a result of it, put an end to anyone ever sitting on David's throne, and at the same time fulfill His promise to David?

Despite the curse, Jeconiah did not die childless. One rabbi explained it by interpreting the word "childless" as meaning "childless from the Kingdom," but not necessarily "childless from sons"[14]. He understood Jeremiah's statement to mean that Jeconiah would not prosper[15], to mean that Jeconiah would be unsuccessful in putting one of his sons on the throne after him.

Regardless of God's initial meaning in this curse, we do know that Jeconiah's grandson Zerubabel was leading the return of the exile from Babylon to Judah (Ezra 2:2). We also know that he was one of their main leaders, once they were back in the Land (Ezra 3:2).

Hagai the prophet referred to him as "the governor of Judah" (Hagai 1:1, 1:14, 2:2, 2:21), meaning that the King of Babylon had appointed him to be a ruler over Judah. Both prophets, Hagai and Zechariah, also encouraged Zerubabel to build the Second Temple and communicated to him that this was God's will for him (Hagai 1:14–15, 2:4).

Zachariah 4:6–10 says:

> "Then he answered and said to me, this is the word of The Lord to Zerubabel saying, not by might or by power, but by my spirit, says The Lord of hosts.
>
> "What are you, o Great Mountain? Before Zerubabel you will become a plain; and he will bring forth the top stone with shouts of grace, grace to it! Also the word of The Lord came to me saying, the hands of Zerubabel have laid the foundation of this house, and his hands will finish it. Then you will know that The Lord of hosts had sent me to you.
>
> "For who has despised the day of small things? But these seven will be glad when they see the plumb line in the hand of Zerubabel—these are the eyes of The Lord that range to and fro throughout the earth."

So now, not only was he ruling in Judah, but also he was in charge of the rebuilding of the Temple in Jerusalem, both of which definitely have something to do with God's Kingdom. And Zerubabel indeed rebuilt the Temple, just as Hagai prophesied (Ezra 5:2, 6:14–22).

In addition, one of the things that God said about Jeconiah when He cursed him, in Jeremiah 22:24, was "As I live, declares The Lord, even so Coniah, if the son of Jehoiakim king of Judah were a signet ring on my right hand, yet I will pull you off."

A signet ring was precious and engraved; it was a ring that signified the Kingdom and all of its rules and regulations. A king did not take off his signet ring because the life of his kingdom was dependent on it. Yet God said that if Jeconiah were a signet ring on His hand, He would have torn it off. In other words, He would have preferred to give up His kingdom (not the eternal one) than to use such a despised signet ring. Pretty strong words! Yet, in despite of this, look at what God said to Zerubabel, Jeconiah's grandson, in Hagai 2:23:

> "On that day, declares The Lord of hosts, I will take you, Zerubabel, son of Shealtiel, my servant, declares The Lord, and I will make you like a signet ring, for I have chosen you, declares The Lord of hosts."

So, using the same language, God made it fairly clear to Zerubabel that He had canceled the curse He had put on Jeconiah, his grandfather. As a result of God's forgiveness, the way was once again open for the promise He had made to David to be fulfilled.

A Messiah will indeed sit one day on David's throne. Therefore, it really did not matter that Matthew had mentioned Jeconiah in Jesus' genealogy since the judgment had been reversed, and Matthew probably was aware of it.

A Messiah will indeed sit one day on David's throne. Therefore, it really did not matter that Matthew had mentioned Jeconiah in Jesus' genealogy since the judgment had been reversed, and Matthew probably was aware of it.

It was much more important that Zerubabel be mentioned, and indeed he is mentioned in both genealogies, because God had chosen to reverse the situation through him.

The rabbis, in an attempt to explain God's forgiveness, suggested that maybe the miserable exile and his suffering perhaps atoned somewhat for Jeconiah's sins. They also talked about the great strength of repentance, which has the power to cancel a negative decree and to cancel an oath—a powerful tool that God gave us that can change death to life and can turn our lives 180 degrees around. It can cancel any verdict against us, as has been demonstrated so clearly in the example of Jeconiah and Zerubabel.

Incidentally, the two different lines of descent of Davidic kings, one through Solomon and the other through Nathan, are well known in Judaism[16].

In summation, both Matthew and Luke provided the genealogy of Jesus through Joseph. In doing so, Mathew established that Jesus was a descendant of David. Joseph was Jesus' legal father. He was a descendant of David through the line of Solomon and, therefore, he was a member of the royal tribe. Jesus being his legal son, by Jewish law, was considered to be his own son and because of it was considered to have the same lineage. And indeed he was recognized by others as Joseph's son (Matthew 13:55).

CHAPTER 2 ENDNOTES

1. The six letter of the Hebrew alphabet is called Vav and it looks like this ו.
2. Josephus, Apion 1:7.
3. The testimony of the XII patriarch, The Testimony of Simon VII.
4. Jerusalem Talmud, Taanit 4:2, Bereshit Raba 98 and 33.
5. The Fathers of the church, Origen, Contra Celsum 1:28, 32, 33,39.
6. Zvi Meir Rabinowitz, Introduction to *Midrash HaGadol* (Book of Numbers), "Sifri Zuta" 75 Mossad Harav Kook: Jerusalem 1983 (4th printing), pp. 7–8.
7. Talmud Bavli, Sanhedrin 10b.
8. Avot de Rabbi Nathan, pp. 6–8, Talmud Bavli, Seder Nezikin.
9. Omission of names in Matthew genealogy can be seen from II Kings 8:24, I Chronicles 3:11, II Chronicles 22:1, 11; 24:27, II Kings 23:34, 24:6.
10. A levirate marriage is commanded in Deuteronomy 25:5-6 and obliges a brother to marry the widow of his childless deceased brother, with the firstborn child being treated as that of the deceased brother, (see also Genesis 38:8) which renders the child the heir of the deceased brother and not the genetic father.
11. Also in Jeremiah 22:30.
12. Hamilon HaChadash, *The New Dictionary*, Abraham Even Shushan, Vol. 3.
13. The Jerusalem Institute of R. Cook commentaries (in Hebrew), on Jeremiah 36:30.
14. Mahari Kara, (in Hebrew) on Jeremiah 22:30.
15. Ibid.
16. *A Rabbinic Commentary on the New Testament*, Samuel Tobias Lachs, p. 2.

CHAPTER 3

ZECHARIAH

LUKE 1:5–25

The first thing Luke discusses in his Gospel is the story of Zechariah and his wife, Elizabeth. As usual, Luke is very careful to make sure that he provides us with an indication of the time. This happened during the reign of King Herod.

Zechariah's name in Hebrew consists of two words and is pronounced as ZECHAR-YA, meaning "God remembers." Elizabeth's name in Hebrew also consists of the two words ELI-SHEVA, meaning "the oath of God."

Both of them were Jewish, Israelites, and from the priesthood family, i.e., they both belonged to the tribe of Levi. Luke described Zechariah as a priest, and indeed he was not the only priest that was called Zechariah in the Bible. I Chronicles 15:24 recorded a priest by the same name who participated in the event of bringing the ark back to Jerusalem at the time of King David. Nehemiah 11:12 also mentioned a priest by that name who lived at the time of the return from Babylon.

Elizabeth is described by Luke as "the daughter of Aaron," which is a strong statement that points to her descent. Incidentally, Aaron's wife's name was also Elizabeth[1]. It is possible, therefore, that this name remained in the family and actually related all the way back to her. It was not obligatory for a priest to marry a woman from priestly descent, although it was recommended[2] and also was often the case[3].

Elizabeth and Zechariah were not only what we describe today with the term "Orthodox Jews," but also they were described here as righteous as far as God is concerned.

Much attention was paid in general to priestly marriages, primarily because of the different biblical rules and limitations concerning who they should marry. As long as the marriage did not conflict with biblical prohibitions, a priest could marry anyone. However, it was stressed that the bride had to be above reproach, a woman who truly deserved to be married to a priest.

Luke described Elizabeth and Zechariah in verse 6 as "Righteous in the sight of God, walking blamelessly in all the commandments of The Lord and in His statutes."

Elizabeth and Zechariah were not only what we describe today with the term "Orthodox Jews," but also they were described here as righteous as far as God is concerned. Why? Because they walked blamelessly in all of God's commandments! What does this mean? It means they kept all of God's commandments and His statutes. In other words, they kept the Torah. Three things to notice here:

1. If Elizabeth and Zechariah kept God's commandments, then obviously anyone can do so. Many times, people had the notion that "no one could have kept the Torah." Here is a very clear record that this is not the case.

   A similar claim was made by Paul in Philippians 2:15, where he stated that as far as the Torah was concerned, he was himself blameless. The whole idea that God gave Israel a whole list of rules and commands, which He knew they could not possibly fulfill, but yet He demanded them to live by them or they would die, really does not put the God of the Bible in a very good light. Does it?

God is a logical God. Just take one look at the universe and it becomes clear, everything has a cause and effect. If we claim that He acted irrationally, we either miss the point or lack understanding of who He is and of the biblical record, or we worship another God, not the God of the Bible.

2. God did not give Israel commandments they could not keep. Take a look at Deuteronomy 30:9–15:

   "For The Lord will again take delight in prospering you, just as He delighted in prospering your ancestors, when you obey The Lord your God by observing his commandments and decrees that are written in this book of the Law, because you turn to The Lord your God with all your heart and with all your soul.

   "Surely, this commandment that I am commanding you today is not too hard for you, nor is it too far away. It is not in heaven, that you should say, 'Who will go up to heaven for us, and get it for us so that we may hear it and observe it?'

   "Neither is it beyond the sea, that you should say, 'Who will cross to the other side of the sea for us, and get it for us so that we may hear it and observe it?' No, the word is very near to you; it is in your mouth and in your heart for you to observe. See, I have set before you today life and good, and death and evil."

   God's words in this text are clear, but there are those who do not want people to realize it.

3. The New Testament does not go against the Torah. Rather, in line with the Tanach (OT), it teaches that God's Torah is good and righteous. According to the description, there is no doubt that Zechariah and Elizabeth were righteous. However, it is possible that Luke wanted to include it here in order to make clear that the couple's childlessness would not be understood by people as a punishment for their unrighteous conduct or sins. Barrenness, unfortunately, was often considered as a sign of God's judgment. This is probably why Elizabeth considered her barrenness to be a disgrace (verse 25).

The couple had no children, and they were already advanced in age. Therefore, the birth of John was a miracle and an answer to a long-standing prayer. The account of John's birth is similar to other biblical accounts of barren women in the Bible. It brings to mind the story of Sarah who at the age of 90 gave birth to Isaac (Genesis 16:1), and the story of Rebecca (Genesis 25:21), and of Rachel (Genesis 30:1), and of Samson's mother (Judges 13:2) and of Hanna (I Samuel 1:2).

The birth of Samuel and Samson both bear a lot of similarities to the birth of John. The birth of Samuel, just like the birth of John, was an answer to prayer. Therefore, the rabbis claimed he was "the righteous child who was granted to parents who came together in holiness"[4].

John also was to become righteous, and indeed he was born to parents who came together in holiness. In Talmudic literature, Samuel is elevated. He is called "The Rabban," meaning "the foremost master." He is considered to be the teacher of all the prophets[5]. His place among the prophets is also recognized in the New Testament—of all of them he is the one who is mentioned by name and was considered to be the first of the prophets, although biblically Abraham was the first of the prophets[6].

Jesus, according to Matthew 11:11, elevated John not only above the prophets but also above anyone who was born of a woman, which literally means everyone!

In Luke 1:5 we are told that Zechariah was a priest of the order or the division of Abijah—in Hebrew AVIYA. This is a reference to the order by which the daily duties were performed by the priests and the Levites in the Temple.

The priesthood was divided into twenty-four groups or courses that were called in Hebrew MISHMAROT, which literally means "watches." Each one of these watches served in the Temple twice each year, for one week at a time[7].

According to the Mishna, it was King David and Samuel who divided the priests into twenty-four courses[8], primarily because there were too many priests in Israel at the time, and they wanted to ensure that each priest, at least once in his lifetime, would have the chance of a quality service in the Temple. During the three pilgrimage feasts of Passover, Pentecost and Tabernacles, all the Mishmarot served together in the Temple for a period of one week for each holiday.

In speaking about Zechariah and the priestly Mishmarot, it requires that we take a short sidestep at this point in order to discuss, to some extent, the time of Jesus' birth. This is because the information that Luke provided here concerning the Mishmar of Aviah serves as a clue to determine, somewhat, the time of year in which Jesus was born.

The Mishmarot started to officiate in the Temple on the first Sabbath of the month of Nisan, which is the first month of the biblical year, and which usually corresponds to the month of April in the Gregorian calendar. The course of Aviah, to which Zechariah belonged, used to be the eighth course in line.

Each course served one week at a time; therefore, the course of Aviah came into service on the tenth week of the year. That was comprised of eight weeks + two extra weeks = ten weeks—an extra week for Passover and an extra week for Pentecost, in which all the courses officiated together in the Temple. Zechariah, more likely, served in the Temple sometime in the middle of the third month on the Hebrew calendar, which corresponded to the middle of June on the Gregorian calendar. Therefore, this was probably the time in which John was conceived.

The priesthood was divided into twenty-four groups or courses that were called in Hebrew MISHMAROT, which literally means "watches."

Six months later, according to the Gospels' report, Jesus was conceived. This was sometime around the middle of the ninth biblical month that corresponded to the middle of December on the Gregorian calendar. Nine months later, Jesus was probably born; that must have been sometime in between the middle of the seventh to the eighth month in the Hebrew calendar that corresponded to September/October in the Gregorian calendar. It appears from this calculation that Jesus was born sometime around the Feast of Tabernacles.

It is important to realize that there is always the possibility that Zechariah performed his duty in the Temple during the second term of the priestly officiating cycle of the year, which would have brought the time of Jesus' birth to be around the Feast of Passover.

When it comes to John's birth, in light of the reference in the text to Elijah, who is expected to come during the Passover service, and taking into consideration the equation of John with Elijah in the Gospels, John was probably born sometime around the Feast of Passover, which means that Zechariah actually officiated in this role in the Temple during the first term of his priestly service cycle that year.

There is no doubt that Jesus was born during one of the pilgrimage feasts, which is the only reason to support the idea that "there was no room in the inn." Some people believe there was no room in the inn because of the census. But the census actually had nothing to do with it. The census was done over property taxes, and as such, according to Roman law, each person had to register for it in the location in which he owned property.

Most people had property wherever they lived, simply because it was hard to travel in those days from one location to another. It was even harder to move all of their belongings from one place to another; therefore, people for the most part stayed where they were. They moved only if they had a very important reason for doing so, such as a forthcoming disaster, famine, or enemy. Therefore, most people registered for the census wherever they lived.

There is no doubt that Jesus was born during one of the pilgrimage feasts, which is the only reason to support the idea that "there was no room in the inn."

But as we know, there were always exceptions. There were those who had inherited property in other towns. This was probably the case with Joseph, who may have inherited a piece of land in Beit Lechem, the lot that Naomi gave as a wedding gift to Boaz and Ruth.

The land must have remained in the family's possession, passed from father to son and more likely ended in Joseph's hand. For this reason, Joseph ended up in Beit Lechem. But other people did not just flock to Beit Lechem to register for the census; therefore, this cannot be the reason why there was no room in the inn. The only logical reason is that Jesus was born during one of the pilgrimage feasts.

During the feasts, according to historical records, between 210,000–250,000 people gathered at the Temple. Small Jerusalem could not possibly accommodate them all. Every house in Jerusalem was full, all the inns, guesthouses and hotels were full, people camped in the streets, so guests filled the neighboring cities, including Beit Lechem.

That must be why the Gospel recorded no room in the inn.

Going back to the birth of Jesus, it would no doubt be important if Jesus were indeed born during the Feast of Tabernacles, known as the Messianic feast in Judaism. This is the time of year that, throughout the generations, Israel expected the Messiah to come. The idea is basically derived from the Scriptures that often equate the Feast of Tabernacles with the Messianic Kingdom of God.

Returning back to our text, David and Samuel did not only divide the priests in Israel to Mishmarot for the work in the Temple, but they also divided the Levites to Mishmarot for ministering alongside the priests in singing, and each course was made of the priests of that course. The Levites were assigned to it as well, and a MA'AMAD of Israelites, meaning "a number of Israelites who were not priests or Levites but were standing ready," would pray while the sacrifices were offered.

Not all the people who made up the MA'AMAD of Israel had to show up in the Temple at the time of the priestly service, but there was always a small representation of them. The rest of the Israelites who belonged to this group gathered during the proper times of the day in their local synagogues and prayed to God to accept the offerings[9].

The Mishna provides us with much information concerning the priests' services and the way they were carried out[10]. Every day in the Temple, there were about 50 priests on duty. They drew lots in order to determine who was going to do which job. Many jobs needed to be done in the Temple. Some examples include inspecting the Temple courts with torches, trimming the golden Menorah, killing sacrifices, taking different parts of a sacrifice to the altar, preparing the altar, sweeping the altar of incense, offering the incense, and carrying it from the main altar to the altar of incense.

Once all the priests had gathered, the head of the Mishmar came in and randomly touched someone's head. That person who was touched was considered to be number one, the leader who then announced that person number so and so was selected for this job or that job.

Counting started from number one and ended at the number he chose, then that person stepped out. The process then started all over again for the next job, and the next. Lots were drawn twice a day. All the different jobs were determined in the morning. However, since Exodus 30:7–8 commanded Aaron to offer the incense twice a day, in the morning and in the evening, a lot was drawn in the afternoon in order to determine who was going to offer the evening incense.

Zechariah was chosen to offer the incense. This was truly a privilege and an honored position. The priest chosen for this task had to be at least 60 years old and one who had never before performed this task. It was bestowed on a person only once in a lifetime[11].

It is not clear whether Zechariah offered the morning or the evening incense since it is not specified in the text. Some people believe it was the morning incense offering at the time of the morning sacrifice. But, more likely, it was the evening incense, which took place at the ninth hour at 3:00 p.m. since the first watch of the day started at 6:00 am; 3:00 pm was the hour that was known as the hour of prayer[12].

Zechariah's job was to burn the incense on the golden altar. He was accompanied by another priest, an assistant who was chosen to go to the altar, climb to the top, stir the fire and take some of the hottest coals. Then he had to go down, pour the coals into a golden vessel that he took to the golden altar, spread the incense on top of the altar, bow down and leave the place[13]. Once the first priest left, Zechariah was left alone to burn the incense, after he received an order to do so from the president of the Sanhedrin.

The term used in verse 9 to refer to the Temple that was translated as "The Temple of The Lord" is the word NAOS in Greek. It literally means "a cell in the Temple"—not the Temple as a whole, but seemingly referring to the Holy of Holies. In classical Greek, this term was used at the time to refer to the sanctuary or a cell of an idol temple where the image of gold was placed, which was a distinguished part from the rest of the structure.

Here it could not possibly refer to the Holy of Holies. It must be some sort of a mistake. If anything, it has to refer to the Holy Place and not to the Holy of Holies since it is known that only once a year one person entered the Holy of Holies and that was the High Priest. Zechariah was not a high priest, and the day was not the Day of Atonement.

Verse 10 reads:

> "And the whole multitude of the people was in prayer outside at the hour of the incense offering."

Once Zechariah and his assistant were on their way to the Holy place and walked between the main altar and the court of the Temple, a large instrument known as the MAGERPHA was sounded in the Temple. The word Magerpha literally means "a garden rack."

According to the Mishna, there were three Magrephot in the Temple: one for gardening, one was a musical instrument in the form of a garden rack, which some people believe was an organ, and the third was some sort of an instrument which, when thrown on the floor, made a terrible noise[14].

In the case of the offering of the incense, it was the musical instrument that was sounded. The rabbis also tell us that when the Magerpha was sounded in the Temple, people in Jericho could hear it[15], and that in Jerusalem it was so loud that people could not hear one another[16].

Zechariah's job was to burn the incense on the golden altar. He was accompanied by another priest, an assistant who was chosen to go to the altar, climb to the top, stir the fire and take some of the hottest coals.

The sound of the Magerpha was a sign for the rest of the priests to assemble—for the Levites to come in and for the Ma'amad of Israel to gather in prayer. This is the multitude that Luke is referring to in this verse. According to the Mishna, all the priests and the people had to leave the court and gather somewhere outside in the area of the main altar at the time of the offering of the incense in the holy place.

This was done in accordance with the command found in Leviticus 16:17 that says, "When he goes in to make atonement in the Holy Place, no one shall be in the tent of meeting, until he comes out…"

Although this Scripture is talking about the high priest, the rabbis decided that no man should be in the place while any offering was given in the Holy Place[17]. Luke's account that the people prayed outside while Zechariah was offering the incense seems to be in line with Temple practices.

Zechariah was to offer a short prayer and leave as soon as he was done; however, according to the Gospels, it did not happen like this. The Gospels recorded that he had an encounter that caused him to tarry. When he finally came out, the people wondered why it took him so long (verse 21).

We do not have a rabbinical record stating that priests officiating in the Holy place should not tarry. Such a reference only exists in relation to the high priest officiating in the Holy of Holies on the Day of Atonement[18].

During that service, the people were worried, not only because of the possibility that God did not accept the sacrifice, but they were also afraid that the High Priest was struck dead.

This is because, according to Jewish tradition, if the priest had done anything wrong in performing his service, or if he was not proper or worthy, God would have struck him dead[19].

Angelology is a phenomenon that appeared in Judaism basically after the Babylonian exile. The Pharisees accepted the idea of the existence of angels, while the Sadducees rejected it.

Even though Zechariah was not the high priest, since he did tarry, it is no surprise that the people were wondering what was happening to him. Perhaps some of them even worried that in light of the tradition, there was the possibility of God striking him if he had done something wrong in his service.

Once he came out, we learn that he was unable to speak (verse 22), which actually hindered him from doing his job. After the offering of the incense, all the officiating priests used to bless the people. The priestly blessing is found in Numbers 6:24–26[20]. Zechariah was unable to do so at this point.

Zechariah tarried because "...an angel of The Lord appeared to him, standing to the right of the altar of incense. And Zechariah was troubled when he saw him, and fear gripped him" (verses 11–13).

An angel of The Lord appeared before him, just like in a similar way an angel of The Lord appeared before Manoach in order to tell him that his wife, who was barren, would now conceive a son[21]. Even though Zechariah was not the high priest, he was still scared to death, probably because he knew what could have happened to the high priest if he was alone in the Holy of Holies and did not perform his duty correctly. And if God did not spare the life of the High Priest, why should he have believed that He would spare his life if he had performed wrongly—not to mention the fear that grips people when they come into any encounter with the divine.

The name of the angel was Gabriel, meaning "God's strength" or "a man of God." In the Bible, of all the angles, only Gabriel and Michael are named[22]. In the Apocrypha others are mentioned. For instance, there is a reference to Rafael[23], to Uriel[24], and to Penuel[25].

Angelology is a phenomenon that appeared in Judaism basically after the Babylonian exile. The Pharisees accepted the idea of the existence of angels, while the Sadducees rejected it. Gabriel described himself in answer to Zechariah's question as "an angel who stands in the presence of God" (verse 19). In Hebrew these kinds of angels are called MALACHAY HA SHARET, meaning "the angels who tend to The Lord, who serve Him directly." In English, people refer to them as Archangels. Seven of them existed, according to Tovit 12:15 and Revelation 8:2.

The angel Gabriel is mentioned four times in the Bible: once here, once when he appeared to Mary to tell her that she would give birth, and twice in the Book of Daniel. Take a look at Daniel 9:21:

> "While I was still speaking in prayer, then the man Gabriel, whom I have seen in the vision previously, came to me in my extreme weariness about the time of the evening offering."

Gabriel appeared in order to communicate to Daniel the prophecy of the seventy weeks. The other reference to Gabriel in Daniel has to do with the end of time.

Zechariah's reaction to Gabriel's appearance is truly fitting to the general reaction one gets in the presence of the divine. Although Gabriel himself was not divine, he appeared in all of these cases as a personal messenger of God; therefore, he was sent by God, empowered by God himself to do his mission. He was God's representative to Zechariah and so Zechariah knowing that reacted instinctively rather than logically.

Zechariah offering the incense was not the only one who saw a divine appearance during his service. The rabbis wrote: "From what place did the angels speak?" R. Nathan said, "From the altar of incense." Simon Ben Asai said, "From the side of the altar of incense."[26]

Gabriel's message to Zechariah was spelled out in Luke 1:13–18:

> "But the angel said to him, do not be afraid, Zechariah, for your petition has been heard, and your wife Elizabeth will bear you a son, and you will give him the name Yochanan. And you will have joy and gladness and many will rejoice at his birth. For he will be great in the sight of The Lord, and he will drink no wine or liquor; and he will be filled with the Holy Spirit, even from his mother's womb.
>
> "And he will turn back many of the sons of Israel to The Lord their God. And it is he who will go before him in the spirit and power of Elijah, to turn the hearts of the fathers back to the children, and the disobedient to the attitude of the righteous; so as to make ready a people prepared for The Lord."

After Gabriel assured Zechariah there was no reason to fear, he proceeded to tell him the reason for his appearance. "Your prayers have been answered"—Zechariah and Elizabeth must have prayed for a child for a long time. At last, God had harkened to their prayer, and a son was going to be born.

"You will call him Yochanan"—this is not the only place in the Bible where God commanded a person to give a certain name to a child. God also commanded Abraham to call his son Isaac in Genesis 17:19. Isaiah 9:5 is another example of a name of a child being determined by God before his birth. And according to the Gospels, God also determined Jesus' name before His birth in Matthew 1:21 and Luke 1:31.

The name Yochanan is a Hebraic name, which means "God pardoned" or "God forgave." Perhaps, in this case, it was alluding to John's futuristic message since we know he called people to repent. And when people repented, God forgave their sins.

"And he will drink no wine or liquor." In other words, John was to become a NAZIR, meaning a Nazarite—someone who is consecrated by a vow to God. The laws of the Nazarites are spelled out in Numbers 6:1–21, and they include the following:

A Nazarite has to abstain from drinking wine. The word used in the Hebrew text is SHECHAR, which usually refers to a stronger drink, hard alcohol. But a Nazarite also had to abstain from vinegar, whether it was made from wine, a strong drink, or grape juice. He also had to abstain from eating fresh or dried grapes.

Some say the term wine refers to new wine, whereas the term SHECHAR refers to an old wine. According to the Talmud, one suggestion is that the fruit that Adam and Eve ate in the Garden of Eden was of the vine, i.e. grapes. Therefore, a man like Noah, who planted a vineyard and later got drunk, should have known that wine leads to transgression.

After Gabriel assured Zechariah there was no reason to fear, he proceeded to tell him the reason for his appearance. "Your prayers have been answered"—Zechariah and Elizabeth must have prayed for a child for a long time.

A Nazarite cannot cut his hair. The rabbis said, "Since he should be holy, he should not be bothered with fancy haircuts, etc..." The laws of the Nazarites are given within the priestly code. And indeed there are many similarities, in particular with the high priest. For the high priest, the head is the focus of sanctity as is the case for the Nazarite who cannot cut his hair. Even the drinking issue is similar, except it is more lenient when it comes to the high priest, who is only to abstain from wine while he is in the sanctuary (Leviticus 10:9).

A Nazarite cannot come in contact with a corpse, much like the high priest. The following are a few more points concerning the Nazarites:

1. The Nazarite period of consecration can be terminated earlier if he gets contaminated.

2. In case of premature termination, the Nazarite is obligated to offer a reparation sacrifice in the Temple. If he completes his consecration period, he pays no penalty.

3. In a case of contamination, the following ritual took place: On the third day and on the seventh day, the Nazarite was to be sprinkled with purification water. The next day, three events had to happen: 1) He had to

offer a purification offering. 2) His hair was consecrated. 3) He began a new Nazarite period.

4. The uncut Nazarite hair was his distinction. The root of the word Nazir is the term NEZER, which often refers to a person's hair and implies the importance of the Nazarite's hair, although it literally means "a crown" in Hebrew.

   Therefore, it is a reference to a royal priesthood. The term Nezer in the Bible referred to the holy crown of the high priest (Exodus 29:6, 30; Leviticus 7:9) and also to the crown of God's anointing oil (Leviticus 21:12). So the idea is that a person's hair is his crown. Since hair usually grows throughout a person's life, it was considered in the ancient world to be the center of man's vitality and life force.

5. If a person took upon himself a Nazarite vow without specifying its length of time, it was considered to be for 30 days.

6. It was customary for the wealthy to help poor Nazarites to purchase their offerings.

7. A man or a woman could take the Nazarite vow.

8. The rabbis said that the vows of the Nazarite could be taken only in the Land of Israel.

People took the Nazarite vow for different reasons. Some took the vow because they wanted to fulfill a wish, such as giving birth to a child, as in the case of Hanna, Samuel's mother. The pious took the Nazarite vow upon themselves in order to have an opportunity to bring a sin offering at the end of the period allocated.

After the destruction of the Temple, many people who mourned over it became ascetics and vowed not to eat meat or drink wine. As a result, the rabbis discouraged people from becoming Nazarites because asceticism is against the spirit of Judaism. At one point they even went to the extent of calling them sinners.

Paul took the Nazarite vow upon himself (Acts 21:20–26) to prove to the Jewish population that he was teaching the Gentiles to keep the Torah and that he himself kept it.

In the Bible there are two other Nazarites mentioned: Samson in Judges 13:7 and Samuel in I Samuel 1:21. Not only do we find similarities between the priests and the Nazarites, but also there are some similarities between the prophets and the Nazarites. Just like the prophets were dedicated at conception, as can be seen from Isaiah's testimony about himself in Isaiah 49:1, and from Jeremiah's testimony in Jeremiah 1:5, so also were the biblical Nazarites dedicated from conception as well.

In the Mishna we find a distinction made between a lifelong Nazarite and Samson. Unlike the lifelong Nazarite, Samson was not permitted even to thin his hair. In addition, unlike the other Nazarites, Samson was permitted to come in contact with the dead. According to the rabbis, this is because the angel did not communicate to his mother that he should abstain from doing so.

> After the destruction of the Temple, many people who mourned over it became ascetics and vowed not to eat meat or drink wine. As a result, the rabbis discouraged people from becoming Nazarites because asceticism is against the spirit of Judaism.

"And he will turn back many of the sons of Israel to the Lord their God..." The term that is used here is LEHASHIV LEV, which literally means "to return a heart." It is a reference to the biblical Hebraic concept of turning back to God, which is known by the term CHAZARA BE TESHUVA, which literally means "returning back with an answer," but it is used idiomatically to mean "repentance."

Often we get the idea that repentance means "saying sorry" or "asking for forgiveness." CHAZARA BETESHUVA means much more. Not only does one have to repent by begging for forgiveness from God, but he also is obligated to make a decision never, ever to return to his folly. Above all, he has to make a decision to return to God wholeheartedly, meaning to make a decision to live and walk, from that point on, according to God's commandments as they are found in Torah.

To return hearts—because repentance is a work of the heart—one has to commit his mind, his heart, his soul, his spirit, all of his being to be used by God in order for him truly to obey The Lord for the first commandment is "You shall love The Lord your God with all your heart..." There is no more important work than to turn people back to God Almighty. CHAZARA BE TESHUVA restores a person back to the presence of God. And, therefore, as a result, in our prayers we can truly say, "CHAZARTI LE FANECHA—I have returned to your presence…"

Today, people who made such a decision are known in Judaism as CHOZRIM BE TESHUVAH. People who had repented from their ungodly ways and made a drastic change in their lives became orthodox and quite often even Chassidic Jews. The most active in this area is the Chassidic organization known as Chabad. They are engaged in active proselytizing work among our people and convince many to turn their hearts back to God.

So, according to this, God bestowed upon John the great honor of turning the hearts of the children of Israel back to Him. He was not the only one who had such a job. There were others. Most of the prophets were engaged in similar work amongst other things, but the closest to John's case is the example of Elijah.

There is no more important work than to turn people back to God Almighty. CHAZARA BE TESHUVA restores a person back to the presence of God.

When Elijah was proving to Israel that Baal was not a God at all and that God alone is a true God, (I Kings 18), he called upon God in verse 37 saying, "Answer me, o Lord, answer me, that the people may know that you, o Lord, are God, and that you had turned their heart back again."

And so it happened. Through the work of Elijah, God turned the hearts of the people back to himself. John, once he grew up, called the people of Israel to repent, to change their hearts and to return fully to God. And just like Elijah needed the power of God in order to do so, John needed it as well.

"And it is he that will go as a forerunner before him"—the first thing to realize is that the words "as a forerunner" do not appear at all in the Greek text, nor in the Hebrew. The NAS translator decided to add them to the text. The Hebrew text simply can be understood as "and he shall go before Him," but it should be understood as "and he will go in His presence," which makes a big difference.

The word LEFANAV in Hebrew could be understood as "before him," but most of the time it is used in the Bible as an idiom. The word comes from the root PANIM, which means "face." So it literally says, "To His face," which makes no sense, unless it is understood in its idiomatic usage, which means "in his presence." The word LEFANAV, in this case, more likely implies both meanings and, therefore, should have been translated as "he will go before in His presence." i.e., he will still go before him, but so close that he will actually be in His presence.

In the Greek text, two words are used: PRO-ELUSETAI and ENORION. The first, PRO-ELUSETAI, is made up of two words: PRO meaning "before" and ELUSETAI, which according to the Greek lexicon comes from the word ELUSIS, which comes from the word ERCHOMAI, means "going" or "coming."

The word ENORION means "in the presence." It is very clear here that the Greek text was trying to be truthful to the Hebraic idiom used in the Hebraic text. So in translating the Greek, it says, "And he will go before, in the presence (of) Him." However, the English, both in the KJB and the American Standard Bible, does not reflect this and the American Standard Bible as I mentioned, added the words "as a forerunner."

Who then was John going to go before? It is a reference to God Almighty and not to Jesus as it is often understood. The text leaves no doubt that John preceded Jesus and even announced his coming. Not that Luke saw him as such. However, Gabriel could not possibly announce to Zechariah that his son would go before Jesus as Zechariah had no clue at that time who Jesus was.

In addition, Gabriel knew quite well that Zechariah would have understood it as a reference to God since he would have connected it with Malachi 3:1 in which God was saying, "Behold, I am going to send my messenger, and he will clear the way before me." The words "before me" are a translation of the Hebraic word LEFANAY, which comes from the same root as the word that is used here. Therefore, it implies "before me in my presence."

"In the spirit and the power of Elijah"—John himself then would not be Elijah, but rather he would come in the spirit and the power of Elijah. What does that mean? Possibly two things:

1. John had the same kind of responsibility that Elijah had, which was to turn the hearts of the people back to God. For this he needed the same power and spirit in order to be able to perform that function. The spirit was, of course, the Spirit of God, who was given to Elijah and according to this text, was also given to John.

2. It is possibly connected to the promise that was given by Elijah to his disciple Elisha that he would receive a double portion of His spirit: "Now it came about when they had crossed over, that Elijah said to Elisha, ask what I shall do for you before I am taken from you. And Elisha said, 'please, let a double portion of your spirit be upon me'" (II Kings 2:9–10).

It is known that the disciples of the prophets were called their sons. They were referred to as "the sons of the prophets," probably because of the Jewish understanding that he who teaches you is considered to be your father. An example of the use of the term "sons of the prophets" can be seen in I Kings 20:35 and also in II Kings 2:12, where Elisha was calling after Elijah when he was taken up to heaven: "my father, my father." As a son, Elisha was to inherit from Elijah the spirit of prophecy and the power that was given to him. Elisha, who was considered to be the first of Elijah's disciples, had exercised his right and asked Elijah to bless him with a spiritual inheritance, according to the share of the first-born son, with a double portion (Deuteronomy 21:17).

Later on we learn that he indeed received it. All of Elijah's disciples were to have a share in Elijah's spirit and power. Therefore, John coming in the spirit and the power of Elijah is more likely a reference to John as being Elijah's disciple. So just as Elijah did certain things, so would John. Elijah returned the hearts of the people to God, so would John. And just like Elijah, he was also commissioned to do the following:

1. "To turn the hearts of the fathers back to the children"—This is another thing that is parallel to the role of Elijah. Malachi 3:24 states this is one of the things that Elijah would do before the coming of God's terrible Day.

   The Talmud related this to Micah 7:6, which says, "For son treats father contemptuously. Daughter rises up against her mother. Daughter-in-law against their mother-in-law; a man's enemies are the men of his own household."

The rabbis understood this to be a reference to Messianic times. Thus Rabbi Nahorai said, "In the generation when Messiah comes, young men will insult the old, and old men will stand before the young (to give honor). Daughters will rise up against their mothers…The people will be dog faced, and a son will not be abashed in his father's presence[27]."

Since this was going to be the case, there was a need for repentance. Repentance for two reasons: 1) if they repented, God would not destroy them—in the case of the terrible day of the Lord. 2) God would go ahead and fulfill his plan—in the case of the coming of the Messiah.

2. "To make ready a people prepared for The Lord"—To be prepared for The Lord is to be not only ready for the work He is going to do, but fitting to be His people as well. King David said that God not only redeemed Israel from Egypt, but also prepared them to be His people forever (II Samuel 7:24).

   Here, the term "The Lord" is a translation of the sacred name of God, which appears in the Hebrew text. This is then again a reference to the God of Abraham, Isaac and Jacob and not to Jesus.

Zechariah had a hard time accepting this message and believing it. After all, he himself said, "He and his wife were old." He reacted similarly to Abraham when he was told that he would inherit the land (Genesis 15:8). Abraham wanted to know how he would know it? Zechariah wondered as well. He was basically asking for a sign, just as Abraham did and just as Gideon did (Judges 6:37–42).

Signs were given to all three of them, but only Zechariah was punished in the process. It is interesting to note that Abraham and Manoach and his wife believed when they were told they were going to have a child. Zechariah had a problem believing it.

The cases of Abraham and Gideon were not concerning something so personal, but rather concerning the nation of Israel. Perhaps this is the reason that both of them had received a sign while Zechariah, although he also received a sign, was punished in the process.

Gabriel answered him in verse 19 saying, "I am Gabriel, who stands in the presence of God, and I have been sent to speak to you and to bring you good news…"

The angel scolded Zechariah about his lack of faith. Incidentally, the word translated here as "in the presence of God" is the same word we discussed before, ENORION, which was translated by the American Standard Bible as "a fore-runner."

It is known that the disciples of the prophets were called their sons. They were referred to as "the sons of the prophets," probably because of the Jewish understanding that he who teaches you is considered to be your father.

The sign that was given to him was the sign of dumbness. Zechariah was not able to speak until the circumcision of his son. When he came out, the people were wondering about his delay, but he was not able to perform his priestly duty and bless them. He had to give them signs as he was unable to communicate orally.

Elizabeth conceived and went into seclusion for five months. We do not know exactly why, perhaps in order not to take part in all the religious activity, which often involved the Kiddush over the wine (the blessings over wine). After all, she was ordered to stay away from it, and it probably would have been hard and uncomfortable for her to explain why she was not participating on a regular basis since people probably would have found it hard to believe that she was pregnant at her old age. After five months, her condition must have become obvious.

CHAPTER 3 ENDNOTES

1. Exodus 6:23.
2. Vayikra Raba 4, Kidushim 4 Hal. 1.
3. Jerusalem Talmud., Taanit 4:11.
4. Tanchuma on Numbers 5:13.
5. Talmud Yerushalmi, Chagiga 77a.
6. Acts 3:24, Heb. 11:32.
7. Mishna, Taanit 4:2; Talmud Bavli, Taanit 2:1.
8. Ibid, 4:2.
9. Mishna, Taanit 4:2.
10. Mishna, Tamid 5:2.
11. Ibid, 6:3.
12. Acts 3:1.
13. Mishna, Tamid 6.
14. Ibid.
15. Ibid, 3:8.
16. Ibid 6.
17. Ibid.
18. Mishna, Yoma 5.1.
19. Ibid.
20. Mishna, Tamid 7:1.
21. Judges 13:3.
22. For Gabriel—Daniel 8:16, 9:21; for Michael—Daniel 10:13, 12:1.
23. Tovit 3:27, Enoch 9:1, 20:7, 40:9; and in the DSS, IQM 9:26.
24. Enoch 9:1, 19:1, 20:2; And in DSS, IQS 3:20.
25. Enoch 40:9.
26. Yalkut Shimoni vol. 1, pg. 113.
27. Bavli, Sanhedrin 97a.

CHAPTER 4

GABRIEL'S MESSAGE

LUKE 1:26–38; MATTHEW 1:18–25

Just as in the story of Zechariah, also here, the angel Gabriel came to deliver the message again. According to Luke, this took place in the sixth month (verse 26). This verse gives the impression that Luke is talking about the sixth month of the year since there are no indications here pointing to the contrary. However, he is speaking about the sixth month of Elizabeth's pregnancy, which becomes clear from the content of verse 36: "And behold, even your relative Elizabeth has also conceived a son in her old age; and she who was called barren is now in her sixth month."

Verse 34 recorded Mary's initial reaction to Gabriel's message: "And Mary said to the angel, how this can be since I am a virgin?" Literally, in Greek, the question appears in the future tense. It says, "How shall this be, since I know no man." Bearing in mind that she was a minor and was described as a virgin, she must have thought about the fact that she had not menstruated yet. Therefore, in her mind, the whole situation was probably impossible. I know no man has a Semitic meaning—I am not involved in a sexual relationship.

Her question "how" does not really make sense, unless it is understood according to the rabbinic meaning of virginity. Asking "how" implies there is a problem. When Gabriel told her the news, she should have naturally assumed she would be taken to Joseph's home, and that is how. But she did not. Rather, she asked, "How" since she knew there was a problem, and it was not the lack of sexual relations, but rather the fact that she had not menstruated yet and, therefore, could not possibly conceive physically.

Verse 36: "And behold, even your relative Elizabeth has also conceived a son in her old age; and she who was called barren is now in her sixth month."

In mentioning the sixth month, Luke provides the element of time, which is very important in order to calculate the time of year in which Jesus was born because it connects both births.

"And Mary said to the angel, how this can be since I am a virgin?" Literally, in Greek, the question appears in the future tense. It says, "How shall this be, since I know no man."

According to verse 26, this took place in a Galilean town called Nazareth—Natzeret in Hebrew. The city of Nazareth, just like the city of Jerusalem, is surrounded by mountains and is located on top of one. In the case of Nazareth, they are the beautiful mountains of Zebulun and Naphtali.

Today, many of these hills are built on with houses, making it at times hard to see the natural beauty of the place, which is actually surrounded by an area that is forested with fig and palm trees.

The town is located not too far, but far enough, from the main road that leads to the coast. In ancient times, the city was removed from the Via Maris (way of the sea), which enable it to maintain a peaceful environment.

Until the fourth century CE, the town was exclusively Jewish[1]. In the fourth century CE, Gentile Christians moved to Nazareth and established churches in the vicinity. The Jewish population of Nazareth maintained a good relationship with the Christian population up to the sixth century CE.

According to rabbinic records, Nazareth used to be one of the priest-centered towns. Priests belonging to the 24 courses—and who did not belong to the course that was on duty in the Temple at the time—used to gather at different towns in Israel for prayer. Nazareth was one of these towns.

Some scholars see a conflict between Luke and Matthew's accounts here. They claim that Matthew implies that Mary and Joseph lived together in Beit Lechem. I have not found any such indication. Matthew chapter 2:1 only indicates that Jesus was born in Beit Lechem and not where Gabriel appeared to Mary.

Luke also wrote in this verse that Mary was betrothed (engaged) to Joseph. Betrothal in Hebrew is the word ERUSIN.

Generally speaking, in the first century, ERUSIN used to take place about one year prior to the marriage ceremony, and it was a binding commitment.

According to the rabbis, the ceremony of betrothal was fundamentally a ceremony of acquisition. This is based on Deuteronomy 24:1 where the Torah speaks about "taking a wife," using the same terminology as was used in purchasing a field[2].

This was to encourage the belief that just as a person could not really divorce himself from the responsibility of attaining his land, he could also not shake off the responsibility to his wife. When the marriage ceremony took place, the acquisition turned into a union.

ERUSIN could only be dissolved by divorce, even though the marriage was not consummated yet. During the period of ERUSIN, the bride remained with her family, until the time of the wedding, when she was taken to her husband's house.

ERUSIN could only be dissolved by divorce, even though the marriage was not consummated yet. During the period of ERUSIN, the bride remained with her family, until the time of the wedding, when she was taken to her husband's house.

We can deduce from Luke's statement that Mary was betrothed as a minor, and more than likely her parents arranged her marriage. According to the Mishna, the age of betrothal at the time was 12 years, 6 months and one day[3].

Mary was described as "a virgin," and it is important to understand the concept of virginity within Judaism of first century Israel in order to grasp

Mary's response to Gabriel's message. According to rabbinic understanding, the word virgin was understood at that time in two different ways:

1. The primary understanding was "a young girl who had not menstruated yet."[4]

   The word BETULAH (a virgin) was not associated with the absence of sex, but rather with a physical inability to conceive. This kind of virginity, of course, did not end with intercourse, but rather with menstruation.

   In the Mishna, the rabbis asked, "Who is a virgin?" Their answer was "Whoever has never seen blood, even though she is married."[5] In the Tosefta, we find the teaching of the late first-century scholar Rabbi Eliezer Ben Hyrcanus who said, "I call a virgin, whoever has never seen blood, even though she is married and has had children, until she has seen the first flow."[6]

   The sages understood that a girl could have conceived while she was still a virgin in respect to her menstruation. In other words, she could have conceived at the moment of her first ovulation. At the time of the first century, of course, physiological knowledge was very limited. The blessing of fertility was always attributed to God. Conception before menstruation was, therefore, considered to be miraculous.

   Philo, the Jewish philosopher of the first century CE, was also familiar with the sages' concept of virginity. He also understood it as an inability to conceive. Philo considered Sarah, in spite of her advanced age and long marriage, to be a virgin because of her inability to conceive.

   He said, "Thus it was when she advanced from womanhood to virginity that Sarah, who according to Genesis 18:11, ceased to be...after the manner of woman, conceived the son of the promise, Isaac."[7]

   Philo also identified Isaac as the son of God; primarily because of God's intervention in his conception[8]. From here we also see that any child that was born miraculously was considered to be the son of God.

   Since, at that time, girls used to get married at such a young age, many of them did not reach the physical maturity needed for marital life.

In order to protect these girls, the rabbis created all sorts of laws concerning the sexual relationship between a husband and a minor wife.

For instance, they forbade sexual relations to take place up until the time the minor had at least three menstrual periods. The Essenes also forbade cohabitation until the girl menstruated three times, and thus proved that she was capable of conception[9].

That is because they believed that sex should be practiced only as a means for conception.

2. The secondary usage of the word virgin was a title given to husbands and wives who did not participate in sexual relations prior to their marriage. Archaeology uncovered Jewish graves in Rome of people who lived during this period. On the graves were inscribed, for example, "here lies my virgin mother, a mother to nine children." Similar inscriptions were found on male and female graves[10].

   If we understand the word virgin to mean "without sexual relationship," Jesus' conception finds no parallel to other miraculous births in the Bible. If, on the other hand, we understand it according to its primary concept of the first century to mean "without menstruation," then it is different altogether.

Therefore, the birth of Isaac, Samuel and John are all parallel examples to the birth of Jesus because their mothers conceived at an old age. In Judaism, there are no expectations for the Messiah to be born of a virgin, and such expectations were never there throughout all history.

One of the reasons that the Ebionites, one of the Jewish sects at the time, were considered by Christians to be heretics was their belief that Jesus was conceived in a natural conception.

Luke did not connect his account of the virgin birth to Isaiah 7:14. However, Matthew did connect it in chapter 1:22, where he said:

> "Now all this took place that what was spoken by the Lord through the prophet might be fulfilled, saying, behold the virgin shall be with a child, and shall bear a son, and they shall call his name Emmanuel, which translated means God with us."

In Isaiah 7:14, the Hebrew word ALMA was translated into the English as "a virgin." Some people have a problem with this because the word ALMA in Hebrew refers to a young woman, more likely older than twelve years old.

The Hebrew ALMA always refers to a young female adult. And although the word sometimes refers to a woman who is a virgin as in Genesis 24:43, it does not carry this meaning inherently. The word is simply the feminine form of the corresponding masculine noun ELEM, which means "a young man." An example of the word ELEM is found in I Samuel 17:56; 20:22.

However, the reality is that when the 70 rabbis translated the Septuagint (LXX), they used the word PARTENOS, in Greek, to translate ALMA in Isaiah 7:14. In all fairness, we need to realize they also used the word PARTENOS in Genesis 34:3, referring to Dinah who was no longer a virgin in the sense that we understand the word today. Thus it appears that the term PARTENOS was used by the rabbis to refer to the different concepts of virginity that existed then.

> The birth of Isaac, Samuel and John are all parallel examples to the birth of Jesus because their mothers conceived at an old age. In Judaism, there are no expectations for the Messiah to be born of a virgin, and such expectations were never there throughout all history.

Luke did not record when the conception took place, nor did Matthew. The next thing they recorded is that Mary conceived and gave birth to Jesus. Although, Matthew stated that the conception was a result of the Holy Spirit (Matthew 1:18).

Mary was betrothed to Joseph, who was from the House of David. In other words, he was from the tribe of Judah. This is all the information Luke gives about Joseph at this point. Matthew provided more information. He recorded in verse 19 that Joseph was a righteous man.

The word used here in the Greek is the word DIKAIOS, which is the word used in the Bible to indicate one who keeps the Torah. So here, Joseph is not called righteous because of the way he treated Mary, but rather it is in order to point out what he was obligated to do according to the Torah.

People probably believed that Mary had committed adultery and that Joseph had no choice but to divorce her. However, perhaps because of his love for her, he wanted to spare her from public shame and from punishment. He, therefore, decided to divorce her quietly, without a public hearing. Joseph would probably have done so if God's angel had not appeared to him in a dream.

The angel's message is communicated in verse 20:

> "But when he had considered this, behold, an angel of the Lord appeared to him in a dream, saying, Joseph, son of David, do not be afraid to take Mary as your wife; for that which has been conceived in her is of the holy spirit."

Carefully examining this text reveals two incorrect translations:

1. The angel did not tell Joseph "to take Mary as your wife" as is translated in the NAS Bible. Rather, the angel told him *"to take his wife Mary."* This is the way it appears in the Greek. It is not surprising that he told him to welcome his wife because it is in line with the Jewish concept of betrothal. The bride is considered to be his wife already during the period of betrothal. That is why termination of a betrothal requires a divorce.

2. The sentence that has been translated as "for that which has been conceived in her because of the Holy Spirit" appears in the Greek as *"for the thing is being conceived in her because of the Spirit, is holy."*

As a result of the dream, Joseph took Mary to his home but refrained from sexual relations with her until she gave birth to Jesus. That means that he did have a sexual relationship with her afterward, which goes against the idea of the perpetual virginity of Mary.

According to Luke's account, Gabriel greeted Mary saying, "Hail, favored one! The Lord is with you." Hail is a translation of the Greek word CHAIRO, meaning "greetings." In Hebrew, Gabriel started by saying, "SHALOM LACH"—"Hello to you," or better still, "peace be unto you."

Favored One is a translation of the Greek word KEXARITOMENEH—simply meaning "charming" or "graceful one." The Hebrew text has the term ESHET HEN—meaning "beautiful woman." The same appears in Proverbs

11:16, which says, "A gracious woman attains honor, and violent men attain riches." In this text, it was translated as "gracious woman."

The English translation here rendered "favored one." This is really not implied by the Greek, but it can definitely come from Hebrew. The term CHEN is also used in Hebrew as part of the idiom MATZATI HEN LEFANECHA, which literally means "I have found favor before you." Biblical examples are too many to mention, but here is one of them: "Noach found favor before The Lord God" (LXX—Genesis 6:9).

It is clear then that the word CHEN was understood here as part of this idiom. Incidentally, CHEN is also the root of the name Chana, and its meaning has to do with beauty, favor and good nature. The words "blessed are you among women" is a later addition to the text and is not found in earlier manuscripts.

Joseph took Mary to his home but refrained from sexual relations with her until she gave birth to Jesus. That means that he did have a sexual relationship with her afterward, which goes against the idea of the perpetual virginity of Mary.

Mary was startled by his words—perhaps because of the presence of the angel, but also because she was probably thinking that he had done that which he should not have done. He was not supposed to greet her at all! No man was to greet any woman at that time[11]. The phrase, "The Lord is with you," of course, does not mean that Jesus is in her, but rather it is a guarantee of God's support for her.

Mary's fear could also be understood in light of her young age. Being so young and having an angel appear to you is frightening enough, but also to be told that you are going to be pregnant when you do not fully understand what that means must be scary.

Gabriel's message is found in verses 31–33:

> "And behold, you will conceive in your womb, and bear a son, and you shall call him Jesus. He will be great, and will be called the son of the most high; and The Lord will give him the crown of his father David."

"You shall call Him Jesus." According to this, God gave him his name before his birth. According to rabbinic writings, different men received their names before birth, including the Messiah. The rabbis said, "Isaac, Ishmael, Moses, Solomon, Isaiah, and the name of The Messiah, whom, May the Holy One blessed be His name...brings quickly in our days[12]."

In Hebrew the name appears today in three forms:

1. Yehoshua.
2. Yeshua.
3. Yeshu.

Two of them, Yehoshua and Yeshua, are considered to be real names in Israel today. The name Yeshu, when appearing in textbooks, is not written in abbreviated form. I suspect the only place to still find it abbreviated is in some extreme, ultra-Orthodox publications. The word Yeshu in its abbreviated form stands for "may his name and memory be blotted out."

As a result, for the most part, people in Israel are not familiar with the abbreviated form. It does not appear this way in textbooks, in newspapers, or in other books, and it is not used this way by the media either. When the New Testament is quoted in textbooks, usually the name Yeshua or Jesus is used. Authors who wrote about their understanding of the first century, such as Professor David Flusser, usually used the form Yeshua in their Hebraic works.

When the New Testament is quoted in textbooks, usually the name Yeshua or Jesus is used. Authors who wrote about their understanding of the first century usually used the form Yeshua in their Hebraic works.

Eliezer Ben Yehuda, who revived the Hebrew language, mentioned Jesus eight times and always used the name Yeshua. The author Shalom Ash, who wrote the book *The Nazarene*, also used the name Yeshua in both his Hebrew and Yiddish texts. When writing about Jesus, Maimonides also used the name Yeshua[13]. In rabbinic literature, both forms of the name are used[14].

Some scholars believe that Jesus' proper name in the first century was indeed Yeshua. However, Christianity had deified the name of Jesus, and that brought about a change in the Jewish relationship to the name of Jesus. One wrote,

"It is no wonder that Jews considered the Christian belief as simple idolatry and were left obligated to apply the Torah in Exodus 23:13 that says, 'Now concerning everything which I have said to you, be on your guard; and do not mention the name of other gods, nor let them be heard from your mouth' to Jesus' name"[15].

A book written in the 18th century provided the following reasons amongst others as to why Jews removed the letter Ayin [ע] from Jesus' name:

1. Most Jews do not recognize Jesus as a Messiah—a savior.
2. Jesus was unable to save himself. Therefore, the letter Ayin [ע] is left out.
3. The Torah commanded Israel to change and defame the name of false gods.
4. In reference to Exodus 23:13, Israel was forbidden to mention the names of other gods[16].

In the first century and also during the Second Temple period, the name of Yeshua was a popular common name. It appears to be a later adaptation of the name Yehoshua. The name Yehoshua includes in it the sacred name of God. It means "God's salvation." The Name Yeshua comes from the same root and means "salvation."

The first time this name is mentioned in the Bible is with Yehoshua Ben Nun (Numbers 13:16). Other people were named Yeshua and Yehoshua in the Bible. The most interesting reference, however, is found in Nehemiah 8:17 where the short form of Yeshua is used to refer to Joshua Ben Nun, thereby providing us with proof that the long form was indeed replaced by the short form.

It is quite possible that in the first century both forms of the name were also in use. According to Professors David Flusser and Joachim Jeramias[17], the letter Ayin [ע] was not pronounced by the Galileans. Thus they pronounced his name as Yeshu, but wrote it as Yeshua. Professor Flusser wrote:

> "The Hebrew name for Jesus, Yeshu, is evidence for the Galilean pronunciation of the period, and is in no way abusive. Jesus was a Galilean, and therefore the A sound at the end of His name, Yeshua, was not pronounced. His full name was therefore Yeshua Ben Yosef."

In the Talmudic sources, which are from a later period, there is a reference to Rabbi Yeshu, who is not to be confused with Jesus[18].

In Matthew 1:21, we find the explanation for the name Yeshua, and we have a Hebraic play-on-words: VE KARATA ET SHMO YESHUA KI HU YOSHIA—"And you shall call his name Yeshua, for he will save his people." This is definitely a Hebraism since biblical and Jewish names are usually a hint at the character of the person and, at times, to his vocation as well.

Even if Mary was to be taken, at this point or shortly after, to Joseph's house, she still could not have sexual relations with him since she had to menstruate at least three times before this could happen. So the statement, "I know no man" should be understood as "I am not involved in sexual relations at this time, nor would I be able to be involved in such relations, at least and at best, for the next three months."

So in order to make her question clear, it should be reconstructed to imply *How can this be since I am not supposed to have sexual relations with my husband until the time I will go to live at his home and once I have menstruated three times?*

Gabriel answered her in verses 35–36:

> "The Holy Spirit will come upon you, and the power of the most high will overshadow you; and for that reason the holy offspring shall be called the son of God. And behold, even your relative Elizabeth has also conceived a son in her old age, and she who was called barren is now in her sixth month."

Gabriel answered Mary giving her two explanations:

1. "The Holy Spirit will come upon you and the power of the Most High will overshadow you"—This is a Hebraic doublet used to emphasize to Mary that all this would happen through the power of the Holy Spirit.

2. The word overshadow in Greek is EPISKIASAY—"to overshadow, to cover or to shelter." Other examples of how this word is used throughout the Bible include Ezekiel 31:3; II Samuel 16:13, 30:6; Isaiah 32:15; Jonah 4:6; Psalm 91:4, 140:8; and Numbers 11:25.

Each example demonstrates how The Lord overshadowed the elders in the desert with His spirit. The word is also used in Acts 1:8 where it is used to describe the coming of the Holy Spirit upon the disciples on the Day of

Pentecost as well as in Acts 5:15 where it is used to describe Peter's shadow falling upon the sick.

The statement that the child will be holy is the same claim that we have seen in Matthew 1:20 in the angel's communication to Joseph. In addition, Jesus is also called holy in Mark 1:24, Luke 4:34, John 6:69 and Acts 3:14.

> VE KARATA ET SHMO YESHUA KI HU YOSHIA—"And you shall call his name Yeshua, for he will save his people." This is definitely a Hebraism since biblical and Jewish names are usually a hint at the character of the person and, at times, to his vocation as well.

"Your relative Elizabeth…" is rather vague since we are not told what kind of relation she was to Mary. Wycliffe popularized the idea that she was a cousin.

It is important to note that Gabriel provided Mary with a direct answer to her real question. Gabriel knew exactly what Mary was asking. Mary's dilemma was the fact she had not menstruated yet—i.e. her womb was not ready to conceive. Gabriel, therefore, gave her the example of her relative Elizabeth, who was much advanced in age.

More than likely, Elizabeth had passed the stage of menopause and, therefore, was not menstruating either. According to first-century Jewish understanding, Elizabeth was no less a virgin than Mary. So Gabriel continued by asking Mary if God was capable of performing this miracle in the womb of her relative. Why did she suppose that He could not perform this miracle in her womb? Nothing is impossible for God. Mary, of course, had no more arguments. She accepted the explanation, and we are told she blessed The Lord.

CHAPTER 4 ENDNOTES

1. Irenaeus, Adversus Haereses (against heresies), p. 30.
2. Genesis 23:13, Abraham purchased the field of Ephron for Sarah's burial.
3. Mishna Kidushin 2:1.
4. Tosefta, Niddah 1:6. Yerushalmi, Niddah 49a.
5. Mishna, Niddah 1:4.
6. Bavli, Niddah 1:6.
7. Philo, De Mutatione Nominum 131.
8. Philo, De Legume Allegoria 3.
9. Josephus, Jewish wars 2, 161.
10. H.J. Leon, *The Jews of ancient Rome*, pp. 130, 232, 274–5 (no. 80).
11. Bavli, Kidushim 70:1.
12. Pirkay De Rabbi Eliezer 32.
13. A.S. Halkin (ed.), Moses Maimonides, *Epistle to Yemen*, N.Y., 1952, p. 12.
14. The name Yeshua was used in Tosefta, Hullin 2, 22, 24.
15. M. J.A. Eisenmenger, Entdecktes Judenthum, Konigsberg, 1711, Vol. 1 pp. 64-67.
16. Baze's, *Jesus the Jew—the Historical Jesus: the True Story of Jesus*, Jerusalem 1976.
17. J. Jeremias, *Neuestamentliche Theologie*, Gutersloh, 1973, Vol. I p. 13.
18. Prof. David Flusser, *Jewish Sources in Early Christianity*, Tel-Aviv, 1989, p. 15.

CHAPTER 5

MARY VISITING ELIZABETH

LUKE 1:39–56

Luke 1:39 says, "Now in these days Mary arose and went with haste to the hill country, to a city of Judah, and entered the house of Zacharias and greeted Elizabeth."

Shortly after her encounter with Gabriel, Mary left to visit Elizabeth. The time element here is not very precise, which is very unlike Luke, who is usually more specific. The term "in these days…" simply implies "at about the same time that these other events happened." Elizabeth, at this point, was already in her sixth month of pregnancy; therefore, her five-month isolation period was over, so she could receive guests.

Mary went with haste, more likely, because Gabriel knew the connection between her and Elizabeth. There is no doubt that his words directed her to Elizabeth. Beforehand, she probably did not know that Elizabeth was pregnant until he revealed it to her. Now she was eager to speak with Elizabeth and could hardly wait to see her. The fact that Mary herself was pregnant perhaps also contributed to her need to get away at this time; however, it was not her main reason since she was not showing yet.

Luke stated that she went to the hill country of Judah. Again his description is vague and not specific, so we cannot be sure of the distance of the location of Zechariah's residence from it. However, it does confirm that Zechariah and Elizabeth were not living in Jerusalem.

This is not surprising since it is a known fact that only a small section of the priests lived in Jerusalem; the remainder lived in the cities of Judah[1]. One of the cities in the hill country of Judea was Hebron, and we know that Josephus testified to its location[2].

However, the city is still located today in the same place, so even without his testimony, we know it is part of the Judean desert. However, we cannot deduce that they lived in Hebron since there were several other cities in the area.

"And it came about that when Elizabeth heard Mary's greeting, the baby leaped in her womb; and Elizabeth was filled with the Holy Spirit."

The term BEIT ZECHARIA, which literally means "the house of Zechariah," was taken by some as a reference to a place that used to be called Beit Zechariah and is mentioned in the Apocrypha[3]. In this case, however, the term applies to their home rather than a place with the same name.

When Mary arrived at their home, she greeted Elizabeth and according to Verse 41, "And it came about that when Elizabeth heard Mary's greeting, the baby leaped in her womb; and Elizabeth was filled with the Holy Spirit."

It appears, just as before, that a revelation was given to Mary by Gabriel concerning Elizabeth's state of pregnancy. Elizabeth was also now given a revelation concerning Mary's state of pregnancy by the Holy Spirit.

In addition, according to this verse, the baby leapt in her womb. The Greek word used here is ESKIRTESEN, which means "jumping" or "skipping." The Hebrew word VAIRKOD means "and he danced," and it is used to express the same idea.

Some people believe this is a reference to the medical term describing the movement of the baby in the womb, which would be typical for Luke to mention, bearing in mind that he was a physician[4]. However, the Hebrew term used here could not be stretched to express this meaning.

Furthermore, the same Greek word is also used in Genesis 25:22 to describe the movement of Jacob and Esau in their mother's womb. This movement was actually a sign to Rebecca to encourage her to go and seek The Lord, which resulted in God's revelation to her concerning the future of her twins.

The leaping of the baby in Elizabeth's womb, likewise, was a sign to her that led to the revelation that was just given to her, indicating that Jesus would be born to Mary.

The fact that the baby leaped with joy indicates, of course, the manner of his behavior and not necessarily his knowledge. Just like Jacob and Esau, who had no knowledge of what was coming upon them when they skipped in Rebecca's womb, neither did John.

Some see this as a fulfillment of Luke 1:15 where Gabriel promised that John would be filled with the Holy Spirit from his mother's womb. The claim is that he had by then already recognized Jesus. This, of course, presents a problem since according to John 1:32–33, John did not recognize Jesus until his immersion (baptism). Elizabeth recognized Jesus at this point because of the inspiration of the Holy Spirit, who filled her at that time, but her revelation must have been personal.

The idea that a baby would leap in his mother's womb or respond to something great that God is doing is not strange at all in Jewish context. Firstly, this is because of the biblical description of Esau and Jacob's behavior in Rebecca's womb. Secondly, this is also because it is according to Jewish tradition.

The rabbis said that "the unborn infants in their mother's womb said 'Amen' to the hymn of praise that was sang at the Red Sea"[5]. The term used in the Hebrew text is MIMKOR ISRAEL, which literally means "from the source of Israel." For example, "Bless the Lord from the source of Israel, from the future infants to be born, who will constitute Israel."

Also, the fact that the baby leapt in the womb presents an argument against abortion. The word used here for baby is the Greek word BREPHOS, which is the same word used in Luke 2:16 to describe a newborn baby. Thus the newborn baby and the unborn baby—both babies—are considered to be fully human.

According to the text, as a result of the inspiration of The Holy Spirit, Elizabeth responded to Mary's greeting with poetry. The word translated as "she cried out" is the Greek word ANEPHONESEN, which literally means "proclaiming." This word is used consistently in the LXX for liturgical music. Examples include I Chronicles 15:28, 16:4–5, 16:42.

Elizabeth's song seems to have a messianic nature. Verse 42 states:

> "Blessed among women are you, and blessed is the fruit of your womb! And how has it happened to me that the mother of my lord should come to me? For behold, when the sound of your greeting reached my ears, the baby leaped in my womb for joy, and blessed is she who believed that there would be a fulfillment of what had been spoken to her from The Lord."

"Blessed among women" in Hebrew is BERUCHA AT, meaning "blessed are you." This is a declaration of a blessing that already exists , rather than the promise of a blessing for the future. Here, Elizabeth recognized the blessing that God had already bestowed upon Mary.

Although Mary is specially blessed among women, she is not blessed above all women. A similar statement was also mentioned in the Bible about other women. For instance, Judges 5:24 says that "most blessed of women is Yael (Jael)…" and the same was also said about Judith in the Apocrypha as well[6].

The expression "fruit of the womb" is a typical Hebraism and a poetic way of describing a child. The same expression can also be found in Genesis 30:2 and in Lamentation 2:20.

In Elizabeth's poem, we have an indication that Jesus was already conceived in Mary's womb. Elizabeth also recognized the blessing that was bestowed upon her, by the fact that Jesus' mother actually came to see her. That in itself showed Elizabeth that Mary was blessed for believing that God would fulfill that which He revealed to her.

Here, the word blessed has a different meaning. In Hebrew, the word ASHRAY is used, which literally means "happy is." The same word is used in Matthew chapter 5 to describe the beatitudes. Happy she must be because this is an indication of another blessing still to come in the future. Elizabeth knew that Mary believed God, by the fact that she came to her. If she had not believed, she would not have shared it with someone else so quickly.

The following section, verses 46–55, is known in the Christian world as "The Magnificent," a poem that Mary uttered in response to Elizabeth's greeting[7].

However, there is a problem with this view since the proceeding phrase, "And Mary said," appears in most of the Greek manuscripts, but not in all of them. Some early manuscripts read "And she said." Some of the old Latin manuscripts have "And Elizabeth said." Elizabeth was also understood to be the speaker by some of the early Church Fathers, such as Irenaeus[8]. She is also the speaker in Jerome's translation of Origen[9]. The Catholic Church attributed it to Mary, but it could have been attributed to Elizabeth since there are some textual and other evidences for it. For instance:

> The expression "fruit of the womb" is a typical Hebraism and a poetic way of describing a child.

1. Generally speaking, the poetry here finds its closest match in Jewish hymns and poems from the period of 200 BCE to 100 CE[10]. It is accepted among scholars that it was literally written in Hebrew and could have been recited by any Orthodox Jew at the time. The song has very little to do with Mary and everything to do with Israel.

2. According to verse 41, it was Elizabeth not Mary who was filled with the Holy Spirit at this point, and so she was the one who was inspired.

3. Mary's reaction to Gabriel's message was limited. It is highly unlikely that she would have come up with such a hymn of praise at the age of twelve, specifically since the revelation actually put her life at risk, which must have confused her. Elizabeth, on the other hand, had much more experience and, in addition, was inspired by the Spirit.

4. There is a strong parallel between this poem and the one uttered by Hanna in I Samuel 2:1–10. There is also a parallel between this speaker's condition and Hanna's condition, a condition of barrenness in both cases that had been removed by God.

5. In verse 48, the speaker refers to her own "low estate," TAPINOSIS in Greek, which means "humiliation, dreadfulness"—"bareness" fits much better than a lack of menstruation[11].

The same word is used in the Tanach in Deuteronomy 26:7 as one of the adjectives describing the suffering of the Israelites under Egyptian persecution. Elizabeth suffered from her barrenness, whereas Mary did not suffer from her young and yet not fully developed condition.

6. Since Mary was already introduced as the speaker, there was no need to mention her name again in verse 56, yet it is mentioned.

7. We find a powerful parallel between Elizabeth and Zechariah since both were the parents of John and if we realize that indeed both of them spoke a hymn of praise as a result of an angelic revelation that was given to them.

Although the majority of scholars accepted the theory that Mary was the speaker in this text, she is by no means considered to be the author of this poem. It is quite possible that the song was a common hymn of praise, spoken by people within Israel who were suffering from one thing or another.

The Psalms of the late Second Temple period are known as "Hymns of Praise"—in Hebrew, HODAYOT. These Psalms are usually divided into three parts:

1. An introduction of some sort—usually praising God.

2. The body of the Psalm—usually spelling out the motives for praising God. It tends to begin with the word "because," and it follows a certain grammatical pattern. The motive lists God's deeds for Israel and His attributes.

3. Conclusion—an undefined part, sometimes it repeats a motive; sometimes it includes a blessing.

In our poem here, we have a similar structure:

In verses 46b–47, we find the introduction—praises to God.

In verses 48–53, we have the body of the song. It begins with the word "for" or "because" and lists the motives for praise. It spells out God's attributes in verses 49–50 and His deeds in verses 51–53.

In verses 54–55, we have the conclusion—a triumph to God's attributes. He has done it according to His promise. Therefore, God is faithful; He keeps His promises.

The poem has many similarities to the Qumranians' war-like hymns, an example of which can be found in their War Scroll[12]. Many of its verses are a direct quotation from the Tanach or a paraphrase of it.

For instance, verse 46 is a paraphrase of Psalm 34:3–4. Verse 47 is a paraphrase of Psalm 35:9. Verse 48 is a quote from I Samuel 1:11. It is also a paraphrase of Genesis 29:32 and 30:13. Verse 49—"Holy is His name"—is a quote from Psalm 119:9.

Verse 50—"And His mercy is upon generation after generation towards those who fear him"—is a quote of Psalm 103:17, which says, "but the loving-kindness of The Lord is from everlasting to everlasting on those who fear him."

In both cases, the Hebrew term CHESSED appears in the text. In Luke 1:50, it was translated as mercy, and in Psalm 103 it was translated as "loving-kindness."

Note that the Psalm says that God's loving-kindness is from everlasting to everlasting for those who fear Him. Incidentally, CHESSED is usually translated in the English Bible as "grace." But the word "grace" cannot be found in the Tanach. People often say there was no "grace" in the Tanach, and that the God of the so-called Old Testament is a God of judgment and vengeance, whereas the God of the New Testament is a God of love and grace.

CHESSED is usually translated in the English Bible as "grace." But the word "grace" cannot be found in the Tanach. People often say there was no "grace" in the Tanach, and that the God of the so-called Old Testament is a God of judgment and vengeance, whereas the God of the New Testament is a God of love and grace.

It is not surprising because most of the time where the word CHESSED appeared in the Tanach, it was translated into English as "loving kindness," which is its actual meaning or as "mercy."

The word CHESSED was translated into Greek as CHARIS, which is a proper translation of the Hebrew word. But when this word appeared in the New Testament, it was translated into English as "grace." As a result there are many instances of the word "grace" in the New Testament yet no instance of it in the Tanach, even though it is a translation of the same word.

In this text we have a declaration that God's loving-kindness was, is and always will be there. Or, if we observe the New Testament translators, we end up with the statement "God's grace was, is and always will be."

This concept of God's loving-kindness and mercy—the so-called "grace" concept—is not a concept that could have been created with the coming of the New Covenant. It is not something new that has not been there before and now exists because of Jesus' works.

This concept of God's loving-kindness and mercy—the so-called "grace" concept—is not a concept that could have been created with the coming of the New Covenant. It is not something new that has not been there before and now exists because of Jesus' works.

We are not in a dispensation of grace now, whereas before it was a dispensation of law. No, this is something that existed from everlasting to everlasting. ALWAYS! It was there for the nation of Israel throughout biblical times. It was there during the first century, and it is here today, and it will continue to be there until the end of time. Any other claim contradicts God's word.

Verse 51 states, "He has done mighty deeds with His arm; He has scattered those who were proud in the attitudes of their hearts." This is a paraphrase of Psalm 89:10, which states, "Thou did scatter Thine enemies with Thy mighty arm."

The phrase "with his arm" is a Hebrew expression that appears in different places in the Bible. It's usually in reference to the Exodus, which more likely is the case here as well. The fact that the word "enemies" was substituted here by the word "proud" teaches us that those who are proud are God's enemies—a lesson that can be deduced also from Isaiah 13:11.

Verse 52 is a paraphrase of Job 5:11. Verse 53 is a quote from I Samuel 2:5 and Psalm 107:9. Verse 54 is a paraphrase of Psalm 98:3. Verse 55 is a reference to the Abrahamic Covenant that is recorded in Genesis 17:7 and 19.

In addition, as was mentioned before, there are many similarities between Hanna and Elizabeth. Both were barren. God, in His mercy, opened their wombs. They both gave birth to a son. Both of their sons were dedicated to God's work and served Him all their lives. Both enjoyed the Holy Spirit. Both mothers expressed their joy and gratefulness in uttering a hymn of praise to The Lord. Finally, Elizabeth's song echoes Hanna's song in many points. As we can see, Elizabeth must have had tremendous knowledge of the Bible since so much of it has been quoted here.

In verse 56, Luke draws our minds back to Mary, who stayed with Elizabeth about three months and then returned home. In relation to Elizabeth's pregnancy, we remember that Mary came to see her when she was in her sixth month of pregnancy (Luke 1:26, 36). If pregnancy lasts ten lunar months, then we realize that Mary must have left her home just before John was born.

More or less, Mary had to leave at this point. Shortly after Elizabeth gave birth, she would be surrounded by all her relatives, who would joyfully gather to see her and the child. The circumcision ceremony, which they would all attend, would take place within eight days. Mary, considering her state, probably started to show at this point; therefore, she would not have exposed herself to public scrutiny.

We are told that Mary went home. It is probably a reference to her actual home. Luke does not tell us exactly when Mary went to live with Joseph. Matthew 1:24 tells us that Joseph took her to his home, after he received a revelation about her pregnancy from the angel of God.

It appears then that Elizabeth uttered the poem we discussed.

However, in our verse here, it was translated correctly as "mercy," probably due to the fact that Jesus had not yet been born.

We have to remember the theology that teaches that the God of the Tanach is a God of anger, judgment and wrath, and that the God of the New Testament is a God of Grace, mercy and love. And also there is the added conclusion that Grace was not mentioned in the Tanach; it only appeared with Jesus. If in our verse this word were to be translated as "grace," it would have implied that grace existed before Jesus came on the scene, which would have gone against this kind of theology. Therefore, we still have the correct translation here.

In line with Jewish custom and tradition, the time came to circumcise the child. We will discuss circumcision to a greater extent when we discuss Jesus' circumcision. John's circumcision took place on the eighth day of his life, according to God's commandment found in Genesis 17:12–13 and Leviticus 12:3. His circumcision was just like Isaac's, who was circumcised on the eighth day in Genesis 21:4 as well as Paul, according to Philippians 3:5.

From the Bible, we know that both men and women were able to perform the circumcision (Exodus 4:25). From Jewish tradition, we know that a Minyan—ten Jewish men—had to be present for the ceremony to take place and that a benediction was going to be pronounced during it.

Circumcision is the ceremony through which the child enters and becomes a part of the covenant of the loving-kindness that God made with Abraham and his seed.

According to Jewish tradition, during the ceremony, the father of the child acts as a high priest offering his child to God in love and gratitude. To Zechariah and Elizabeth, this ceremony must have been very important since they were miraculously given a child in old age; therefore, they had much to be thankful to God.

But there was a problem because the ceremony involved the participation of the father. The circumciser would start the ceremony by pronouncing the following blessing: "Blessed are you Lord our God, who has sanctified us by His commandments and given us the law of circumcision." The father of the child would continue with the next blessing: "Blessed are you Lord our God, who has sanctified us by His precepts and had commanded us to enter the child into the covenant of Abraham our father." But Zechariah could not speak; therefore, he could not participate according to custom.

From Jewish tradition, we also learn it is customary to name the child during his circumcision ceremony. The claim is that Moses was named on this occasion as well[13]. The reason the name of the child is given to him during this ceremony is because God changed Abram and Sarai's names to Abraham and Sarah during Abraham's circumcision[14]. Therefore, the rabbis said a child should be named during that time, and this has been the custom throughout most of the Jewish generations.

However, this was not always the case. In the patriarchs' time, they often named the child at birth[15]. The Gospel of Luke is the only Jewish record we have attesting to the custom of naming the child during the circumcision ceremony, which was customary during the first century CE. We do know from other Jewish sources that this custom was practiced a few centuries later, two to three centuries later.

Here we are dealing with John's circumcision ceremony, and the time had arrived to perform it. And as already mentioned, naming the child was a part of the ceremony. Since the circumciser could not have asked Zechariah because he was dumb and deaf, presumably the relatives decided to call the child Zechariah after his father.

The custom of naming a child after a relative was, and still is, quite popular in Judaism. Naming a child after a father was not as popular as naming the child after a grandfather, specifically among the priests[16], which is what we are dealing with here.

Circumcision is the ceremony through which the child enters and becomes a part of the covenant of the loving-kindness that God made with Abraham and his seed.

Even so, we do have documents from the first couple of centuries CE, mentioning people who were named after their father[17]. We also know this was the case in Josephus's family as well since both his father and brother were named Matthias[18].

In the Bible, examples of naming children after relatives is found in I Chronicles 23:21, 23; 7:20–21; 5:35, 36; and Genesis 11:24, 26. According to Jewish tradition, the custom of naming children after their relatives goes all the way back to the sixth century BCE, when Egyptian Jews used to do it. The custom is still practiced in Israel today, although not so rigidly. Native-born Israelis today use their imagination to name their children; they name them after the flowers, the trees, the mountains and the seas of the land.

Nowadays, when children are named after relatives, it is more common for them to be named after a dead relative than a living one. The relatives are usually close relatives, such as a grandparent or a parent. There are two reasons for this: 1. To commemorate the dead. 2. To honor the dead relative.

The naming of the child after a parent is seen as another way of obeying the commandment to honor thy father and mother.

Perhaps the relatives in our text suggested naming him after Zechariah because he could not have provided the name he chose, and naming him Zechariah would bring honor to him. Elizabeth, who knew exactly what the name of the child should be, stopped the relatives' objecting to the name they had chosen by providing them with the name he should be called, according to Gabriel's Instructions—Yochanan!

Yochanan is a good priestly name[19]. The name Yochanan literally means GOD PARDONS. In hindsight, we know that John's name was definitely an indication of what he was going to do since he claimed again and again that repentance would lead to God's forgiveness.

"Our God and God of our Fathers, rise up this child to his father and mother, and let his name be called in Israel Yochanan Ben Zechariah (John the son of Zechariah). Let his father rejoice in the issue of his loins and his mother in the fruit of her womb..."

Amazingly, the family did not accept Elizabeth's words, claiming that no one in the family had this name; therefore, there was no reason for her to give the child this name. As a result, they became engaged in making all sorts of signs to Zechariah in order to ask him what the name should be because he was deaf and dumb. It was obviously clear to them that Zechariah had heard nothing of the discussion that had just taken place and had no idea of Elizabeth's wishes.

Zechariah then asked for a tablet. Once they gave it to him, he wrote, "Yochanan is his name." The relatives were amazed. Why? Perhaps because he could not have heard Elizabeth, and yet he requested the same name. Surely, at any given time during the pregnancy, he could have communicated to Elizabeth the encounter he had with Gabriel.

There must have been some sort of a communication system used during that period, so even if there was no appearance of an angel, they could still have agreed upon the name given to the baby. Perhaps they were surprised at the insistence of the parents to call him by a name not before used in the family.

With this one act of obedience, the judgment of dumbness was forthwith removed from Zechariah. He was suddenly able to speak and could fulfill his part in the circumcision ceremony of his son. This in itself must have been somewhat of a shock for the relatives. Zechariah's last words were those of unbelief, now his first words were words of praise. He had learned his lesson.

The ceremony would now have taken place with all of its benedictions. After the circumcision took place, the congregation must have responded according to custom, saying, "As he had been made to enter the covenant, so may he also be made to enter into the study of the Torah, huppa[20], and performance of good deeds[21]." The ceremony most likely ended with the blessing over a cup of wine, followed by a prayer for the baby receiving his name.

An example of such a prayer is "Our God and God of our Fathers, rise up this child to his father and mother, and let his name be called in Israel Yochanan Ben Zechariah (John the son of Zechariah). Let his father rejoice in the issue of his loins and his mother in the fruit of her womb..."

The result of Zechariah regaining his ability to speak was that fear struck those who were present. Shortly afterward, that fear spread to the rest of the nearby community as the whole area heard what had happened. Verse 65 tells us the whole area of the Judean Mountains knew about it. Fear—most likely because of divine intervention—is a common motif within the Bible. In most public interventions of God, people are struck with fear.

Verse 66 says, "And all who heard them kept them in mind, saying, 'what then will this child turn out to be?' for the hand of The Lord was certainly with him."

"What" rather than "who" the child will be is simply a Hebraism. This is how it is communicated in Hebrew. The realization and the expectation were already there for God had a special mission for this child—who, although just born, had the Hand of The Lord with him. This can be seen as a fulfillment of Gabriel's promise that the child would be filled with "The Shechina" (the presence of God) from his mother's womb. He had just been born, and yet it was evident that God was with Him. Zechariah provided the answer to their question later in verse 76.

Zechariah, at this point, was touched by God himself. And just like his wife, Elizabeth, previously (1:41), he now also proclaimed a song, or as it appears in the original languages, a prophecy. The prophecy had many things in common with Elizabeth's song, which shows us that it was indeed drawn from a common source. And just like Elizabeth's song, the prophecy resembled the hymns of praise that were popular during the Second Temple period. It is a HODAYAH[22] as such. It is also divided into the same structure of three parts that we saw with Elizabeth's song[23]:

1. An Introduction—praising God, verse 68.

2. The body of the HODAYAH—listing the motives for praising God. This section is also divided into three parts:

   A. The things that God has done for the Nation of Israel are reasons to praise Him, verses 69–71.

   B. God's faithfulness to fulfill His covenant with Abraham is also a reason to praise Him, verses 72–75.

   C. The calling of John to bring knowledge concerning the forgiveness of sins to the people is also a reason for praising God, verses 76–77.

3. The Conclusion is usually an undefined part. In this case, it provided more reason for praising God, and it also repeated one of the Messianic promises, verses 78–79.

   The prophecy begins in verse 68 when Zechariah was blessed by the God of Israel because, in the original languages, "He had visited his people and redeemed them." The English translation (NAS) says, "for He has visited us and accomplished redemption for his people."

   Although this can be understood as two different groups—US and HIS PEOPLE—the verse actually refers to the same group of people, the nation of Israel. Here, the term "visited" is a translation of a Hebrew term HU PAKAD ET AMO, literally meaning "He looked upon; He watched over, He considered, He regarded," and finally "He visited."

This expression also appears in Exodus 4:31, where it was translated as "concern," and also in Ruth 1:6, where it says "God had visited His people in providing them with food." Also in Psalm 106:4, it says, "(God) visit me with thy salvation." This does not imply an actual visit of God, but rather it communicates that God remembered them, was concerned for them and, therefore, did something wonderful for them.

In the text here, the term PAKAD is mentioned twice: 1) In sending redemption to the people—in this verse, and 2) In raising the light from on high—in verse 78. In the Qumran writings, we find a similar understanding. They spoke about their group in terms of "God had visited us and rose up the teacher of righteousness…"[24].

Here again the term "visited" is understood as "done something great for us." The language of this verse, as in the rest of this prophecy, is very biblical and resembles Psalms 41:14, 72:18, 106:48 and I Kings 1:48. The redemption mentioned here is redemption from "our enemies," meaning Israel's enemies as verse 71 communicates and also Psalm 11:9. This is not referring to eternal life, but rather to a deliverance from our physical enemies.

Verse 69 continues with the description of God's deeds for Israel. Literally, it says: "He raised for us a horn of salvation in the house of David his servant." Here again, "us" is a reference to Israel. Zechariah is very much a part of the nation of Israel and sees things in terms of the covenants and promises of God to the nation. The expression "horn of salvation" is a metaphor for a victorious Messiah, a reference to the king that Israel has expected to come throughout history and still expects today.

The expression "horn of salvation" is a metaphor for a victorious Messiah, a reference to the king that Israel has expected to come throughout history and still expects today.

The phrase "David His servant" is not common in the New Testament. The only other place we find it is in Acts 4:25. The expression here is often used in Jewish writings, in particularly, in Jewish prayers. For instance, in I Maccabees 4:30 and in the eighteenth benediction, the prayer known as the Shmone Esray[25], states, "Speedily make to shoot forth the branch of David, thy servant, and exalt his horn by thy salvation, for in thy salvation we trust all the day long. Blessed are you Lord our God who causes to spring forth the horn of salvation."

There is a reference here to the Davidic covenant God made with Israel. Biblical references that resemble this verse are Psalm 119:9, 132:16–17, 18:3; Ezekiel 29:21 and I Samuel 2:10.

Verse 70 is similar to the following references: II Chronicles 36:22; Acts 1:16, 3:18, 3:21, 4:25.

Verse 71—the phrase "salvation from our enemies" is a reference to God's deliverance from the enemies of the Nation of Israel, usually Gentile pagans. Biblical references are Isaiah 49:6; Song of Solomon 10:9; Psalm 106:10, 18:18.

Verse 72—we have the phrase "To show mercy towards our fathers." Mercy again here, just like in Elizabeth's song, is a translation of the word CHESSED. It is translated correctly in this context, probably for the same reason mentioned earlier. So it refers to loving-kindness in remembering the covenant God made with Israel. It is because of God's love, and not because they deserve it—they do not—but regardless, God keeps His word to them.

The term ANATOLE, at times, appears as one of the names of the Messiah—for instance, in Zechariah 3:8 and 6:12. The Hebrew word in these two references is TZEMACH, which literally means "a branch."

The term "holy covenant" started to appear in Jewish literature during the Second Temple period[26]. The covenant here is a reference to the Abrahamic covenant as the next verse 73 indicates.

In the end of verse 72 and the beginning of verse 73, we have a play on words with the names of Zechariah and Elizabeth. ZECHAR YAH is made up of two words in Hebrew, meaning "God remembers." In verse 72 we read, "to remember His holy covenant."

Elizabeth's name is also made up of two words in Hebrew, meaning "The oath of God," and in verse 73 we read, "the oath which he swore to Abraham."

"To deliver us from the hands of our enemies" is again a reference to the enemies of Israel—verse 74. This deliverance takes place in order for us to be able to serve God all the days of our lives. The term "holiness" is probably a reference to Temple worship, and the term "righteousness" here is a reference to the keeping of the Torah. The Bible teaches that righteous are those who keep the Torah.

The same idea is also expressed in the writings of the Qumran community. God fulfills the covenant and delivers the people, so they may serve Him[27].

It also reminds us of the redemption from Egypt, where God redeemed the people in order for them to serve Him.

Other biblical references that express similar ideas are Psalm 18:18; Joshua 24:14; I Kings 9:4–5.

The attention in the text now was shifted back to John. In verse 76, we are told that John would be called "the prophet of the Most High," and in a later text, we learn that John was the last of the prophets (Luke 16:16).

The expression "you will go on before The Lord to prepare his ways" is made in reference to the God of Israel, just as we saw in verse 17. The word LIFNAY is used in the text idiomatically and it means "In His presence." So John would go in the presence of God to prepare His ways. Here Zechariah answered the people's question concerning the child.

Verses 78–79 refer to the Messiah. The term that was translated as "sunrise from on High" appears in the Greek as the word ANATOLE, which means "rising" or "east." The term sun was added here to the text, perhaps because the term is often used in connection with the sun. But ANATOLE can also mean "coming up" or "shooting up."

The term ANATOLE, at times, appears as one of the names of the Messiah—for instance, in Zechariah 3:8 and 6:12. The Hebrew word in these two references is TZEMACH, which literally means "a branch." The term ANATOLE appears as a branch also in Jeremiah 23:5. In Matthew 2:2, the term ANATOLE—rising—was translated as "east." The word probably refers to some sort of light, not necessarily to the sun, but something from above as it rises from on high. That it refers to light is quite clear from the verse that follows.

The coming of the Messiah is used here as a conclusion for these prophecies. In verse 80, Luke is speaking again about John.

We are told that John grew up in the deserts and lived there until the time came for him to appear to Israel as a prophet.

Some people think that John was raised by the Qumran community since there is a reference here to deserts. This idea is unfounded. John may have had some contact with them, but there is no record in the Gospels anywhere that John was a member of the sect or even any sect. Josephus, who was familiar both with the Qumran community and with John, never mentioned any connection between them.

In addition, we know that the Qumran community was adamantly against the Temple worship in Jerusalem, so surely the fact that John was the son of a loyal Temple priest and possibly a Temple priest-to-be would not have contributed to their willingness to accept him as a member of the sect.

We know that the Qumran community was adamantly against the Temple worship in Jerusalem, so surely the fact that John was the son of a loyal Temple priest and possibly a Temple priest-to-be would not have contributed to their willingness to accept him as a member of the sect.

Others believe that the years in the desert totally secluded him from the community of Israel. Was this the case? Did he not attend Temple service? Was he not celebrating the feasts? Was he disobedient to God's commandments? I truly doubt it. He probably had contacts with local synagogues in the desert, and more likely he attended the Temple services during the feasts just like the other priests who lived in the hill country of Judea, and who yet came from there to the Temple in order to perform their services.

It is possible that the term "deserts" here is metaphoric and, in essence, communicates that. As far as his prophetic role was concerned, John was in the desert until the time for him to fulfill his calling arrived. But even if he had truly spent most of his time in the desert, it does not mean that he spent all his time there.

CHAPTER 5 ENDNOTES

1. Nehemiah 11:3, I Maccabees 2:1.
2. Josephus, *War of the Jews*, Book 4, 9:7.
3. I Maccabees 6:32.
4. Colossians 4:14.
5. The Targum on Mimkor Israel, Psalm 68:27; Sota fol. 2.3.
6. Judith 13:18.
7. For much of the information concerning the structure of this poem I am indebted to Raymond E. Brown, who discussed it in his book "The birth of the Messiah," pp. 354-365.
8. Irenaeus, Adversus Haereses, Book IV, 7.1.
9. Origen, Luc. Hom. 7.
10. Brown, Raymond, *The Birth of the Messiah*, p. 349.
11. Ibid, p. 335.
12. DSS, IQM 14:4–15.
13. Pirkay De Rabi Eliezer 48 (27c).
14. Genesis 17:12-15.
15. Ibid, 4:1, 21:3, 25:25-26.
16. I Maccabis 2:1–2; Josephus, Vita I.1.
17. Wadi Murabba'at legal document, in which we read about Eliezer the son of Eliezer and Judah the son of Judah. Also, Tovit 1:9, Josephus, Ant. 14:1, 3, 20:9.1.
18. Nehemiah 2:13, 42; I Maccabees 2, 2:1–2.
19. Josephus, *War of the Jews*, Book 4. 3.9.
20. The wedding canopy.
21. Talmud Bavli, Shabbat 137b.
22. A thanksgiving song.
23. For much of the information concerning the structure of this poem I am indebted to Raymond E. Brown, who discussed it in his book "The birth of the Messiah," pp. 380–392.
24. DSS, CD1 5–12.
25. "The eighteenth benediction" which is a Jewish prayer from the first century CE.
26. I Maccabees 1:15, 63.
27. DSS, 1QH XVII: 14.

CHAPTER 6

THE BIRTH OF JESUS

LUKE 2:1–7:

The Year of the Census

Christian scholars and historians have written much concerning the year in which Jesus was born. Generally speaking, it is not so easy to determine the year, primarily because there are problems regarding the information Luke provided in this particular section. We will discuss these shortly.

When we examine the historical data, despite some difficulties, it appears to indicate that the year in which the census took place in Israel was 8 BCE. This, however, presents a problem for scholars who have striven to maintain the year 30 CE as the year of Jesus' death and also to maintain the traditional view that Jesus died at the age of 33 or 34 years old.

Many attempts have been made to find an earlier date for Jesus' birth—a date that would fit the traditional assumption that he died approximately at the age of 33, in the year 30 CE. Why is there a need to stick to this age? I have no clue!

Examining both the biblical and the historical data, we can conclude that the evidence points to a birth date of 8 BCE and a crucifixion date of 30 CE. This can be supported firstly by the New Testament record, secondly—to some extent—by the historical information we have, and thirdly by some of the writings of the early Church Fathers whom we should expect to be more acquainted with Jesus' age at the time of his death than the medieval, reformed or modern Church.

Luke 2:1–2 says:

> "Now it came about in those days that a decree went out from Caesar Augustus that a census will be taken of all the inhabited earth. This was the first census taken while Quirinius was governor of Syria."

The phrase "In those days," according to Luke 1:5, is a reference to the days that Herod was the King of Judea.

The verse goes on to tell us that "A decree went out." The Greek word translated here as "a decree" is the word DOGMA, which I am sure you recognize. Dogma in Greek means "an opinion; a thought that something is true, a resolution."

Examining both the biblical and the historical data, we can conclude that the evidence points to Jesus' birth date of 8 BCE and a crucifixion date of 30 CE.

From the second meaning listed here, another word developed—DOGMATIZO in Greek, meaning "to lay down a decree." At best we can understand it as a resolution to take a census, which came out from Augustus, not as a decree or an edict. This is important because there is no evidence from secular history that a decree went out from Augustus approximately at the time of Jesus' birth to take a census in Israel. Perhaps this is Luke's way of communicating that a vote concerning it was taken in the Roman senate.

The phrase "From Caesar Augustus" refers, of course, to Emperor Augustus who was born as Gaius Octavius in 63 BCE and died in 14 CE. He received the title of divinity "Augustus" from the Roman senate in 27 BCE. He was the founder of the Roman Emperor titles, and he ruled over the Mediterranean world until 14 CE. During his reign, Diaspora Jews got along with him quite well because he allowed them to study the Torah and, to some extent, he respected their practice of keeping the Sabbath[1].

Augustus must have been an excellent administrator and organizer. He took a periodic census, or registrations, for the purpose of future taxation and also for taxing property. The periodic censuses were conducted of the colonies in order to make the collection of taxes more accurate and more efficient. By having a regular assessment, Augustus knew what amount of tax money individuals in the different territories owed to Rome.

In order to pay the tax on a property, one had to register wherever one had property[2]. That is why verse 3 states, "And all were proceeding to register for the census, everyone to his own city." This was also the reason that caused Joseph to return to Beit Lechem (verse 4).

During the reign of Augustus, three censuses took place in the Roman Empire, although none were taken of the whole empire. They took place in 28 BCE, 8 BCE and 14 CE. Historically, we know that censuses took place in Egypt every 14 years[3].

We do know from Acts 5:37 that a census did take place in Israel and according to Josephus, the year was 6 CE.

Although there is no historical evidence that the same happened in Israel, it is logical this was the case since we are dealing with the same general area of the Middle East. We do know from Acts 5:37 that a census did take place in Israel and according to Josephus, the year was 6 CE. This census was resented and resisted by the people. Fourteen years before, in the year 8 BCE, we know that a census took place.

This is most likely the census that Luke referred to in chapter 2.

Incidentally, Tertullian mentioned that a census took place during the years 9 and 7 BCE. Therefore, a census date of 8 BCE fits the information he provided. Tertullian, of course, saw no discrepancy between his statement and the Gospel record. No historical evidence whatsoever exists of a census taking place around 4 BCE.

The statement "Of all the inhabited earth…" is a translation of the Greek word OIKOUMENEN, which means "inhabit" or "occupy." At best we can translate it as "all the inhabited area." The same word was also used in Acts 11:28, and there also it was translated as "earth," but it should have been translated as "the inhabited area."

Luke told us "this census was taken while Quirinius was the governor of Syria." This is where the main problem lies. According to Tacitus and others, Quirinius did not begin to govern Syria until 6 CE[4]. He ruled over Syria during 6 and 7 CE, during which time he conducted a census. This is the census that is mentioned in Acts, which took place in 6 CE. Such a late date for the birth of Jesus cannot be considered because King Herod had been dead almost 10 years by that time.

Some scholars came to the conclusion that Luke was telling us that the census took place before Quirinius was the governor of Syria. But then we need to ask ourselves, why did he mention him at all?

We know that Augustus appointed Quirinius as an adviser to Gaius Caesar. As a result, he came to Syria and spent several years there before 4 CE. Quirinius served for 20 years, from 12 BCE to 6 CE. And although there is no evidence that he conducted an earlier census, it is possible that because he was in charge of Syria's defense and foreign policy, he supervised a registration for tax purposes in Herod's territory for Augustus in 8 BCE. This then would be considered the first census as Luke indicated, whereas the census that he conducted in 6 CE would have been the second.

Outside of this possible explanation, there is no better solution, other than reaching the conclusion that Luke got confused with the historical data.

One further possibility is that the word translated as "while" by the NAS in this text is the Greek word PROTOS, which literally means "first." We have other words connected to it, such as PROTEROS, which means "earlier than," and PRO, which means "before." Therefore, some scholars came to the conclusion that Luke was telling us that the census took place before Quirinius was the governor of Syria. But then we need to ask ourselves, why did he mention him at all?

Leaving behind the problem of the census, let us concentrate on the year that Jesus was born. Bear in mind the information we do know, namely, that

Herod the Great was alive at the time of Jesus' birth. In order to see things more clearly, we need to look in reverse chronological order at the following events:

Herod died sometime in March/April of the year 4 BCE.

Early in 5 BCE, he left Jerusalem because he was banished to Gaul. He never returned to Jerusalem because he died in exile. So from here, we already see that Jesus could not have been born after 6 BCE.

From the record of the story of the wise men, which is found in Matthew, we know that the wise men came to visit Jesus approximately two years after His birth.

From the record of the story of the wise men, which is found in Matthew, we know that the wise men came to visit Jesus approximately two years after His birth. We will cover this in detail later. For our purpose here, however, we need to realize that they did not come to a manger but rather a house (Matthew 2:11). Nor did they see the "baby" Jesus but rather the young child (ibid.)—a word that can be understood to refer to a toddler or a child of about two years of age.

Since Herod was still in Jerusalem at the time of their visit, the wise men must have come to Jerusalem sometime around 6 BCE or even 7 BCE.

That would mean that the killing of the children and the flight to Egypt took place around the same period of time. This would indicate that Jesus must have been born around 8 BCE or 9 BCE.

This date is supported by the Gospel account, and it also fits the information that a census took place in 8 BCE. It also fits Tertullian's statement that a census took place between 9 and 7 BC. Perhaps the census began in 9 BCE and lasted until 7 BCE.

The Counter Argument

The main argument against an 8 BCE date is the fact that it brings Jesus' age to thirty-nine or forty at the time of his death. As was mentioned earlier, traditionally, the Church assumed that he was thirty-three years old when he died. Although the date goes against Church tradition, it does not contradict the data we find in the Gospels nor does it contradict the historical record.

The only possible objection to this idea is Luke 3:23, which says, "And when he began his ministry, Jesus himself was about thirty years of age…"

The word translated in this verse as "about" is the Greek word HOSAY, which does not only mean "about," it also means "as if, as though, like and about." Possibly then, it could indicate he was not in his early thirties, but rather he was in his thirties. In his thirties would allow for the age of thirty-nine.

> Traditionally, the Church assumed that Jesus was thirty-three years old when he died. Although the date goes against Church tradition, it does not contradict the data we find in the Gospels nor does it contradict the historical record.

Although there is no linguistic evidence available to support this reading, this kind of an understanding fits better the historical data and the Gospel record. Understanding this verse to mean "about thirty years of age" enables us to understand that in light of the historical data and the information in Matthew, Jesus could not have been born after 8 BCE.

Therefore, it would indicate that he died in the year 24 CE. But there is no dispute concerning the year of his death. It is known to be 30 CE. This is incidentally the only text in the Gospels that mentions Jesus' age.

There is another text, which comes close to indicating Jesus' age, and it is actually supportive of the possibility that Jesus was approaching forty at the time of his death. The text is found in John 8:57, after Jesus made the statement that Abraham had seen his day. The leaders of Israel are said to have answered him, "You are not yet fifty years old, and have you seen Abraham?"

They were in the midst of a heated discussion, in which the leaders tried to say anything they could think about to prove him wrong and to show that he did not know what he was saying. When they made this particular statement, they tried to belittle him—specifically, his age. If indeed he was in his early thirties, why did they not say, "You are not yet forty years old?" Surely they did not want to add to his age when they wanted to belittle it.

But if they indeed knew him to be about forty years old, give or take, then it makes sense that they asked what they did: "You are not yet fifty." They may have questioned whether he was already forty years old or not, but they knew without a doubt that he was younger than fifty.

It was this verse, John 8:57, which led Irenaeus, one of the Church Fathers, to the understanding that Jesus was past the age of forty at the time of his death[5].

The Significance of this Date

After considering the historical, biblical and patristic evidence of Jesus' date of birth to be 8 BC and accepting the year 30 AD as the date of his death, we come to the conclusion that Jesus was 39 years old at the time of his death—i.e., He was in his fortieth year. If this was indeed the case, is it significant? The answer is probably.

We often hear that the number 40 in the Bible is a significant number, but we do not always understand what it stands for or why it is significant. In checking the references to the number 40 in the Bible and elsewhere, the question is answered. A definite pattern can be noted. For instance:

1. The rain fell on the earth for forty days—and then it stopped (Genesis 7:17).

2. The Children of Israel were to be slaves in Egypt for 400 years (10 x 40)—and then redeemed (Genesis 15:13).

3. The Children of Israel were to spend forty years in the desert—and then the promised land (Numbers 14:34).

4. Moses spent forty days and forty nights with God on Mount Sinai—and then brought the Torah, which was a gift of love from God for the redeemed community (Exodus 34:28).

5. Goliath challenged the armies of Israel for forty days before David came, slew him and brought relief to Israel (I Samuel 17:16).

6. David ruled over Israel for forty years and then came Solomon and the building of the Temple (II Samuel 5:4).

7. Elijah fled for forty days and forty nights before God met him on Mount Horeb (I Kings 19:8).

8. Jesus was tested for forty days in the desert before his ministry started (Luke 4:2).

9. Pregnancy that runs full term, something else that God designed, lasts for nine months, or thirty-nine weeks, with birth occurring on the fortieth week.

10. From all these references, and I am sure we can find more, and also from life examples, we can see that all indicate a pattern of trial or hardship for a period of thirty-nine days or years, and then redemption, or relief, or provision, or something that puts an end to suffering or longing, like in the case of David and Solomon. The number forty in the Bible, therefore, stands for deliverance.

After considering the historical, biblical and patristic evidence of Jesus' date of birth to be 8 BC and accepting the year 30 AD as the date of his death, we come to the conclusion that Jesus was 39 years old at the time of his death.

11. God still uses this system, did you know? God does not change. Here are two examples that I personally experienced in my own life: **Our educational company, H.I.M, started shortly after Danny and I got married. Our wedding was one long chain of miracles. We did not have any money, we had no idea how we would make it, but we knew it was the will of God. Two hundred people were invited, and God performed one miracle after another, and the wedding came together beautifully; He planned every detail.**

    Once it was over and we started our lives together, we found out that we had no money for food, rent or for anything else. Somehow, someone offered us a short-term house-sitting opportunity in a beautiful Beverly Hills apartment, but there was no food. I do not know how we managed, moving from one location to another, but we did. Altogether, we were in this situation for 80 days (2 x 40). Relief came on the eighty-first day. One of the churches I taught in paid our first month's rent for a new apartment. This was the end of this initial trial. That day was the evening of the Feast of Tabernacles, and God had made this wonderful provision for us on the eve of the provision feast.

12. In 1991, during the Gulf war, Saddam Husain attacked Israel with Scud missiles. He launched forty Scuds. Thirty-nine of them fell in Israeli territory, one fell in Jordan, and the war was over—on the feast of Purim, the day on which we celebrate God's victory over our enemies. Nothing is coincidental; God works out His patterns, which He sets in motion in the Bible, even still today.

It is interesting to note that Jesus is often connected and compared with two particular individuals in the Bible: Moses and David. The number forty is also connected to both of their lives. As we mentioned previously, David ruled over Israel for forty years, and Moses was forty years old when he left Egypt. He spent another forty years in Midian, and then he led Israel for another forty years.

Jesus was probably in his fortieth year when He died. His life mission, among other things, opened the door of redemption for the Gentile world.

CHAPTER 6 ENDNOTES

1. Encyclopedia Judaica, Vol. 3, "Augustus," p. 853.
2. Brown, Raymond E. *The Birth of the Messiah*, p. 549.
3. Jack Finegan, *Light from the Ancient Past: The Archaeological Background of the Hebrew-Christian Religion*, Volume II, p. 258.
4. Josephus, Antiquities XVIII, 1.1.
5. Irenaeus, *Against the Heretics II*, xxii 6.

CHAPTER 7

THE SHEPHERDS

LUKE 2:8–20

Verse 8 reads: "And in the same region there were some shepherds staying out in the fields, and keeping watch over the flock by night."

"In the same region" basically means "in the same area." It refers here to an area geographically close to Beit Lechem. The name "Beit Lechem" literally means "the house of bread." At this point, the shepherds were not in Beit Lechem itself as is clear from verse 15, which states that after hearing the angelic message, the shepherds decided to go to Beit Lechem.

Beit Lechem is a town located in Judea, five miles south of Jerusalem, 2500 ft. above sea level. It is surrounded by fertile fields. Historically, the town dates way back to the days of our forefathers. According to Genesis 35:19, Jacob buried his beloved wife, Rachel, in the area of Ephrata/Beit Lechem, and her tomb is still there today.

In time, Bethlehem became the center of the tribe of Judah. The town was inhabited by the descendants of Peretz, the son of Tamar and Judah. Among them were Boaz, Jesse and David. Many biblical events took place in the city as well, two of which include: 1) The story of Boaz and Ruth took place in the fields of Bethlehem. 2) Samuel anointed David to be a king in the city (I Samuel 16:1–13).

At the end of King Saul's reign, Bethlehem was occupied for a short time by a Philistine garrison. Bethlehem in biblical times was a fortified city (II Samuel 23:15). King Rehoboam, son of King Solomon, fortified the town in order to protect the approach to Jerusalem (II Chronicles 11:5). There was the return to Bethlehem of the exiles from Babylon (Ezra 2:21; Nehemiah 7:26). The city continued to be inhabited by Jews until the time of Bar Kochva.

In 135 CE, a Roman garrison was stationed in the city in order to put an end to the remnant of Bar Kochva's army[1]. At a later period, a Gentile population settled in the town and erected a Temple to Adonis (Tamuz)[2].

Jesus was born in Bethlehem, according to the information found in this and other chapters. According to Christian tradition, he was born in a cave-stable. The location of this cave—east of the city—was first mentioned by Justin Martyr (155–160 CE). By the time of Origen, who lived in the third century, a site for the cave was determined[3]. Today, we have the same understanding, and the same site is presented as the authentic birthplace of Jesus, although we cannot be sure that this was indeed the place.

Jesus was born in Bethlehem, according to the information found in this and other chapters. According to Christian tradition, he was born in a cave-stable.

After Constantine became the ruler of Rome, Queen Helena, his mother, erected a church over the cave. This church was destroyed by the Samaritans in 529 CE, but it was rebuilt shortly afterward. The church still stands there today. In the 5th century, Jerome settled in Bethlehem. He lived there for thirty-three years (387–420 CE). He built a monastery there, and he also prepared his Latin translation of the Bible, which eventually became the basis for the Vulgate. Jerome was assisted by some Jewish scholars who lived in villages surrounding the city of Bethlehem.

During the early Arab period, Bethlehem remained intact and suffered no damage. Tancred the crusader took over the town without any opposition during the first crusade in 1099 CE. Baldwin I and II, the crusader kings of Jerusalem, were crowned in the church of Bethlehem.

The Crusaders built a fort in the town, which was destroyed in 1489. The church, however, remained in Christian hands throughout all the turmoil. It was in Christian hands during the rule of the Mamluks and the Turks, and even through the rule of different Muslim leaders, in spite of their oppression.

Christian leaders constantly reduced the size of the entrance to the church for security reasons. As a result, today it has a low and narrow opening.

In the middle of the 19th century, Turkish officials demanded a division of the church authorities among the different Christian groups abiding in Bethlehem. This division still operates today.

In 1949 the town became part of Jordan and with it Jewish residency in the city was forbidden. Today, Bethlehem is basically a Christian town. Until 1947, seventy-five percent of the town's population was Christian. The remaining population was Muslim. But after 1948, this changed as a result of the influx of Arab refugees from Israel to the city. In 1967, during the Six Day War, Bethlehem surrendered to Israel without a fight. According to a census taken in that same year, the population of the town was 27,000, of which 14,000 were Christians, mainly Roman Catholic and Greek Orthodox, along with some Protestants and Armenians.

Since the shepherds were not inside Bethlehem, we should ask ourselves where were they? It appears they were in a field outside of town.

The town of Bethlehem has very close economic ties with Jerusalem. Its inhabitants mainly grow olive groves, vineyards and fruit orchards. In addition, the town caters to Christian tourism. It has several small hotels and restaurants, and a number of workshops producing Christian souvenirs. Bethlehem is also a market town for the local Bedouins, who come here to trade their wares for local goods. The main building in the town is, of course the Church of the Nativity.

Since the shepherds were not inside Bethlehem, we should ask ourselves where were they? It appears they were in a field outside of town. Not too far out, the field of MIGDAL HA EDER was located.

Migdal Ha Eder in Hebrew means "The Tower of the Flock." We cannot be sure exactly which structures were there or what the place looked like, or even how it operated. We do know, however, that it had fertile grazing fields. Migdal Ha Eder was a shepherd's station that raised different kinds of lambs. One type of lamb was particularly important—the lamb destined to become a Passover sacrifice in the Temple.

According to the Mishna, Migdal Ha Eder was a town between Bethlehem and Jerusalem[4], and it is mentioned twice in the Bible, both times in a close proximity to Bethlehem. Firstly, in Genesis 35:21, just after Bethlehem is mentioned in Genesis 35:19. It is also found in Micah 4:8, followed by a reference to Bethlehem in Micah 5:1.

The place was well known in temple times. The rabbis used to say if one found a stray animal in the area between Jerusalem and Migdal Ha Eder, and it was suitable to become a Passover sacrifice[5], then it could be used for this purpose, provided it was found thirty days before the feast[6].

At that time, there was a general prohibition against raising lambs in Israel because they would eat the seeds of the land of Israel[7]. The leaders said the land should be reinhabited and replanted. Therefore, they instructed the people to raise lamb in Syria or in the deserts of Israel, a reference primarily to the Judean desert.

Despite this prohibition, it appears that some people did raise animals around their homes. These animals were known as BAITIYOT, meaning "homely." Since animals were already raised in town, the rabbis allowed the people to use them for slaughtering and consumption[8]. They also mentioned the MIDBARIYOT, meaning "the desert animals," were not suitable for consumption, but suitable for sacrifices.

When the rabbis talked about the Midbariot, they defined them as "Those are the sheep of the wilderness; i.e., those who go out to pasture about the time of the Passover and are fed in the field and return home upon the first rain"[9].

The first rain, according to the rabbis, came as an answer to the prayers for rain, which took place around the third of Heshvan. This date corresponds in the Gregorian calendar to about the middle to the end of October[10].

Other sheep may have been in the fields elsewhere in Israel all year round. According to Edersheim, this Mishnaic reference has to do specifically with the Midbariot, or as he called them, Temple flocks[11].

The time when the sheep were out in the fields of Bethlehem or Migdal Ha Eder should be taken into account when one calculates the time of Jesus' birth. The sheep were out on the field between the end of March and the end of October. Therefore, Jesus was probably born during that period of time.

According to Jewish writings, Migdal Ha Eder also refers to:

1. The anointed one of the flock of Israel—the Messiah[12].
2. The Temple (Rashi).
3. The tower of David.
4. Migdal Ha Eder is also a reference to Jerusalem itself, which is considered to be a tower to the flock—the flock is Israel.

Genesis 35:21, which mentions Migdal Ha Eder, does not say much about It, but simply states, "Then Israel (talking about Jacob) journeyed on and pitched his tent beyond Migdal ha Eder." Based on this statement, the writers of the Targum said, "Migdal Ha Eder, the place from which it will happen that the King Messiah will be revealed at the end of days"[13].

A copy of this Targum was found in the first cave of the Qumran community. Bearing in mind the nature of the Targums and its development, this Targumic understanding was most likely circulating at a much earlier date. And so possibly there was something of an expectation that the Messiah would actually be revealed there.

The shepherds who watched over the Temple flocks on the field of Migdal Ha Eder were not ordinary shepherds. When one thinks of shepherds, usually the picture of King David as a shepherd comes to mind. Sometimes, the picture of the Bedouins in Israel comes to mind as well. All this helps to form a shepherd's profile that probably does not fit them at all.

They are usually described as uneducated ragged men, poor and nomadic. At times, they are said to have been very simple but honest people. Although no documents exist describing the Temple shepherds, certain things are dictated by logic. Shepherds in general were considered to be below the level of lawbreakers by the rabbis. According to the Talmud, the early rabbis added them to the list of those who were considered to be unfit to serve as judges or witnesses since they frequently grazed their flock on other people's lands[14].

It is clear this refers to shepherds who raised their sheep in the regions of their own towns, despite the prohibition—i.e., they raised their flocks on the Land. We know that the rabbis had no objection to raising sheep in the desert, where it did not infringe on anyone's land. Ordinary shepherds came under rabbinic criticism because of their isolation from religious life; rabbis did not think shepherds could possibly live according to the Torah.

There were no rabbinic objections to the shepherds of Migdal Ha Eder. They raised their flocks in a designated place. Unlike ordinary shepherds, they were not nomads. The grazing fields were all around the area. There must have been structures built next to the fields as provision and shelter for the animals during the rainy season, when they were to remain indoors. Since these shepherds did not wander from place to place, they could have fully exercised a religious lifestyle.

There was a need to find hundreds of thousands of sacrificial animals every year. Just to find suitable animals, adhering to all the specifications required for the Paschal sacrifice alone, was a major task.

Neither were they uneducated; it is more likely the opposite was true. They were probably highly educated and must have been trained in the rabbinic academies of the time.

Most of the animals sacrificed in the Temple came from Migdal Ha Eder. There was a need to find hundreds of thousands of sacrificial animals every year. Just to find suitable animals, adhering to all the specifications required for the Paschal sacrifice alone, was a major task. The leaders of Israel must have realized the difficulty in going out into the fields hoping to find thousands upon thousands of suitable one-year-old sheep. In order to have enough lambs to sacrifice every year, they had to be raised, and they had to be raised in such a way that they would indeed be fit to be sacrificed in the Temple.

For this purpose, they must have trained the shepherds. Everything about each animal's life would have been important. How much time it spent out in the field, and how much time it spent indoors. What sort of a feed it received at each stage of its development. The shepherds needed to know this information. Today, there is no need to provide animals for sacrifices; therefore, no such system exists anymore. But we continue to have kosher laws in place, which in a sense dictate a similar situation.

It takes much more than the difference between a cow and a pig to determine whether the animal is kosher or not. For instance, the Bible dictates rules and regulations concerning the slaughtering of the animal. The rabbis devised a complete system of raising kosher animals. Everything about the animal's life is important; how much time it spends indoors and outdoors. What it is fed in each stage of its life, and so on.

Shechinah is the visible manifestation of God's presence on Earth. When the presence of God is manifested to man in whatever form, man expresses major fear. It is the fear that comes as a result of truly experiencing the presence of Almighty God.

Today, In order to ensure kosher laws operate properly, rabbinic academies train kosher inspectors. These are specialty rabbis who are trained just like any other rabbi. This is probably the closest example of the operating of the sacrificial system during Temple time.

Since they raised the Temple flocks, they were Temple shepherds, and they probably received their income from the Temple authorities, as well as room and board. Therefore, they were probably not poor.

According to Luke, it was to these shepherds that the angel of The Lord appeared, verses 9–11:

> "An angel of the Lord appeared to them, and the glory of the Lord shone around them, and they were terrified. But the angel said to them, 'Do not be afraid. I bring you good news that will cause great joy for all the people. Today in the town of David a Savior has been born to you; he is the Messiah, the Lord.'"

So, it was not only the angel of The Lord who appeared to the shepherd, but we also read that "the glory of the Lord" was there all around them shining on the field. The phrase "Glory of the Lord" is KEVOD ADONAI in Hebrew and is a reference to the Shechinah. This phrase is found also in Exodus 16:7, 10; 24:17; 40:34; Psalm 6:3; Numbers 12:8 and many other passages. The Shechinah is the visible manifestation of God's presence on Earth. This is, incidentally, the first time the phrase appears in the Gospels.

And as we often see in the Bible, when the presence of God is manifested to man in whatever form, man expresses major fear. It is the fear that comes as a result of truly experiencing the presence of Almighty God. And although we are experiencing only a tiny fraction of His greatness, we still tremble in fear when His presence is evidently around us. And so it appears to have been the case here. The Shechinah was present and the shepherds were frightened.

The core of the angelic message was the announcement that a Messiah had been born. The child, we are told, was an heir to David's throne. The term "Lord" in this place is not a reference to God. In both languages, Hebrew and Greek, the word is not capitalized. In both languages, the word appears in lower case. In Greek the word can mean "Master" and even "sir." In Hebrew the word in this text is ADON and not ADONAI, indicating in this case to mean "a master" rather than God. So it is talking about the Messiah, the Master.

"The city of David" was identified by the shepherds in verse 15 as the city of Bethlehem. The phrase "city of David" can also refer to Jerusalem, but the shepherds knew this was not the case here because they more likely associated the birth of the Messiah with Bethlehem. It was a common notion in first-century Judaism that the messiah would be born in Bethlehem.

Micah 5:2 predicted that the birth of the Messiah would be in Bethlehem. The Targum referred to this text also as about the Messiah[15] and rabbinic commentators did as well[16]. In addition, the Talmud stated that the Messiah would be born in a royal castle of Bethlehem[17]. Everywhere, the message was the same.

Not only were the shepherds told that Jesus was born, but they were also told how to find him. Verse 12 says, "And this will be a sign for you; you will find a baby wrapped in cloths, and lying in a manger."

Other translations use the term "swaddling clothes." Swaddling clothes were strips of material that were connected with a tie and were used for wrapping around the baby in order to keep him warm. The term in Hebrew is CHITU-LIM, which literally means "diapers."

Wrapping a baby with swaddling clothes was not a sign of poverty, as some have believed, but rather of a baby well taken care of. In the Apocrypha work *Wisdom*, King Solomon states, "I was carefully swaddled and nursed, for no king has any other way to begin at birth"[18].

Swaddling clothes are also mentioned in Job 38:9, which uses a birth metaphor: God described to Job how He wrapped the sea in thick darkness like a mother would wrap a newborn in swaddling clothes. It is also mentioned in Ezekiel 16:4.

"Lying in a manger"—The word in Greek is PHATNE and in Hebrew, EVUS. Both refer to a crib-like shaped horse feeder. They were usually made of stone and were found, as expected, in stables. Since they were shaped like a crib, it was perfect for laying down a newborn. The term EVUS appears also in Job 39:9, Proverbs 14:4 and Isaiah 1:3.

Stables could be made of wood or stone. By the middle of the second century, some Christian scholars had already decided that Jesus was born in a cave. But this idea has no foundation and is not supported by the text.

All we know is that he was born in some sort of a stable as he was laid in the manger.

Some believe today that the manger was a SUKKA, but there is no linguistic relationship between the word sukka—which mean a tabernacle—and the word evus—which means a manger, which is an animal feeder. The word sukka does not appear in this text at all. The sukka idea is an extension to the belief that Jesus was probably born during the feast of Sukkot. Some support this notion with John 1:14, which says, "…and the word became flesh and tabernacled among us…"

Since it says that "he Tabernacled among us," they concluded that he must have been born in a tabernacle. In English, the word Tabernacle means "a Sukka or to dwell." In Hebrew, the word Tabernacle is a "Sukka." The term "he dwelled," on the other hand, is the word SHACAN, which is the root of the word Shechinah. The same idea is also found in II Corinthians 4:5–6. John's statement, therefore, cannot be stretched from its meaning of a dwelling to the meaning of a manger, which is, as we have seen, a horse feeder.

Verses 13–15 states:

> "And suddenly there appeared with the angel a multitude of the heavenly hosts praising God, and saying, 'glory to God in the highest, and on the earth peace among men with whom he is pleased.' And it came about when the angels had gone away from them into heaven, that the shepherds began saying to one another, let us go straight to Bethlehem then, and see this thing that has happened which The Lord has made known to us."

The first thing to notice here is that not only the angel of The Lord and the Shechinah appeared to the Shepherds, but also a multitude of heavenly hosts. And all of them were present right down on earth, in the field of Migdal Ha Eder, praising God. Luke makes it clear they were not in heaven but down on earth, also in verse 15, where he wrote about their departure to heaven.

The idea of angels praising God is common in Judaism. It appears in the Tanach and also in Jewish literature that describes the reaction of the angels to God's creation. They said they sang a hymn of praise, a hymn to the creator[19].

"A multitude of the heavenly hosts" corresponds to the Hebrew term TZEVA SHAMAIM or TZAVA SHEL MA'ALA, which means "a heavenly army" or "the army of above." This term appears in the Bible also in I Kings 22:19, Jeremiah 19:13, Hosea 13:4, and II Chronicles 33:3.

The angels' praise is recorded in verse 14, which is known as the "Gloria"; however, it is actually part of a Jewish liturgy known as the KEDUSHA, meaning "holiness." It seems that Luke was familiar with some form of the Kedusha prayer, whether written or oral.

> Wrapping a baby with swaddling clothes was not a sign of poverty, as some have believed, but rather of a baby well taken care of.

Christian scholars often assume that all the passages expressing praises and holiness must have come from a Jewish/Christian source. They find it difficult to believe that such passages could have been communicated by non-Christians.

In reality, though, most of these passages, including this one here, existed decades before any believer in Jesus existed. They stem from mainstream early Judaism. Perhaps, it would be helpful to realize that everything that came into Christianity, such as the concepts of the God of the creation, Messiah,

Holy Spirit, baptism, repentance, loving-kindness (known in Christianity as "Grace"), atonement and much more, all came directly from Judaism, and it had been a part of Judaism for hundreds of years before Christianity arrived on the scene.

The term "Glory to God in the Highest" does not appear in the Tanach, but it is found often in the Jewish Apocrypha[20].

The idea of angels praising God is common in Judaism. It appears in the Tanach and also in Jewish literature that describes the reaction of the angels to God's creation.

"On the earth peace for men with whom he is pleased"—there are different translations of this. Some have translated it as "on the earth peace for men of good will."

The first translation appears to be more faithful to the Greek text and also to the Hebraic idiom translated here, which is BENAY RETZONO, literally meaning "the sons of his will"—i.e. those who do His will, those who are part of His Kingdom. The same term is also used by the Qumran community[21] to refer to their members only.

The shepherds went to Bethlehem and found Jesus, just as they were told. They communicated to the parents and whoever else was around what they had seen and heard. We are told in verse 18 that Mary kept these things to herself. In verse 20, we see the shepherds praising God for revealing to them all these wonders—meaning, revealing to them that which He was doing.

CHAPTER 7 ENDNOTES

1. Lamentation Raba 1:15.
2. Jerome, Epistle to Paulinus.
3. Origen, Contra Celsum I 51.
4. The Mishna, Shkalim 7 (4).
5. Passover sacrifices had to have certain qualification. For instance, they had to be males, one year old only, without blemish, according to the specifications found in Exodus 12:5–6.
6. The Mishna, Shkalim 7 (4).
7. Ibid, Baba Kama 7 (7).
8. Ibid, Beitza 5 (7).
9. Ibid, 40:1.
10. Ibid, Taanit 1 (3).
11. Alfred Edersheim, *The life and Time of Jesus, the Messiah*, p.187.
12. The Targum on Genesis 35:21.
13. Targum pseudo-Jonathan on Genesis 35:21.
14. Talmud Bavli, Sanhedrin 25b.
15. Targum pseudo-Jonathan on Micah 5:2.
16. Pirkay De Rabbi Eliezer, chapter 3.
17. The Yerushalmi, Berachot 2:3.
18. Wisdom of Solomon 7:4-5.
19. Jubilees 2:2-3, DSS 11Qpsa 96.
20. I Esdras 9:8, IV Maccabees 1:12.
21. DSS, 1QH 4:32-33; 1QH 11:9.

CHAPTER 8

CIRCUMCISION, REDEMPTION AND PURIFICATION

LUKE 2:21–40

We covered circumcision to some extent when we dealt with the circumcision ceremony of John. I would like to add further information concerning it now. Circumcision is a covenant that God made with Abraham and his descendants. It is an act of voluntary obedience to God and accepts the privileges and the obligation of the Abrahamic covenant. Circumcision is an operation of removing part of or the entire foreskin that covers the glands of the penis[1].

In Judaism, circumcision began to be accepted with the covenant that God made with Abraham, who circumcised himself at the age of ninety-nine years old (Genesis 17:11–12). At the same time, he also circumcised Ishmael and the males in his household. One year later, Isaac was born and he was circumcised on the eighth day of his life, in accordance with God's commandment. According to rabbinic tradition, Abraham circumcised himself on the 10th of Tishray, a day which eventually became known as the Day of Atonement.

The commandment of circumcision is considered to be very important in Judaism. The rabbis said, "Were it not for the blood of the covenant, heaven and earth would have not existed"[2].

One cannot find a stronger statement than this! And indeed, the punishment for not obeying this commandment was KARET, meaning "cut off." In other words, whoever did not obey was cut off from the community of Israel (Genesis 21:4). In the rabbinic world, this was translated as "Excision at the hand of heaven from the community." In other words, it was not the leaders who cut the people off.

According to the rabbis, circumcision existed before God commanded it to Israel. It became rooted in Israel and was considered to be a religious practice as God commanded, and also it was and is considered to be something that characterized the Israelites. In Exodus 12:44 and 48, it states that only the circumcised could partake of the Paschal sacrifice. Circumcise here refers to an Israelite since foreigners were not allowed to participate in the sacrifice, nor were they allowed in the Temple, where the ceremony was carried out.

In Judaism, circumcision began to be accepted with the covenant that God made with Abraham, who circumcised himself at the age of ninety-nine years old (Genesis 17:11–12).

Joshua circumcised the Israelites before they entered the Land of Israel. During their years of wandering, the children of Israel were not circumcised because of the dangers of the journey (Joshua 5:2).

Later on, under the influence of Queen Jezebel, circumcision was stopped in Israel for a period of time (I Kings 19:14). Elijah complained about it to God in I Kings 19:10 and 14, thus he was considered to have been instrumental in restoring it, and he is called "The herald of the covenant." Therefore, in many synagogues today, there is a chair known as "the chair of Elijah," which is placed at the circumcision ceremony, it is left unoccupied for Elijah.

According to some rabbinic Midrashim, after Elijah complained to God, He expected Elijah to attend all the circumcision ceremonies in the future. Elijah is also considered to be "The angel (messenger) of the covenant" of Malachi 3:1 and the angel guardian of the Jewish child.

During the time of the prophets, the term "uncircumcised" became an idiom for "rebellious of the heart" and for those with a "hard to hear ear" (Ezekiel 44:9; Jeremiah 6:10). Jeremiah said that "All the nations were uncircumcised in the flesh, but the whole houses of Israel were of an uncircumcised heart" (Jeremiah 9:25)—i.e., the house of Israel was a rebellious nation.

The word "uncircumcised" in Hebrew is AREL. At times, it is attached to another word and forms an Hebraic idiom, as in the term AREL SEPHATAIM, which is used in Exodus 6:12, 30, where Moses told God that he was unable to speak to Pharaoh because he did not have a fluent speech. The term literally means "uncircumcised lips," but it is used idiomatically to mean "unable to speak clearly."

During the time of the prophets, the term "uncircumcised" became an idiom for "rebellious of the heart" and for those with a "hard to hear ear" (Ezekiel 44:9; Jeremiah 6:10).

The fact that it was used as an idiom for a rebellious heart does not affect in any way the physical commandment of God given to the nation of Israel. Israel was to be both circumcised in the flesh and have a circumcised heart, not one or the other. Circumcised heart then, does not replace circumcision.

During Hellenistic times, circumcision was neglected to some extent[3]. Many Jews wanted to participate in the Greek sport games, which were conducted in the nude. Some of them underwent painful operations in order to remove the marks of circumcision.

Antiochus Epiphanies was the first ruler who prohibited circumcision[4]. Mothers who had circumcised their sons during his rule suffered martyrdom[5]. After the Maccabees won their victory, King John Hyrcanus forced the conquered Edomites to undergo circumcision[6]. The second person to prohibit circumcision was the Emperor Hadrian. This was one of the reasons that led to the Bar-Kochva rebellion.

With the rise of Christianity, circumcision became initially the difference between Jewish followers of Jesus and Gentile believers, and eventually the difference between Christianity and Judaism.

Circumcision of the child was and still is the responsibility and obligation of the father[7]. It is not considered to be a sacrament in Judaism.

Any child born of a Jewish mother is a Jew, whether he is circumcised or not.

Although anyone can perform a circumcision, it is preferable that it is performed by a MOHEL, who is loyal to the Torah. A Mohel is a person who is trained in the technique of circumcision and has rabbinic approval. Mohels are considered to be craftsmen.

The circumcision operation is performed on the eighth day after birth, ideally early in the morning in order to imitate Abraham's eagerness to fulfill the divine commandment. Circumcision can also take place on the Sabbath or a festival[8]. If the child is of poor health, the ceremony should be postponed until he recovers. According to Jewish law, if the child was born circumcised, miraculously, the ceremony still needs to take place on the eighth day. This is done by puncturing the skin and drawing one drop of blood.

In 1843, the leaders of the Reformed movement in Frankfort wanted to abolish circumcision. Their dispute, which lasted for twenty years, eventually spread to the U.S. They listed five reasons for their objections:

1. It was commanded to Abraham but not to Moses. It is not distinctive to Israel since the descendants of Ishmael also practice it.
2. It is mentioned only once in the Torah and not repeated in Deuteronomy.
3. Moses did not circumcise his own son.
4. The generations of the desert were not circumcised.
5. There is no initiation of daughters into Judaism.

All these objections were answered by Orthodox Judaism. Today, most reformed Jews do circumcise their children.

Many people circumcise their children today. For instance, the descendants of Ishmael circumcise their children, but they do not do it on the eighth day, instead at the age of 13, the same age that Ishmael was circumcised. In the US, for years now, male babies are circumcised in a hospital, usually on the third day after birth, for health reasons.

Some Muslim countries and also some African tribes circumcise girls as well. Female circumcision is unbiblical and brutal. In an attempt to stop girls' circumcision, in the past, different groups called for the abolition of circumcision in the US. Today, they claim other reasons for their conviction that circumcision must be stopped.

These people consider male circumcision to be mutilation as well and are very concerned because the child, being only a few days old, cannot give his consent. If circumcision becomes outlawed, it would make the life of Jews in the US impossible.

In Genesis 17:12-13, circumcision was made obligatory for all children of Israel—all the Jews. Christians misunderstand this point due to a misinterpretation of Paul's letter to the Galatians. Paul, of course, wrote this epistle to Gentiles—not to Jews! Paul himself was not against biblical circumcision. In Acts 16:1, Paul circumcised Timothy for the sake of the Jews. He did so because Timothy was a Jew, born to a Jewish mother and, therefore, he was obligated by the Torah to be circumcised. It was the right thing to do so.

The Abrahamic covenant is still in effect today, and so the commandment of circumcision given to the descendants of Abraham, Isaac and Jacob is still obligatory for all Jews. So all of the descendants of Jacob, whether followers of Jesus or anyone else or not, should circumcise their male children on the eighth day, so they may keep their part in the covenant of blood that God made with them originally.

Genesis 17:13 states that the commandment is for BRIT OLAM—an everlasting covenant with regard to its duration. And, of course, everlasting means what it says—everlasting. The obligation for all Jews to circumcise their children does not end with the birth of Jesus as Paul makes clear in Acts 16 and 21.

Incidentally, there is no indication anywhere in the New Testament that Gentile followers of Jesus, by becoming believers, also become Jews. If this were the case, Gentile believers would be obliged to get circumcised, and Paul would have treated Titus' situation the same way as he treated Timothy's.

The New Testament does not support the idea that is voiced at times by Christians who claim, "We are all Jews now!" Some Gentile believers call themselves "spiritual Jews." But this is an incorrect usage of the term. A Gentile believer can only be a spiritual Gentile! A spiritual Jew is a Jew who has circumcision, both of the flesh and of the heart. A spiritual Jew cannot be a Gentile, just as a spiritual woman cannot be a man. She is either a woman or a man, but she cannot be both. We are either Jews or Gentiles, but we cannot be both.

Throughout the New Testament, there are two complementary principles on this issue:

1. Jews should circumcise their children.
2. Gentiles should not be circumcised in an attempt to attain a higher status before God because in one's status before God, being a Jew or a Gentile is irrelevant.

In testament to these principles, Paul circumcised Timothy who was Jewish, but refused to circumcise Titus who was not Jewish. It is also important to note that in every mention in the New Testament of people being exempted from the requirement of circumcision, it was Gentiles who were exempted, not Jews.

The Circumcision of Jesus

The New Testament cannot go against God's commandment in the Tanach. Thus Jewish followers of Jesus were never exempted from the commandment of circumcision. They are still descendants of Abraham, Isaac and Jacob. They are still Jewish and their Jewishness still has meaning no matter whom they follow, not to mention the fact they are still members of the covenant that God made with Israel. Therefore, they are under obligation to fulfill their part in it. Otherwise, they would be guilty of violating it.

Thus Jewish followers of Jesus were never exempted from the commandment of circumcision. They are still descendants of Abraham, Isaac and Jacob.

Just as Gentiles do not become Jews if they became followers of Jesus, so also Jews do not become Gentiles if they become followers of Jesus. Many pastors and lay Christians put this idea forward. However, it is a damaging and a very confusing theory.

Being a Jew means being part of the covenantal society. It means that one is a part of the covenant that God made with Israel and, therefore, a Jew is obligated to keep its commandments all of his life. The so-called "law" spells out the terms of this covenant! One cannot claim he is part of this covenant but not obligated to keep it.

This kind of claim is unbiblical! In the Bible, God obligated all the descendants of Abraham, Isaac and Jacob to keep the terms of this covenant.

The church claims it is no longer under the Law and, therefore, there is no need for anyone to keep these old customs. Now they are free!

Think about it. Free from what? Free from the Word of God? Free from His commandments? I thought it was the truth that sets man free! Is truth not spelled out for people in the Word of God? How ironic!

The reality is that the church and the Gentile world were never "under the Law"! They were never part of this covenant that God made with Israel. They are not a party to this contract and, therefore, they should not worry about keeping its terms because it does not obligate them! And, therefore, they should not be concerned with it.

Being a Jew means being part of the covenantal society. It means that one is a part of the covenant that God made with Israel and, therefore, a Jew is obligated to keep its commandments all of his life.

Here we are at Jesus' circumcision, and just like John, Jesus was also circumcised and named on the eighth day after birth. This is all that Luke tells us. He hardly pays any attention to Jesus' circumcision. Some Christians say that Jesus' circumcision calls attention to his solidarity with the human race. But the human race was not circumcised! Nevertheless, it definitely established his solidarity with the Jewish people, and his identity as a Jew. And if he were not a Jew, no one could have claimed that he was the Messiah. This whole concept of Messiah is a Jewish concept. There was no such thing as "a messiah" in the pagan mind.

Luke moved from the circumcision ceremony directly to the purification and the redemption ceremonies, although there was a gap of thirty-two days between the circumcision of Jesus and his redemption ceremony. He discussed both the redemption and the purification ceremonies in verses 22–24:

> "And when the days of their purification according to the Law of Moses were completed, they brought him up to Jerusalem to present him to The Lord. (As it is written in the law of The Lord, every first born male that opens the womb shall be called holy to The Lord). And to offer a sacrifice according to what was said in the law of The Lord, a pair of turtledoves, or two young pigeons."

There are several problems with this section. We have a bit of confusion between the two different ceremonies commanded in the Torah. Luke seems to have mixed up the ceremony of the redemption of the first-born son with that of the purification of the mother.

To begin, Luke used the word "Their" purification rather than "Her" purification, implying that both parents and even all three of them needed purification. Whereas, according to the Torah, only Mary needed it. He also gave the impression that they went to the Temple for the ceremony of the redemption of the first-born son. Whereas, only the purification ceremony demanded appearance in the Temple.

Taking a child up to Jerusalem for the redemption ceremony is not found anywhere in the Tanach, or in the Second Temple period literature or in the Mishna. Not to mention that a trip from Galilee to Jerusalem would have been difficult and would have put the child's survival in danger.

Luke also did not mention the main point of the redemption, which is the use of money. He instead mentioned the sacrifice, which is not connected to this ceremony, but rather to the purification ceremony. All of these anomalies have led different scholars to the conclusion that Luke possibly misunderstood the tradition, or that he misread the laws of the Torah.

It is quite possible that Luke did not have an accurate understanding of the customs as many scholars believe today. He was a proselyte to Judaism, was not raised as a Jew, and only had book knowledge of the Bible[9]. Edersheim claimed that it was quite possible that the purification and redemption ceremonies could be combined[10], although there is no support for this in Judaism or in any literature of the time.

The Redemption of the First Born Son

We have here two distinct ceremonies—the first one is known as PIDION HABEN—the redemption of the first-born son. The ceremony usually takes place a month—thirty-one days—after the birth of the child. It is only the first-born son who goes through this ceremony.

Exodus 13:1, 12 require that all first-born sons be consecrated to God because He had saved the lives of the first-born Israelites in Egypt. As a result, the first-born of Israel was to spend his lifetime serving God. In time, the tribe of Levi took over this service and rendered it—the service of the first-born—unnecessary.

This change was recognized legally in Numbers 8:15–16, which made a provision for first-born sons to be bought back from The Lord for the sum of five silver shekels. Although the money was to be paid at the Temple, there was no obligation to bring the child there. The price was due on the thirty-first day of the child's life. So, in fact, Joseph and Mary were ten days late here, but that was not unusual.

At the time of the ceremony, the child had to be healthy and without any blemishes because all first-born sons were initially intended for the priesthood. The main point and purpose of this ceremony was for the father to purchase his child from the priest, and it could be any priest, for the sum of five shekels. Mothers did not have to attend this ceremony, but they usually did if they could.

The Purification of the Mother

The second ceremony is the ceremony of the purification of the mother. According to the Torah, Leviticus 12:2–8, a woman who gave birth to a son, was considered to be ritually unclean for 40 days, and only after that period could she enter the Temple. So technically speaking, Mary could not have come to the Temple before this point. A mother who gave birth to a female child was considered to be ritually unclean for 80 days, twice as long.

When the time elapsed, the mother was to bring to the Temple a sacrifice for a burnt offering—a one-year-old lamb—and one young pigeon or a turtle-dove for a sin offering and give it to the priest at the door. If she could not afford the lamb, which was much more expensive, she was to bring instead two pigeons or two turtledoves. This offering was called KORBAN ANI—the sacrifice of the poor (Leviticus 5:7). Here we learn that Joseph and Mary were very poor at this point.

In order to prevent the poor from being exploited by the people who bought and sold sacrifices in the Temple, there was a special provision for the purchasing of the birds for sacrifices. In the Temple were thirteen horn-shaped chests into which people used to put money for various purposes.

> According to the Torah, Leviticus 12:2–8, a woman who gave birth to a son, was considered to be ritually unclean for 40 days, and only after that period could she enter the Temple.

The third chest was for the payment for the purchasing of the birds. Those who needed this sacrifice would place money in this chest.

The Temple officials would then take the money from the chest and offer the amount of the sacrifice on behalf of the people. This was the cheapest available sacrifice, and it was done in this way in order to maintain the dignity of the poor and also to prevent uncleanness in Israel. If the poor could not afford this price either, they were to give whatever they could, and the Temple officials would cover the rest.

Each day at a given time, an organ was sounded in the Temple, indicating that the time had arrived for the incense to be lit in the golden altar. The women who were to be purified that day were then escorted to one of the gates of the Temple that was located higher than the women's court, indicating they were to be honored for bringing another child into the house of Israel. Mary was among them on that day.

For My Eyes Have Seen Thy Salvation

In the Temple in Jerusalem, they met a man named Simeon. We do not know who he was, and from the way the text talks about him, he appeared to be unknown. In other literature[11], it is stated that his age was 112, but we cannot know if this was indeed the case. There is no doubt, though, that he was old in age.

Simeon is described as someone righteous and pious, someone who had lived his life according to the Torah. He is also described as one who was looking forward to the consolation of Israel—or in Hebrew, NECHAMAT ISRAEL. This is a reference to the Messiah since the Messiah is often referred to in a similar terms.

In rabbinic writings and also in the Targums on the Books of Isaiah and Jeremiah, he is called the MENACHEM—he who consoles or comforts. These two terms come from the same root NICHEM, meaning HE COMFORTED. This text is saying then that Simeon was waiting to see the consolation of Israel—i.e., he was waiting to see the Messiah.

We are told that he was under the influence of the Holy Spirit. And indeed the Holy Spirit is often mentioned in rabbinic writings as speaking to individuals or speaking through them[12], just as it can be seen in the Tanach with the prophets and in the Gospels with both Zechariah and Elizabeth as discussed in the previous chapter.

"Now Lord, thou dost let Thy bond-servant depart in peace, according to thy word."

It was by the Holy Spirit, according to Luke, that Simeon was promised he would not die before seeing The Lord's Anointed. This must have been important to Simeon, probably his heart's desire, which God apparently granted him.

This was translated as "The Lord's Christ," but it literally means "The Lord's Anointed"—i.e., he who was anointed by God. The same term is also used in I Samuel 24:7,11; 26:9,11,15, and 23 and in other literature as well[13]. In verse 27 we learn, literally, that the Spirit led him to the Temple.

In verse 29, when Simeon saw the child, he took him into his arms and blessed him, saying, "Now Lord, thou dost let Thy bond-servant depart in peace, according to thy word." Simeon is simply saying that he can now die in peace because God had fulfilled what He promised to him. Because Simeon blessed them, some have believed that he was a priest, but this idea is unfounded.

Simeon then sang a song, "For my eyes have seen Thy salvation." The same phrase appears in Genesis 46:30, where it is spoken by Jacob/Israel. It looks like we have a bit of comparison here since the Targum on this verse stated that Jacob, although he was speaking to Joseph, was looking forward to the redemption that God would bring his people[14].

This salvation, Simeon said, was prepared before all peoples and, of course, the salvation of God is for all people.

He went on to say, "A light of revelation to the Gentiles and the glory of Thy people Israel."

This is going to touch all people because it is going to have an effect on both groups of people that existed—the Gentiles and Israel—the Jews—a revelation to the Gentiles and a glory for the people of Israel.

Notice the order here, first to the Gentiles and then to the Jews. This child. according to Luke, will be an amazing revelation for the Gentiles, and he will eventually become the Glory of Israel. We see this pattern communicated again and again in the Gospels.

There are two parts to this song, and in between we have Jesus' parents' reaction. That brought some scholars to the conclusion that the song was redundant and probably a later addition. However, the first part, verses 29 through 32, communicates the good things the child would do and bring, whereas the second part, verses 34 and 35, communicates the negative things that would follow.

Incidentally, we find a real parallel to the positive part here in the first-century work known as the "Psalms of Solomon."[15] It also echoes Isaiah 52:9–10, 49:6, 42:6, and 40:5. All of these Scriptures communicate the theme of seeing salvation for all people, a light to the Gentiles and Glory to Israel. The light is to come to the Gentiles, but they are to come to Jerusalem, for Israel is God's people.

The parents are said to be amazed, and obviously they were amazed at the good and great things that this son was going to do, and probably very sad about the negative things they learned were also a part of his future role.

The fact that the parents were amazed at all is puzzling. Did they not remember what the angel told them at the stable? Could Mary have actually forgotten what Gabriel told her, or did they have a hard time believing it, in spite of the miraculous birth? Well, we will never know why they reacted this way.

In the second part, we hear that Jesus would cause many to rise and fall in Israel; many would stumble because of him. He would be a cause for conflict, something we know to be true, even today, as families fight bitterly over the question of his Messiahship.

Verse 35 is obscure. It is not clear about what the "sword" that is going to go through Mary is. The Church Fathers came up with all sorts of ideas, none of them sound and none supported by the text. The only possibility I can see is that we have here a symbolic language describing the pain that she is going to experience at the premature death of her son.

Anna from the Tribe of Asher

In addition to meeting Simeon at the Temple, they also met a woman named Anna from the Tribe of Asher. The Tribe of Asher was not one of the main tribes nor did it dwell in Judah, but rather in western Galilee. Anna then is obviously not in her home territory. She probably moved into the area of Jerusalem in order to be near the Temple.

The fact that the Tribe of Asher is mentioned here goes against the idea of British Israelism, which claims that ten tribes were lost and actually developed into Gentile nations. Those who hold to this theory can also tell you what nations the tribes became. The claim is they got lost after the exile of 722 BCE. Only two tribes remained, Judah and Benjamin, which were attached to Judah and Levi. Well, here we are in the first century CE, and it appears that Asher was still around! The biblical data we have renders this theory false.

> "A light of revelation to the Gentiles and the glory of Thy people Israel."

According to the text, Anna was worshiping day and night in the Temple. This is probably a reference to her participation in the prayers of the people attending the daily sacrifices. Anna is described here as a "prophetess." She is the only woman who is described as such in the New Testament, other than Jezebel who called herself a prophetess in Revelation 2:20. Even so, there are several references to women who prophesied among them (Acts 2:17, 21:9; I Corinthians 11:5). In the Tanach, the following women carried this title: Miriam, Deborah, Hulda and Isaiah's wife.

According to the information given here, Anna must have been 103 years old. She was twelve when she married. She lived with her husband for seven years, and she was a widow for eighty-four years. The words she spoke were not recorded for us.

In summing up this section, we see that Luke mentioned the Torah here three times in verses 22–24, 27 and 39. He was obviously emphasizing the Jewishness of Jesus, as well as communicating that everything that Jesus would do in the future—all the great things that he was destined to perform—would be made possible through his obedience to God and to His Torah.

Luke also mentioned the Holy Spirit three times in verses 25–27 in reference to Simeon. So he provided a description of two prophets—Simeon and Anna who were predicting the future greatness of the child. So at the end, the story implies that we have two witnesses as the Torah and the Prophets came together in order to confirm Jesus' role in the future.

CHAPTER 8 ENDNOTES

1. Judaica, Vol. V, pg. 567, circumcision.
2. Talmud Bavli, Shabbat 137b.
3. Jubilees 15:33-34.
4. I Maccabees 1:48.
5. II Maccabees 6:10.
6. Josephus Antiquities, 13:257.
7. Shulchan Aruch YD 260:1.
8. Shulchan Aruch YD 260:1.
9. Brown, The Life of Christ, p. 449.
10. Edersheim, *The Life and Times of Jesus the Messiah*, Book II, p. 194.
11. The Gospel of Pseudo-Matthew 15:2.
12. Bamidbar Raba 15:20; Midrash on Ruth 2:9.
13. Psalms of Solomon 18:8; 17:36.
14. M. McNamara, the NT and the Palestinian Targum to the Pentateuch (Analecta Biblica 27: Rome, Pontifical Biblical Institute, 1966), pp. 243-245.
15. Psalms of Solomon 17:34-18:8.

CHAPTER 9

THE WISE MEN VISIT

MATTHEW 2:1–12

Mathew is the only Gospel writer who recorded the visit of the wise men, just as Luke is the only Gospel writer who recorded the story of the shepherds. This is interesting since Matthew apparently wrote to the Jews, and yet he recorded the first Gentiles who came to pay homage to Jesus.

This chapter is presented in two parts. Firstly, the text is covered verse by verse. Secondly, the general story of the wise men is discussed.

Verse 1—The first thing that appears is the affirmation that Jesus was born in Bethlehem, as expected. As mentioned before, the rabbis recognized that Micah 5:1–2, which is quoted here in verse 6 and which predicts that a ruler will be born in Bethlehem, is a reference to the Messiah[1].

Matthew used the phrase "Bethlehem of Judea" probably in order to make a distinction between this town and Bethlehem in the territory of Zebulun (Joshua 19:15–16). Perhaps he also mentioned it because he wanted to emphasize that Jesus was a descendant of the tribe of Judah.

"In the days of Herod the King"—This is a reference to "Herod the Great," who lived from 73 BCE to 4 BCE. He founded the Herodian dynasty, which ruled Israel from 37 BCE to 70 CE. He himself ruled over Judea from 37 BCE until his death. He was the second son of an Edomite named Antipater.

Herod was born in southern Israel. His father, Antipater, was an Idumæan (an Arab from the region between the Dead Sea and the Gulf of Aqaba). Antipater was a man of great influence and wealth who increased both by marrying the daughter of a noble from Petra in southwestern Jordan, which was at that time the capital of the rising Nabataean kingdom. So, Herod was of Arab origin on both sides, although his ancestors converted to Judaism[2], so he was raised as a Jew, but he never practiced Judaism.

Although we know nothing about his youth, it is clear that he started the struggle for power early in his life. In 47 BCE, Antipater appointed him as governor of Galilee. He crushed the revolt that was led by Hezekiah against Antipater, and he put to death, without trial, all the rebels.

For this he was tried before the Sanhedrin in Jerusalem. He would have been put to death, but somehow he managed to slip out of the city when Hyrcanus ll interrupted the session.

He escaped to Syria, and there the Roman governor appointed him to be a governor of Coele-Syria in Samaria. At that point, Herod was able to return to Jerusalem and threaten his enemies. Later, he was appointed King of Judea in Rome by Octavian.

When Herod came to power, he took absolute control over the government by putting to death 45 members of the Sanhedrin who were supporters of the Hasmoneans.

In 37 BCE, he laid a siege to Jerusalem using a mercenary's army that he himself put together along with an army sent to him from Rome. Jerusalem held against them for five months, but at the end of that summer, it fell into their hands. When Herod came to power, he took absolute control over the government by putting to death 45 members of the Sanhedrin who were supporters of the Hasmoneans. This, of course, destroyed the political power of the Sanhedrin. He also took upon himself the appointment of High Priests. During his rule, he arbitrarily chose them and dismissed them.

Slowly, he gathered control over other territories in the area, and by 19 BC he had control over the whole region that previously was under the rule of the Hasmoneans. At that time, he was considered to be one of the most powerful monarchs in the area and was given the title "Herod the Great."

Rome controlled him but when it came to internal affairs, he was given unlimited authority. He had power in four areas: administrative, judicial, financial, and military with maintenance of his own army. In these areas, he did what he pleased and answered to no one, not even Jewish law.

His government, officials, counselors and army were all Hellenistic in nature and primarily made up of Gentiles.

Even though he married the Hasmonean daughter Miriam, he still feared them and saw them as a threat to his throne; therefore, he put to death all the members of the Hasmonean house. He even accused his own wife of adultery, put her before a court which found her guilty, and executed her at the age of twenty-nine. Later in 7 BCE, Herod also executed his and Miriam's two sons: Alexander and Aristobulus. He also executed his son Antipater a few days before he died in 4 BCE.

Upon his death, his kingdom was divided among three of his remaining sons: Archelous, Herod Antipas, and Phillip.

Herod was an energetic and efficient administrator. He was a talented diplomat and knew how to influence people. He ruled with cruelty. During his reign, he destroyed the internal organization of the Jewish community.

In practice, he did away with the authority of the Torah; he wanted to bring the land of Israel fully into Hellenistic culture. In order to do so, he built all sorts of Hellenistic buildings like theatres and gymnasiums. He did this not only in Israel but also in Syria and in Greece. He built many cities of which Caesarea was just one example. He built many palaces for himself in many different cities, and he also built many fortresses, of which the most well known are the Fortress of Antonia and Masada.

As already mentioned, Herod was the son of Antipater, an Idumæan[3]. According to Josephus, the Idumæans were brought under subjection by John

Hyrcanus towards the end of the second century BCE and were obliged to live as Jews, so they were considered to be Jews[4]. Yet Antigonos called Herod a half Jew[5].

In order to show his loyalty to Judaism and to gain favor with the people, Herod wanted to enlarge and embellish the Temple, but the mountain on which Solomon built the first Temple and on which Zechariah and Haggai built the second was just too small for his plans. That did not stop Herod. He dramatically increased the size of the Temple mount by constructing huge encasement walls and filling them with pure dirt, creating a large trapezoid. He was then able to proceed with his architectural plans to enlarge the Temple and its courtyards.

But this did not help him. The people never forgot the murders of the leaders and his other atrocities. As a result, the Temple became known in history as Herod's Temple, even though Zerubabel built it in 520–516 BCE. The rabbis noted the beauty of the Temple[6] but claimed that Herod constructed it in order to atone for the sages of Israel whom he had slain[7].

Verse 1 continues using the phrase "Magi from the East." The word Magi seems to have originated in Babylon. The English word Magic, as is evident, comes from this word. We find this word not only in the New Testament, but also in the LXX (Septuagint) version of the Tanach and in Jewish writings[8]. It was also used by Josephus and by Philo[9] in two ways: referring to evil and also to good.

As a reference to evil, it is used primarily to refer to the practice of magical arts. It is used in this manner also in Acts 8:9 and 13:6, 8. The word is rarely used in a positive sense. When it is, it refers to pagan priests/sages who had knowledge in some areas, but who were also influenced by many superstitious beliefs.

Initially, the Magi were Zoroastrian priests. In time, the word Magi came to mean a master of divination. Eventually, it became a general term for magicians and sorcerers.

In the Septuagint version of the Book of Daniel (2nd Century BCE), the Magi are described as flourishing in every corner of Babylon. Along with the enchanters and astrologers, they competed over their ability to interpret dreams (Daniel 1:20, 2:2, 4:7, 5:7). The Book of Daniel actually defines

Magi, referring to wise men as "magicians, conjurers, and those who practice divination" (Daniel 4:6–7, 5:7).

The term then relates to those who had evil occupations—in the arts of magic and witchcraft. Interestingly enough, myrrh and incense were also used in the practices of incantation.

Matthew's Magi are described in a positive light. They are decent people and actually represent the best of the pagan culture that came to seek the King of the Jews. Thus they represent the Gentile world.

Throughout the narrative of the birth of Jesus, there is a comparison between Jesus and Moses, which starts here and continues throughout Jesus' life. This comparison must have been emphasized in light of God's promise to Israel to raise unto them a man like Moses.

The Book of Daniel actually defines Magi, referring to wise men as "magicians, conjurers, and those who practice divination" (Daniel 4:6–7, 5:7).

In a future volume of this book series, I will provide a comparison between the two. Until then, as we progress, I will keep pointing out the things in common that happened in relation to both of them.

There is also somewhat of a comparison here with the Magi. Just like the magicians in Egypt were defeated by Moses' demonstration of power, so also the Magi in our story are led to kneel at the feet of Jesus. This symbolizes the surrender of their improper practices.

"From the East"—there is no indication in this text as to their original location. The word that was translated here as "East" is the word ANATOLE in Greek, which literally means "rising."

Since the sun rises in the East, it seems to have become a synonym. "In the East," at the time, was primarily a reference to Babylon. And in Babylon lived a very large Jewish community. This is important because they came seeking the Jewish king.

Information and knowledge concerning the Messiah they could only have obtained in a Jewish community. There were no expectations or knowledge among the Gentile nations of a coming deliverer to Israel.

In Babylon, there was also a great interest in Astrology, so Magi had originated and prospered there. Thus it appears that the Magi came from Babylon.

Verse 2—They asked, "Where is the king of the Jews?" The phrase "King of the Jews" is used in the New Testament only by Gentiles. The Magi used it here. Later, it was used by Pilate and the Roman soldiers (Matthew 27:3; Mark 15:26; Luke 23:3, 38; John 19:19). It is interesting that Herod carried the same title; he too was known as "King of the Jews." That might explain his anger when they came looking for the King of the Jews, and they were not looking for him.

The appearance of a star at the birth of a hero, or a holy man, or a great leader, seems to be commonplace in many legends.

Continuing, they said, "We saw his star in the East"—i.e. we saw his star at its rising. The word "star" here is ASTERA in Greek and it means "star, bright and light." The appearance of a star at the birth of a hero, or a holy man, or a great leader, seems to be commonplace in many legends. For instance, it was predicted that Alexander the Great was destined to conquer all of Asia, from the appearance of a bright constellation on the night of his birth[10]. This can also be found in Jewish sources where we read about a star appearing during Moses' birth. It is also said that a star stood above Jerusalem shortly before the destruction of the city, indicating the coming of an important event[11].

His star is a reference to Numbers 24:17, where the star of Balaam is mentioned. This star was always understood in Judaism to be a reference to the Messiah. At one point, the verse was understood as a reference to Bar Kochva, who led an unsuccessful rebellion against Rome in 132 CE.

Rabbi Simon Bar Yochai used to say, "My teacher Akiva would expound: 'A star rises from Jacob—Kotziba rises from Jacob.'"

Rabbi Akiva, when he would see Bar Kotziba, would recite, "This is King Messiah"[12]. The name Bar Kochva means "son of a star." His name originally was Bar Kochva, but it was changed by people to Bar Koziva, meaning "son of deception" to indicate that he was not the Messiah.

Later on we see that the star they saw in the East reappeared to the Magi when they left Herod's palace, and it directed them to Bethlehem. It seems that the Magi did not need the star to lead them to Jerusalem since it was very well known. But they needed the star to direct them to Bethlehem, which was, until that time, an unknown little town.

The star, according to verse 9, led them to the house where the child was. It was very common at the time to hear about stars leading people to one place or another, but a star leading to a house was, even then, an unusual thing. The whole idea of a star hovering over a house presents a celestial phenomenon unparalleled in astronomical history. This, of course, cannot happen without the universe being disintegrated.

"And came to worship Him"—The word translated as "worship" is the Greek word PROSKUNEO, which literally means "to bow down." This statement is, therefore, better translated as "came to pay homage to him" as one would do to a king—paid respect, rather than the idea of a worship of divinity. At this point, there was not even an inkling in anyone's mind concerning worship. Jesus was only a baby. Although he may have been considered to be the Messiah by his mother, in Jewish context, which it was, it is God who is worshipped and not the Messiah.

The Messiah is considered to be His messenger who will bring the world back to worship God fully. Christianity at this point had not yet evolved, so there was no question of deification either. The account of the wise men does not meet the Jewish expectations of the nations paying homage to the Messiah.

Verse 3—"Herod was troubled and all Jerusalem with him." No doubt that Herod was troubled. Any mention of the Messiah would have presented to him a threat to his throne. And, as we have seen before, he was paranoid when it came to his power.

As for "all Jerusalem," the people must have feared Herod's reaction because they knew him too well and could then anticipate that this would lead to a disaster of some sort. Someone could be killed as a result. And indeed we are told that Herod killed the children of Bethlehem.

Christian scholars often state that Herod was afraid that a Messiah would arise and conspire with the Jews to kill him. This kind of statement presents sheer ignorance of Judaism, not to mention an unbalanced perspective of the Jewish history of the time.

Verse 4—"And gathering together all the chief priests and scribes." This is a reference to some of the Sanhedrin members, whom Herod summoned to him. The term "chief priests" in plural is not necessarily a mistake. The term also appears this way in Josephus and in the Mishna. It is usually in reference to what is known as "the worthy class."

The priests had different classes:

Cohanay Am Ha Aretz—Literally means "the priests of the simple people"—those who were not educated in the rabbinic academies. They were descendants of a priestly family but were not necessarily devoted to religion. Among them, some were ignorant and poor.

Cohanay Hedyotot—"Idiots or private priests." They were educated, but they were of a lower order.

The worthy priests—included the high priests, the Segan (literally means "the priest in the second place after the high priest," the head of the courses, the heads of the families in every course, the presidents over various offices in the Temple and the Levites.

So these were the priests, and with them were also the Scribes, who were scholars. They were the public notaries in the Sanhedrin. They transcribed the Torah, the phylacteries, the mezuzahs, and they wrote bills of contract and divorce.

The Greek word translated as "all" here is the word PAS, which also means "every," which is a better translation in this case. It should have been translated as "and gathering together every chief priest and scribe."

Some scholars rightfully claim that Herod could not possibly have summoned to him the entire Sanhedrin because of the strong opposition that existed between him and them—not to mention the large size of the Sanhedrin, which had 70 members. There was no need to summon them all since bringing in their leaders was sufficient. Most likely, Herod summoned every chief priest—and we know that there were 2 of them at the time—and some of the scribes. There were not that many scribes in the Sanhedrin; therefore, it is safe to assume that the party was made out of no more than ten people.

The people of Israel knew where the Messiah was to be born, but the Gentiles did not, nor did Herod, who remained an Edomite in his heart.

Verses 5–6 are a quote from Micah 5:1–2, in a Targumic manner—i.e., it is a paraphrase.

Verse 9 indicates they left Jerusalem, but not necessarily by night as is commonly assumed.

The people of Israel knew where the Messiah was to be born, but the Gentiles did not, nor did Herod, who remained an Edomite in his heart.

Moving now to the story itself. In the past, people used to argue over the question of whether or not the Magi were Jews or Gentiles. There is really no reason for questioning it because the word Magi itself refers most of the time to a Gentile, although there is one reference in Acts to a Jewish Magi (Acts 13:6–8).

It is important to mention that the Book of Daniel pretty much defines the Magim as Gentile magicians as well. More likely than not, they were Gentiles; therefore, an attempt to answer the following questions is made:

1. What was their motive in visiting a Jewish king?
2. What was their source of knowledge concerning the time they should look for the new-born Messiah and concerning the sign they saw rising?

Perhaps more legends have been developed concerning the story of the visit of the wise men than any other section of the New Testament; here are some of them:

1. There were three wise men.
2. They came to a manger.
3. They arrived twelve days after Jesus' birth.
4. They saw a sign in the stars, which told them that the Messiah was to be born.
5. They followed a star from the East.
6. Stars in the sky can identify houses by hovering over them.
7. They did not know any Scriptures.

8. They had no contact with the Jews.
9. They saw the newborn baby Jesus.
10. The wise men visited Jesus at night.

There are more legends, but these will suffice to make the point. Of course, these assumptions find no support in the Gospels.

How many wise men were there? No one knows! The New Testament does not specify. According to the text, there was more than one; the plural form is used here, but that is all. Any number will do.

The Gospels place the visit of the wise men about two years after the visit of the shepherds. How do we know? Verse 11 states they came to a house and not to a manger. The same verse also says they saw "the young child" not the "baby."

The story here is about a group of Magi. They probably were astronomers from Babylon who arrived two years after Jesus' birth, looking for him, saying they had seen his star rising when they were in Babylon.

Both Hebrew and Greek have different words for a baby, a small child, and a toddler, just like English has. The word used here in the Greek is PEDIYON, which refers to a child of least two years of approximate age. This is not the same word used in Luke 2:16 to describe the new-born baby; there the word is BREPHOS.

Jesus' age at the time of the visit of the wise men is also evident from Herod who based the age of the infants he ordered to be killed on the information he had received from the wise men. Verse 7 states that Herod called the wise men secretly and investigated through them the time that the sign appeared. Verse 6 then communicates that he killed the children based on the information they gave him.

Some scholars have found it difficult reconciling the account of Matthew and the account of Luke concerning the birth of Jesus. They say that in Luke, the family went from Nazareth to Bethlehem, and Jesus was born in a stable. In Matthew, the family went from Bethlehem to Egypt, and Jesus was born in a house.

The assumption here is that all this happened within the same time frame. But understanding that this had happened two years after Jesus' birth will help to reconcile the chronology here.

Joseph and Mary came from Nazareth to Bethlehem before Jesus' birth. Mary gave birth in Bethlehem shortly afterward in a stable of some sort. At a later point, they probably took over the property that belonged to them in Beit Lechem, and now they lived there in a house. Two years later, the wise men arrived for a visit, which was followed by an escape of the family to Egypt.

The story here is about a group of Magi. They probably were astronomers from Babylon who arrived two years after Jesus' birth, looking for him, saying they had seen his star rising when they were in Babylon.

Based on this sign, they made a deduction that they are to go to Jerusalem. Nothing in the text indicates they had followed the star to Jerusalem. In verse 2 they stated, "we saw his star rising and we came…" It appears that once they saw the star, they knew their destination was Jerusalem.

Some of the information given here perhaps provides us with an idea of the possible nature of this star. As we saw earlier, the word used here can mean star but also brightness, or just light.

The text indicates that the sign they saw appeared, disappeared and then reappeared. It was there in Babylon, and then it disappeared. About two years later, it reappeared in Jerusalem and directed them to Bethlehem, where it hovered over the family's house. It is clear that we are not dealing here with a neutral star since stars perhaps appear and disappear, but they do not reappear. Stars cannot direct people by moving from one place to another. Neither can they hover over houses without putting an end to our universe.

Since this is not a neutral phenomenon, we should ask ourselves if there is anything in the Bible that fits in with the description of this strength of light. And the answer is yes—the Shechina (the manifested presence of God). The Shechina can appear, disappear, and reappear. The Shechina can direct people to a place, which is obvious from the fact that it guided the Israelites in the desert for forty years. The Shechina can hover over houses; after all, it hovered over the mercy seat and over Jerusalem. The Shechina usually appears as a bright light. In conclusion, by analyzing the information in the text, it appears it was the Shechina and not the stars that guided the wise men to the house.

There are still some questions that need to be answered. For instance, why should Gentiles want to come and pay homage to a Jewish King? After all, Israel is the least of all the Nations (Deuteronomy 7:7). And secondly, how did they recognize that the appearance of the light was a sign for the birth of the Jewish King?

The first thing to remember is that these men were from Babylon. A book had been written in Babylon that predicted the date of the death of the Messiah. It is the Book of Daniel. Daniel chapter 9 states that the Messiah will be "cut off"—ICARET. Cut off is a Hebraic idiom, implying that a death will occur before the age of fifty, not from natural causes but rather by a violent death.

Daniel also provided the time element that would pass until the anointed one would be cut off. Anyone then could have calculated the time, deducting about fifty years and start looking for a sign that would indicate his birth.

But why should Gentile Magi be interested in the Book of Daniel in the first place? Well, the book was written both in Hebrew and in Aramaic, with a large section of the book in Aramaic, the language of the Babylonians. So there was no barrier of language. Daniel himself was associated with the Babylonian wise men. When he was just a little boy, Nebuchadnezzar took some Jewish children to his palace to raise them in order to be his counselors. Among them were four boys—Daniel and the other three who ended up in the fire.

The king made sure they received the best education possible. At the time, astronomy and astrology were considered to be respectable science, and so these were a part of their curriculum. In time, they grew up and one day the king, who was a true wise guy, came and assembled them all. He had a dream and he expected them to tell him what the dream and its meaning were. He gave them three days to come up with an answer or off with their heads.

Needless to say, they were terrified. Daniel went and prayed to the God of Israel, the God of Abraham, Isaac and Jacob; and God gave him the dream and its meaning. Daniel, therefore, had saved the neck of the wise men in Babylon. As a result, he must have been a very important figure to them. He did some other extraordinary things as well. Daniel was respected by them and through him, they learned about the God of Israel. Anything that Daniel wrote, they would have read, and perhaps even kept a copy of it in their records.

So from Daniel they learned the element of time, but how did they know what sort of sign to look for? This they had taken from another Babylonian wise man—another Magi, Balaam. In Numbers 24:17, Balaam prophesied, "I see him but not now, I behold him but not near. A star will come out of Jacob; a scepter will rise out of Israel…"

This is then the first record of homage paid to Jesus by Gentiles. As a mark of their respect, they brought him gifts: Gold, frankincense, and myrrh. All were expensive gifts worthy of a king. Two of the gifts are mentioned in Isaiah 60:6. It is interesting that Isaiah 60:1 speaks about the gifts that the Gentile nations would bring to the Jewish King.

Daniel chapter 9 states that the Messiah will be "cut off"—ICARET. Cut off is a Hebraic idiom, implying that a death will occur before the age of fifty, not from natural causes but rather by a violent death.

According to Jewish tradition, also the nations will offer gifts to the messiah[13]. Generally speaking, it was common custom to bring gifts to a king when visiting him. When King Herod completed the building of Caesarea in 10–9 BCE, many envoys from different countries came to Israel with gifts[14]. And when the Queen of Sheba came to visit King Solomon, she also came bearing gifts.

The gifts they brought may have represented the riches of their country. But there is no doubt that gold represented riches because it appears in this sense in many places in the Tanach. People used to collect it and keep it in their homes in coins and bars. It was kept as an assurance for hard times.

The city of Babylon, where the wise men must have come from, had plenty of it. In the city was a golden image of Baal and a golden Table—both weighing more than 50,000 lbs. of solid gold. Also the city had two golden lions and a solid gold human figure that was 18 feet high[15]. It is not surprising that Isaiah the prophet called Babylon "the golden city" (Isaiah 14:4).

So they brought gold, which was considered to be the most valuable gift at the time. Both myrrh and frankincense were used extensively for healing purposes. Both are considered to be biblical medicines. We do not know in what form these were given, although it is probably safe to assume they were in a form of oils or spices.

This is still the case today. We know today that frankincense oil offers a variety of health benefits, including helping to relieve chronic stress and anxiety, reducing pain and inflammation, boosting immunity and potentially even helping to fight cancer.

Myrrh was used in the Bible as a spice and as a natural remedy. It is mentioned in the Bible more than 150 times. Myrrh oil has been used for thousands of years in traditional healing therapies and in religious ceremonies. Myrrh oil has many benefits; it is a potent antioxidant and it has anti-cancer, antibacterial, anti-fungal and anti-parasitic benefits. Historically, myrrh was used to treat wounds and prevent infections.

CHAPTER 9 ENDNOTES

1. Midrash on Lamentation Raba 1:6; Yerushalmi, Berachot 2:4.
2. http://ngm.nationalgeographic.com/print/2008/12/herod/mueller-text, also: King Herod: A Persecuted Persecutor : a Case Study in Psychohistory, pp. 19–20 P:22.
3. Josephus, " Bellum Judaicum," I, vi, 2.
4. Josephus, Antiquities, XIII, ix.
5. Josephus, Antiquities, XIV, xv, 2.
6. Talmud Bavli, Baba Batra 4a.
7. Numbers Rabah 4–14.
8. Talmud Bavli, Shabbat 45a, 75a; Sota 22a; Yoma 35a; Sanhedrin 30a, 98a.
9. Philo, De Legibus Specialibus III 18; #100.
10. Cicero, De Divinatione 1:47.
11. Josephus, Wars of the Jews VI 5:3.
12. Talmud Yerushalmi, Taanit 4:9, Lamentation Raba 2:20 (5a).
13. Bereshit Raba 78.
14. Josephus, Antiquities XVI; V.1;#136–41.
15. The history of Herodotus, Book 1, pp. 178–186.

CHAPTER 10

FLIGHT TO AND FROM EGYPT, AND BETHLEHEM MASSACRE

MATTHEW 2:13–23

According to verse 13, once the wise men departed, the angel of The Lord appeared to Joseph in a dream and commanded him to take the boy and flee to Egypt because Herod wanted to kill the child.

Verse 14 states:

> "And he rose and took the child and his mother by night, and departed for Egypt; and was there until the death of Herod, that, what was spoken by The Lord through the prophet, might be fulfilled saying, 'out of Egypt did I call my son.'"

It is interesting that the wise men and Joseph both were warned in a dream. Joseph obeyed the angel's instructions to the letter. A journey to Egypt could have been costly, but the gifts of the wise men would have helped them to accomplish it.

There are several possible reasons for selecting Egypt and not another place:

1. A thriving Jewish community lived and functioned in Alexandria. Taking into consideration the need for Jews to live according to God's commandments, it is important for Jews to live within a Jewish community or nearby. Even today, this is an important factor to be taken into consideration by an Orthodox Jew who wants to move. At the time, it was much more important as any other Jewish lifestyle, but Orthodoxy was not accepted by the Jewish leadership.

2. Herod's power did not reach into Egypt. Egypt had been under Roman control since 30 BCE. It became a perfect refuge for everyone escaping the persecution and terror of Herod in Israel. This was not only true at the time of Herod, but also in earlier periods, according to biblical text. Jeroboam fled to Egypt when King Solomon wanted to put him to death (I Kings 11:40). Uriya the prophet is another example. He also escaped to Egypt when King Jehoiakim wanted to kill him (Jeremiah 26:21). We also have non-biblical examples. For instance, in 172 BCE, the high priest Onnaias IV fled to Egypt, escaping from Antiochus Epiphanies[1].

3. Egypt was an easy country to escape to. All anyone had to do was to cross the border to enter into Gaza, which at that time was considered to be Egyptian territory and under Roman control. Of course, we have no evidence that this is indeed what they did, since no Egyptian town is mentioned by name. Although some Jews lived in Gaza, there is no record of a Jewish community living there at the time. Gaza under Roman control prospered and was fanatically devoted to her Cretan god Marnas[2], hardly a place for a righteous Jewish family to live in.

According to Matthew, the family remained in Egypt until the death of Herod in order for the words of the prophet to be fulfilled. Matthew then quoted the prophet Hosea chapter 11:1, which says, "When Israel was a youth I loved him, and out of Egypt I have called my son."

It is clear that the prophet is talking about the nation of Israel and not about the Messiah. This is also evident from the rest of the context of chapter 11. We know from different texts that Israel was called God's son, but perhaps most classic is Exodus 4:22 where God Himself declares, "Thus says The Lord, Israel is my son, my firstborn."

The prophet did not foretell the coming of the Messiah out of Egypt. What then was Matthew saying? Some believe that Matthew was confused and did not understand the bible well. But it is possible that somewhere in Matthew's mind there must have been a comparison between the Messiah and the nation of Israel.

This idea of the existence of a comparison between the Messiah and Israel stems from Scripture and was also held by the leaders of Judaism who applied Exodus 4:22 to the Messiah as well[3].

The rabbis understood Israel's history to be always pointing to the Messiah, and that is what made them believe there would be a parallel between what happened to Israel and what will happen to the Messiah.

There is a connection in Jewish thought between what is known as the "first redemption"—the redemption from Egypt—and the "final redemption"—the Messianic redemption.

From the Bible, we know that both Israel and the Messiah are called God's servant (Isaiah 49:3, 49:6); both are also called God's son. The rabbis referred to the Messiah by calling him Ephraim. In the Bible, Israel is also called Ephraim[4].

In addition, there is a connection in Jewish thought between what is known as the "first redemption"—the redemption from Egypt—and the "final redemption"—the Messianic redemption. Just as God redeemed Israel from Egypt in order to make it a nation unto Him, so also He would bring about the Messianic redemption and make it once again one nation under God.

As noted before, a comparison was made between Jesus and Moses. There is a continuation of this thought here. The rescue of the child Jesus from the hands of Herod reminds us of the rescue of Moses from the hand of Pharaoh.

Jesus seems to relive, in some ways, the history of the Nation of Israel. So in addition to the parallel with Moses, we have also the parallel with Israel. Not only is he referred to as the Son of God, just as Israel is, but also he was going to be led into the desert for 40 days, just as Israel was led into the desert for 40 years. And just as the desert served as a preparation for Israel before entering into the Promised Land, so also Jesus' time in the desert served as preparation before he entered his service. The fact that the Gospel writers pointed out that his life was equated with the history of the nation of Israel shows there was a full and intimate identification of Jesus with the Nation of Israel.

Once Herod realized he was deceived, more accurately, the word in Greek EMPAIZO has a tone of mockery and ridicule. The same word also appears in Matthew 27:29, 31, and 41 where it talks about the mocking of Jesus by Roman soldiers. According to verse 16, Herod slew all the male children younger than two years old in Bethlehem. Although this action is entirely within Herod's character, this incident was not recorded in the historical accounts from that time.

The double use of the word "all" in verse 16 gives the impression that Herod slew a large number of children; however, different scholars have calculated the possibilities and came to the conclusion this was probably not the case. Due to the high rate of infant mortality at the time, if the total population of the city was 1000, with an annual birth rate of 30, the number of the male children younger than two years of age would have been about twenty[5].

As time passed, stories circulated concerning the number of children slain by Herod, constantly escalating. The Byzantine liturgy set the number at 14,000, the Syrian calendar of saints set it at 64,000. At one point, the number was even equated with Revelation 14:1–5 and was set at 144,000 since there is no question whatsoever that the children Herod killed were Jewish and virgins.

Incidentally, the comparison between Jesus and Moses is continued here. Herod killing the children in Bethlehem reminds us of Pharaoh killing the Israelite infants in Egypt. Both kings were afraid of a Jewish redeemer king.

As noted earlier, there is no historical record of this event. Josephus documented very carefully the last few years of Herod's reign, concentrating mainly on his brutal deeds, yet he did not mention the massacre.

At the time, Josephus was writing for the emperor Titus, who had a Jewish mistress named Bernice, a descendant of the Hasmoneans, who were Herod's enemies. It was in Josephus' interest to blacken Herod's name. If indeed it was a very small number of children who were killed, perhaps Josephus did not hear about it. It is logical to think that if he knew about it, he would have mentioned it.

Matthew describes the reaction to Herod's action in verses 17 and 18 by quoting Jeremiah 31:15:

> "Thus says The Lord, 'a voice heard in Ramah, lamentation and bitter weeping. Rachel is weeping for her children; she refuses to be comforted for her children, because they are no more.'"

This quote, just as the previous one, also does not refer to the slaughter of the children in Bethlehem, but rather to the captivity and deportation of the northern tribes of Israel by the Assyrians in 722–721 BCE. Matthew somehow connected in his mind this verse to the events in Bethlehem. Perhaps he connected it by making a comparison, just as Rachel—meaning Israel—wept over the loss of the northern tribes, so also Israel was weeping over the loss of the children in Bethlehem. However, the number of people who died is not comparable!

Rachel herself is associated with Ramah because she was buried on the way to Ephrata after she died (Genesis 35:19, 48:7). We are given the exact location of her tomb in I Samuel 10:2, which places it in the territory of Benjamin at the border of TzelTzach. This location is near Bethel, about eleven miles north of Jerusalem. Ramah is located about five miles from Bethel. Ephrata, which is also mentioned here, is associated with Bethlehem. So perhaps, by way of location, it became connected in Matthew's mind. And so, he was not too concerned about the real fulfillment of this prophecy.

Reading Jeremiah chapter 31 in context reveals a message of hope for the nation of Israel. God communicated to Rachel (Israel) to stop her weeping since her children would return home. At a later period, the rabbis claimed that Rachel had a successful role of intercession on behalf of those seeking to have children[6].

Matthew, on the other hand, did not communicate a message of hope, nor do we know if he contemplated at all the future of these children. In Christendom, at a later time, the children of Bethlehem became Christian martyrs and saints.

Once Herod died, the angel of The Lord appeared to Joseph again in a dream and said to him according to verse 20, "Arise and take the child and his mother, and go into the land of Israel; for those who sought the child's life are dead."

Note that it does not say the land of Palestine, but the Land of Israel. The land of Israel always appears in the Bible under this name—the name God had given it. At no time did God consider it to be the Land of Palestine. This is incidentally the only place in the New Testament where this expression appears. God then did not send Joseph to the land of Palestine, but rather to the land of Israel.

In the Tanach, this name is consistently used to describe the land of Israel. Christians should be aware of it and use the correct name as well. As we have seen here, God did not change the name. It was changed by the anti-Semitic emperor Hadrian who gave Israel the name Palestine. He wanted to rename the land because he had hatred towards Israel and wanted to eradicate any mention of its existence. He called Israel Palestine-Syria, and he also changed the name of Jerusalem to Aelia Capitolina.

The Church of Rome followed his lead and started to refer to the land by this non-biblical name—Palestine. As a result, most Bible maps of Israel today have titles such as "Palestine at the time of Christ." They prefer to use this product of hatred rather than the name God gave it. It makes as much sense to talk about Palestine during the time of Christ as it does to talk about Jesus' death in the city of Aelia Capitolina. But the Church did not go that far.

Once Herod died, the angel of The Lord appeared to Joseph again in a dream and said to him according to verse 20, "Arise and take the child and his mother, and go into the land of Israel; for those who sought the child's life are dead."

The text goes on to say, "For those who were seeking the child's life"—which is a reminder of God's words to Moses in Exodus 4:19; it is almost a direct quote. The death of Pharaoh freed Moses to begin his mission, which eventually led him to Israel, just as the death of Herod seemed to have freed Jesus to return to Israel and eventually to start His work.

Joseph followed the angel's directions again and returned to Israel. But he did not return to Judah since he had heard that Archelous was ruling in Judah. So he decided to go instead to Galilee.

As noted before, when Herod died in 4 BCE, his kingdom was divided into three parts and given to his three sons. Archelous and Herod Antipas got Judea, Samaria, Idumea, Galilee and Perea. Their half-brother Philip got the region east and north of the Sea of Galilee—The Golan Heights.

Archelous was the least liked of the three sons because he was a dictator and used tyrannical tactics in his rule. Some Jewish deputies went to Rome to protest against him becoming a ruler. In their objections, they mentioned that he ushered in his reign with a massacre of 3,000 people[7].

Despite this, Archelous became ruler of Judea, and he reigned over it until his brutality became intolerable. As the result of a request by his subjects, he was deposed by Rome in 6 CE[8] and was exiled to France (Gaul). Rome then established direct Roman control over Judea through consulate officials, one of which was Pilate.

By going to Galilee rather than Judea, Joseph avoided Archelous. The Galilee ruled by Herod Antipas was much quieter politically. He ruled from 4 BCE to 39 CE, then he too was deposed by Rome. He was the ruler who put Yochanan Ha Matbil (John the Baptist) to death.

By going to Galilee rather than Judea, Joseph avoided Archelous. The Galilee ruled by Herod Antipas was much quieter politically.

Matthew summarized this section in verse 23:

> "And he came and resided in a city called Nazareth, that what was spoken through the prophets might be fulfilled, 'he shall be called a Nazarene.'"

So Joseph decided to go back and live in Nazareth, his and Mary's hometown (Luke 1:26). According to Matthew, this was in order for the prophecy to be fulfilled. Notice that Matthew is not referring to any particular prophet; he talks about the prophets in plural. The statement is not a quote of any known passage of the Scriptures. Many attempts have been made by scholars to explain what Matthew was referring to here.

The five most common explanations often put forward are as follows:

1. Matthew had some known prophetic passages in mind, but was combining them loosely, paraphrasing possibly Isaiah 4:2, which talks about the branch of The Lord that one day will be beautiful, and Judges 16:17 in which Sampson speaks about the fact he was a Nazarene from birth.

2. This combination might work in Greek, but definitely not in Hebrew—the original language of the Tanach. The word translated as a branch in Isaiah 4:2 is not the word NETZER in Hebrew as was assumed by those who hold this theory. The word TZEMACH literally means a plant, but can also be translated as a branch.

3. This word has no linguistic relation to the word NETZER; therefore, it cannot be used in Matthew's quote concerning a Nazarene. Most of Matthew's quotes are faithful to the Hebraic text of the Tanach and not to the LXX; Matthew would have known the difference between a TZEMACH and a NETZER.

4. Some claim that Matthew was quoting a part of the Tanach that existed at the time, but somehow got lost and is no longer available. Chrysostom made this suggestion and also implied that Matthew was using the term "prophets" very loosely because this term refers to a particular section of the Tanach. It seems that he did something similar in chapter 13:35, where he used the term "prophet" to refer to the Psalmist. However, we know that many of the Psalms are prophetic; therefore, in this particular case, it might be justified.

5. Another possibility is that Matthew was quoting from a non-biblical book, although the rest of his quotes are biblical. This suggestion is highly unlikely.

Matthew quoted a part of the text without knowing where it was located, and so he spoke vaguely about it. Or he did not intend to quote specific texts, but simply wanted to communicate the general idea. This explanation seems to be quite popular.

Another possibility is that Matthew was referring to the whole group of prophets in general; therefore, the question that needs to be asked is what did the prophets communicate concerning the Messiah? One thing said is the Messiah would be lowly and despised. Those who hold to this idea see here a connection to the town of Nazareth, which was not held in great esteem. So by calling the Messiah a Nazarene, Matthew is communicating the prophetic idea that the Messiah would be lowly.

This also begs the question why should the Messiah be called a Nazarene? Quote or no quote, what did Matthew have in mind? And again we find several suggestions for this.

Some say Matthew believed that Jesus would take upon himself the vow of a Nazarene. But Jesus did not do this, and there is no indication that he was expected to do so. The term NAZIR in Hebrew does not work since it comes from a different root. It comes from NEZER—a crown—rather than NETZER—a branch—something that is not apparent from the Greek.

Matthew thought he would be called a Nazarene because of his residence in Nazareth.

Matthew called him a Nazarene in association with the word NETZER—a branch—in Isaiah 11:1 which says, “a branch shall come out of Jesse...” In Hebrew, the word NATZRI—a Nazarene—and the word NETZER indeed come from the same root and can be associated. But Matthew could not have attributed it to the prophets in general because they often used the word TZEMACH rather than NETZER. Nevertheless, both words were used also in Jewish tradition to refer to the Messiah. For instance, Rabbi Joshua Ben Levi said, “Tzemach is the name of the Messiah”[9].

The word NAZARENE, as it appears in this verse, is definitely derived from the town of NATZERET, just like the word MAGDALENOS is derived from MAGDALA, and the word GADARENOS derived from GADARA.

The term NAZIR in Hebrew does not work since it comes from a different root. It comes from NEZER—a crown—rather than NETZER—a branch—something that is not apparent from the Greek.

The word also refers to a sect; it appears in this sense in Acts 24:5 referring to Paul as the head of the sect of the Nazarites. In Hebrew, Christians are called NOTZRIM, and we know they were also called this in earlier times because the Talmud referred to Jesus as “Jesus the Nazirite”[10]. In Acts, it must mean then, “the sect of those who followed the Nazirite.”

Matthew could hardly refer to Jesus in this sense since Jesus did not follow Himself.

Some say Jesus was called a Nazirite because he belonged to some pre-Christian group known by this name. We have no evidence of this idea, other than some obscure reference to an unimportant writing to a group that was related to John the Baptist and was called NASORAYYA, meaning "observant." This idea is speculative.

CHAPTER 10 ENDNOTES

1. Josephus, Antiquities, XII, ix 7; #387.
2. Encyclopedia Judaica, Vol. 7; Gaza, p. 340.
3. The Midrash on Psalm 2:7.
4. Pesikta Rabati 161–162.
5. Brown, Raymond E., *Birth of Messiah*, p. 204.
6. Bavli, Sota 1:99.
7. Josephus, War II, VI 2; #89.
8. Ibid, Antiquities, XVII xiv 2; # 342–44.
9. Talmud Yerushalmi, Berachot 2, 5a (12); Midrash, Lamentation Raba 1:16.
10. Talmud Bavli, Berachot 17b; Sota 47a.

CHAPTER 11

JESUS' CHILDHOOD IN NAZARETH

LUKE 2:40

The Gospels are rather quiet when it comes to the childhood and the youth of Jesus. The only record of all his years of development is his visit to the Temple at the age of twelve, which is discussed in the next chapter. We also do not have any record of the type of schooling Jesus received as he was growing up. Nevertheless, we have a fairly good idea of what it was probably like from the information available from Israel at that time.

From the first days of the child's life, he was surrounded by a religious atmosphere at home. His earliest training would have come from his mother. As he watched and observed, he gained education from the celebrations of the different holidays at home concerning the history and the traditions of Israel. Even when the child could not yet understand, he grew accustomed to the mezuzah on the door, the prayer shawl, the phylacteries, the Sabbath celebrations, the daily prayers and the visits to the Synagogue—all of which contributed to his education.

In addition, as soon as the child was able to speak, he was taught the Hebrew alphabet, so he could read the text as soon as possible. The letters would be drawn on a board repeatedly until the child was familiar with them.

Word association was introduced as well. For instance, they would say the letters Alef (א) and Beit (ב) are the initials of OHEV BINAH, literally—loving understanding. Gimel (ג) and Dalet (ד) are the initials of GEMOL DAY, which literally means "give enough," but it is used idiomatically as "be benevolent to the poor." Hay (ה) and Vav (ו) signify the name of God almighty. When the child had mastered letters, the text was introduced and the boy was made to read it out loud.

The Gospels are rather quiet when it comes to the childhood and the youth of Jesus. The only record of all his years of development is his visit to the Temple at the age of twelve.

When he reached the age of three, his father started teaching him the Scriptures as he was under obligation to do so. At this point, he would have been taught things such as the Shema—Deuteronomy 6:4: "Hear, o Israel! The Lord our God, The Lord is one!" And also a personal text of a few verses, which began, ended or contained the letters of his name. Then he would be taught some hymns, in particular, the psalms for the days of the week, or festive psalms such as the Hallel, which is a prayer that covers Psalms 113–118.

At the age of five or six, the child would go to school. Education was compulsory for boys older than six years of age. Israel was the first nation in the world to establish compulsory education for children, and for well over a millennium remained the only nation doing so.

The first attempt to establish a school was made by Simeon Ben Shetach in the first half of the first century BCE, but it was Joshua Ben Gamla who actually made a comprehensive effort and succeeded in establishing schools all over Israel, three years before the destruction of the Temple[1]. In towns where there was no school, the children learned from the head of the local Synagogue.

Education played a very important role in Judaism and still does today. It was considered unlawful for a family to live in a town that did not have a school[2].

Such a place the rabbis said deserved to be destroyed and excommunicated from Israel[3]. Although there were many schools in Jerusalem in 70 CE, when the Temple was destroyed, tradition has it that the city was destroyed because of the lack of attention paid to the education of the children[4]. So great was the importance that the leaders of Israel attributed to education.

Concerning education Josephus said:

> "Above all we pride ourselves on the education of our children, and regard as the most essential task in life the observance of our laws and of the pious practices based there upon, which we have inherited[5]."

The rabbis ruled that the Bible should be the exclusive text for children age five to ten. At the time, the knowledge of God meant everything to a pious Jew. The rabbis said:

> "These are the things of which a man eats the fruit in this world, but their possession continues for the next world: to honor father and mother, pious work, peacemaking between a man and a man, and the study of the Torah, which is equivalent to them all[6]."

The study of the Bible for children started with the book of Leviticus. The reason for this, according to the rabbis, was that "Children are pure and sacrifices are pure, let the pure come and occupy themselves with things that are pure[7]."

After that, they continued to study the rest of the Torah, then they studied the prophets, and finally they studied the writings. From the age of ten to fifteen, they studied the Mishna. At the end of this period, the boys were expected to participate in theological discussions of the type that usually occupied the rabbis in their religious academies. At the age of thirteen, a boy was expected to study for his Bar Mitzvah.

At the age of fifteen, he was to study the Halachot, which are rabbinic legal decisions. At the age of eighteen, he was to be prepared for his marriage. At twenty, he was to pursue a vocation[8]. Some say this type of education dated from a few decades later, and there are plenty of other references to the rabbinic education at the time that confirm it.

After five or six years of education, if a child did not show much interest or ability, he would not have to continue in his education. Instead, he would need to acquire a profession, an education that usually came from his father because he was obligated to ensure that the child would grow up to be financially independent and secure. The rabbis said:

> "Let a man deal gently with his son till he comes to be twelve years old; but from that time (assuming he was not cut out for studying) let him descend with him into his way of living: That is let him diligently and with severity (if need be) keep him close to the way, rule, or art, by which he may get his living[9]."

Twelve appears to be an important age; various things took place when the boy reached this age. The learning of a profession was just one of them. It was at this age also that he started to train to fast for an hour at a time—gradually increasing the amount of hours—in order that he might be able to fast on the Day of Atonement once he reached the age of thirteen. He is obligated by the Torah to do so.

Other than the education a child should have, a lot of attention was also given to things connected with it. For instance, the Talmud discusses the class size. It states that "The maximum number of elementary pupils that should be placed under one teacher is twenty-five. If there are fifty, an additional teacher must be provided. If there are forty, a senior student should be engaged to assist the teacher"[10].

The rabbinic teaching in schools was marked by much care, wisdom and accuracy. The love of learning was instilled in children because of the deep-rooted consciousness in Israel that its actual existence was dependent upon the diffusion of knowledge.

This understanding is illustrated by the rabbinic teaching on the passage of I Chronicles 16:22, which says, "Touch not my anointed and do my prophets no harm." "My anointed" are the school children; "My prophets" are the scholars. The world only exists through the breath of school children. We may not suspend the instruction of children, even for the rebuilding of the Temple[11].

Children would gather in schoolhouses or synagogues in their own towns. Initially, they all stood in a circle facing the teacher, or they all sat on the floor facing him. In regard to the pecking order, there was no difference between a teacher and a pupil.

School hours were fixed and were shortened during the summer. The teacher himself was held in high esteem. Not everyone could be a teacher. In order to be qualified, the teacher had to be experienced, he had to be a married man, and he had to be patient because they said that "a hasty tempered man cannot teach"[12].

In addition, a teacher had to have the highest moral and religious qualifications. The ideal standard for a teacher is described in Malachi 2:7: "For the lips of a priest should preserve knowledge and men should seek instruction from his mouth; for he is the messenger of The Lord of hosts."

The teacher was considered in some ways to be above the parent and was often called the child's father. According to the rabbis, the natural father only brings the child into this world, whereas he who teaches him brings him to life in the world to come, eternal life[13]. Therefore, the teacher is often considered to be more important.

In fulfillment of the commandment "...you shall teach them diligently to your children and shall talk of them when you sit in your house and when you walk by the way and when you lie down and when you rise up" (Deuteronomy 6:7). Joseph was obligated to teach Jesus not only a profession, but also the Torah.

"...you shall teach them diligently to your children and shall talk of them when you sit in your house and when you walk by the way and when you lie down and when you rise up" (Deuteronomy 6:7).

Some people question Joseph's ability to do so because he was a carpenter and probably uneducated. Perhaps they are right, but we should not forget that he was a pious man. As such, he must have known the Scriptures.

If Joseph was not able to teach him, then Jesus, more than likely, would have attended the local school. And if there was no school in Nazareth, it was the duty of the leader of the local Synagogue to teach him. That Joseph taught him a profession is apparent from the Gospels.

Some claim that John 7:15 gives the impression that Jesus was uneducated, but all it reveals is that the leaders were surprised at his knowledge because he had not been educated in their academies. Perhaps they were surprised that such knowledge came out of Nazareth since the town had a bad reputation.

Joseph must have died when Jesus was still young. We do not know at what age, though. We have no reference to Joseph after they visited the Temple when Jesus was twelve years old. But he would have been around for a while. Jesus often talked about a Father's love, and although we know that he referred to God, He must have remembered Joseph's love towards him and had warm memories of him. Relationships between fathers and their sons are fashioned in Judaism after the relationship of God to His children—Israel.

Jesus often talked about a Father's love, and although we know that he referred to God, He must have remembered Joseph's love towards him and had warm memories of him.

After Joseph died, Jesus—being the eldest son—was obligated to support his widowed mother and his younger brothers and sisters. These years must have been difficult for him because Israel, at the time, suffered under heavy taxation imposed by the Romans, which they were all obligated to pay. Jesus must have worked and studied to meet his obligations.

CHAPTER 11 ENDNOTES

1. A. Cohen, *Every man's Talmud*, p. 174.
2. Talmud Bavli, Sanhedrin 17t.
3. Ibid. Shabbat 4.5.
4. Ibid, ibid 119b.
5. Josephus, Against Apion 60.
6. Talmud Bavli, Pe-ah 1:1.
7. Midrash, Leviticus Rabah 7:3.
8. Pirkay Avot 5:21.
9. Talmud Bavli, Ketuvot fol. 50.
10. Ibid., Baba Batra 21a.
11. Ibid. Shabbat 119b.
12. Pirkay Avot 2:6.
13. Talmud Bavli, Nedarim 81a.

CHAPTER 12

JESUS VISITS THE TEMPLE

LUKE 2:41–50

Verse 41 states that Joseph and Mary went to Jerusalem every year to celebrate Passover. This statement shows the deeply rooted level of religious conviction they both had. It tells us a lot about their loyalty to God. In Exodus 23:17, God commanded all Jewish males to appear before Him in the Temple—three times a year, during the feasts of Passover, Pentecost and Tabernacles. Although this command should have been fulfilled, some of the rabbis took into consideration the hardships of accomplishing it and interpreted it differently.

A journey from Galilee to Jerusalem was time consuming and costly, and on many occasions even dangerous. A journey from the Diaspora was all of the above, and so much more. The rabbis, therefore, did not interpret this verse literally. Instead of the word YERAEH, which literally means "he shall appear," they understood it to say REIYAH, which literally means "an appearance."

In other words, they claimed that the verse does not necessarily obligate everyone to appear each time in the Temple. Instead, when they do appear, they bring with them a sacrifice. With this interpretation, the people could avoid having to make this journey every year.

Women, of course, were not obligated to go to Jerusalem because the command only obligated males. However, they were not excluded either, so many of the women did go, and Mary was among the faithful who chose to do so.

They went up to the Feast of Passover. Passover and HAG HA MATZOT—the feast of unleavened bread—were initially two separated feasts. Passover falls on the 14th of Nissan (Deuteronomy 16:4; Exodus 12:6), and the feast of unleavened bread starts on the 15th of Nissan and lasts for seven days (Exodus 12:13, 23:15, 34:18). In time, Passover and the feast of unleavened bread became one, and the name Passover was applied to both (Ezekiel 45:21–25)[1].

In Exodus 23:17, God commanded all Jewish males to appear before Him in the Temple—three times a year, during the feasts of Passover, Pentecost and Tabernacles.

The term "they went up" is an idiom, and within Israel it is used to describe holiness. As the Land is God's land it is a Holy Land. One is said to go up from the Diaspora to Israel. The pilgrims always went up to Jerusalem, regardless of where they came from.

In Israel, they were referring to them with the Hebrew word OLAY REGEL, which literally means "those who go up by foot." Today, anyone who immigrates to Israel is still going up. The term is "Aliyah," and the understanding is that he is going up a step from other lands to the Holy Land. Within Israel, one is going up from any place in Israel to Jerusalem, as Jerusalem is the Holy city. And within Jerusalem, one is going up to the Temple Mount, which is the mountain of The Lord.

At this particular time when Joseph and Mary went for the feast, Jesus was twelve years old. Some think Jesus went for his Bar Mitzvah ceremony, but this was not the case since Bar Mitzvah takes place at the age of thirteen. The rabbis claimed that before the child reaches thirteen years of age, he should be brought to the Temple that year in order to observe the festive rite[2].

They also said a child who did not need the ministering of his mother could be expected to observe the Torah at an earlier stage. This is particularly important in light of the requirement for all men to appear in the Temple during the feasts[3].

So, in accordance with this understanding, Joseph and Mary must have brought Jesus to the Temple at the age of twelve. Luke here demonstrates a good understanding of Jewish customs.

They stayed in Jerusalem (verse 43) until the days were fulfilled, and then they started to make their way back to Galilee. "Until the days were fulfilled"—some say it is a reference to the whole feast; therefore, they could have stayed in Jerusalem for the whole seven days. Others believe they stayed for about three days, until the first day of what is known as CHOL HAMOED, which literally means "the unholy part of the appointed time." The secular part of the holiday, a time that is understood to be "not a holiday and not a regular day" is called by some MOED KATAN, meaning "a small holiday," of which there is a whole tractate under this name in the Mishna. And in Israel today, we treat it as a half holiday; people work only half days during this time.

The term "they went up" is an idiom, and within Israel it is used to describe holiness. As the Land is God's land it is a Holy Land. The pilgrims always went up to Jerusalem, regardless of where they came from.

The mention of returning home with company, more or less, implies they stayed for the whole feast. The word fulfill means "to fill to the full," which also implies they stayed for the whole time. And being in Jerusalem for the final day of the feast, which was considered a full holiday, was part of the obligation.

Those who objected claimed that Jesus would not have been found among the scholars if the holiday were over because they would have gone home. But, of course, they forget there were always some rabbis and scholars who lived and taught in Jerusalem, some of whom met regularly for discussions in the Temple area.

The parents went "a day's journey," verse 44, which was anywhere between ten to thirty miles, before they noticed Jesus was missing. Could such devoted parents be so irresponsible and careless when it comes to their children? How did they lose him? Well, it was not hard to do.

Jesus appears to have been mature for his age and probably quite independent. When people made their plans to travel for the feasts, each town came together in a large group and made preparations to travel together. Camping places would have been decided and arranged by organizers beforehand. As they progressed towards Jerusalem, they met with other large groups from different towns who also traveled together, and gradually they became a larger and larger crowd.

The return journey would have been similar, starting together, slowly progressing through each town, with each group of people departing to their homes. It was truly a large assembly of people.

Within the town crowds, people knew one another very well. They were also responsible for one another. These are manifestations of the principle of collective responsibility Israel shares. All are responsible for one another because all belong to one big family called Israel—all are brothers and sisters. The children of any given town would have also known one another very well because they grew up together, studied together and attended the same synagogue. In addition, they often had other family relatives living in the same town, so they too would be very familiar with them.

When people made their plans to travel for the feasts, each town came together in a large group and made preparations to travel together. Camping places would have been decided and arranged by organizers beforehand.

In this kind of environment, there was no need to keep an eye on the children, especially at the age of twelve when they preferred to play with their own age group. All that Jesus had to remember was the time his group was leaving and where it was meeting.

We should not forget that as a boy of twelve, he was already working, and girls at this age were already getting married. Unlike children of today, they were much more mature. Jesus chose not to appear at the rendezvous on that particular day, but his parents could not have realized it. They found out he was missing, more than likely, when it was time to camp for the night, and he had not shown up as he was supposed to.

After Mary and Joseph realized no one had seen him, they decided to return to Jerusalem to look for him, and it took them three days to find him. He was discovered in the Temple, among the teachers of the Torah, learning and asking questions. We do not know exactly where in the Temple he was. Some suggest he was found in one of the three courts. Others think he was in the Temple synagogue. We really do not know. According to the Mishna, the members of the Temple-Sanhedrin would come out on feast days and Shabbats to the terrace of the Temple in order to teach there[4]. It is possible that Jesus' parents came to pray in the Temple on the Shabbat once they were already in Jerusalem and unexpectedly found him there.

The rabbis made every effort to give people an opportunity to participate in a discussion. When a question was asked, the young were given the first opportunity to answer. Jesus then would have been given an opportunity and would have been encouraged to show his ability[5]. And indeed he must have demonstrated great wisdom and ability as they were amazed. Children at the age of twelve were not yet expected to carry their weight in a rabbinic discussion since they were only supposed to enter into such a discussion at the age of fifteen. Perhaps this was the reason for their great amazement.

"Why have you looked for me—did you not know that I had to be in my Father's house?"

There are stories within Judaism about other boys who had exceptional knowledge and wisdom. The rabbis claimed that King Solomon was only twelve years old when he presided as a judge in the case of two women claiming the same child. There is a story about Rabbi Ishmael that tells about how Rabbi Joshua discovered him when he was a child. This happened in 70 CE, sometime after the destruction of the city. The child was in prison, and Rabbi Joshua was visiting there. A discussion developed between the two, during which Ishmael demonstrated great wisdom. As a result, Rabbi Joshua decided to ransom him. In time, Ishmael became a great rabbi and scholar[6].

Jesus' mother scolded him, but many believe she was out of place here and should not have done so. But a mother's heart is a mother's heart. She must have been very scared and very worried. They looked for him for three days, so surely she was suffering terrible thoughts of what might have happened to him.

Once they found him and were no longer concerned for his safety, and being poor as they were, the thought of money spent unnecessarily during this time surely then bothered her as well.

Yeshua answered, "Why have you looked for me—did you not know that I had to be in my Father's house?" The Greek says, literally, "you (pl) not know that in the Father I must I?" The words house or business do not appear in the text. In other words, we do not know exactly what he said; it is too cryptic. Possibly, he meant to say to his parents, "Why have you looked for me—you should have known that I would be in the Temple." His parents did not understand what he said. But if he did say that, they should have known he would be in the Temple. We cannot help but wonder then how is it that Mary had forgotten all that had transpired during the time of his birth.

CHAPTER 12 ENDNOTES

1. Josephus, Antiquities VI 9.3, XX 5.3.
2. Talmud Bavli, Yoma 82a.
3. Ibid, Chagiga 1:2.
4. Mishna, Sanhedrin 88d.
5. Talmud Bavli, Sanhedrin 36b.
6. Talmud Bavli, Gittin 58a.

CHAPTER 13

A SUMMATION OF JESUS' EARLY LIFE

LUKE 2:51–52

> "And he went down with them and came to Nazareth; and he continued in subjection to them; and his mother treasured all these things in her heart. And Jesus kept increasing in wisdom and stature, and in favor with God and men."

These two verses are a summation of a period of about thirty years of Jesus' life, of which we know nothing other than what has already been discussed of his education. It is interesting to note that only three points regarding Jesus are communicated here:

1. He grew up and developed in Nazareth.
2. He was subject to his parents during these years.
3. He grew in wisdom and found favor before God and men.

The first point is merely an historical fact that helps us understand his background. The third point helps us understand that the years in Nazareth were actually part of the preparations for his future. It is the second point that gives important information. Food for thought and instructions for living! Jesus lived in subjection to his parents. So according to Luke, as powerful as he was, Jesus submitted to his parents' authority. Why?

1. Because it was fitting for him to do so. "Honor your father and your mother" is considered by the Jewish people to be one of the most important commandments in the Torah. We regard it as a very serious obligation of children toward their parents—not to be taken lightly. The commandment in Exodus 20:12 is "Honor your father and your mother that your days may be prolonged in the land which The Lord your God gives you."

   This is the first commandment, which carries with it something of a reward, and it is actually the only one within the Ten Commandments that does so. The first four commandments relate to the relationship between God and men. The last five commandments relate to the relationship between men and men. The fifth commandment, which we are dealing with here, relates to both the relationships between God and men and relationships between men and men.

   The rabbis thought the natural father of the child was a symbol of our Heavenly Father. Our Heavenly Father is our first Father while our biological father is our last father. So, just as we are to honor our earthly father, we are also to honor our Heavenly Father.

   They said there are three partners in the making of man: God, his natural father and his mother. From his parents, he received his physical body, but his soul and his spirit came from Hashem (The sacred name of God). It is as if the Almighty is saying, "You are to honor me, but I also want you to honor them who had participated with me, to some extent, in your creation." Of course, since this is God's will, when we honor our parents, we also honor God[1].

   As we do so, we will be rewarded since God promised to prolong our lives in the land. This was understood to be a two-fold blessing: 1) A communal blessing for the Nation. As long as Israel honors their parents, they will be able to dwell on their land—the land of Israel. 2) A personal blessing. When one honors his parents, his life on earth will be prolonged as well.

Jesus obeyed the Torah; the Gospels give the impression he kept it to the letter. There was no other way for him but to be subjected to his parents as The Torah expected him to do so. Had he not done so, he would have gone against God's will and against the Torah. That would have constituted a sin and would have jeopardized his future mission.

It was not only strangers who came to know him as a respected teacher and spiritual leader in Israel, but also some of his half brothers. Had they of known him to rebel against their parents, breaking one of the most important commandments, they would never have followed him.

And in addition, when it comes to the question of being chosen to be a Messiah, Judaism teaches that the Messiah would glorify the Torah. He would bring it to its highest place. No one who went against the Torah, therefore, would have been considered by the people in Israel to be a Messiah.

2. It is also interesting that throughout all of these years, only one example was communicated here for his disciples to follow—the fact that he subjected himself to his parents. It could have been left unsaid, but it was not. This surely gives us an indication of the importance of this commandment and its fulfillment to God. Jesus—who was the example for all his disciples—honored his parents. He kept the Torah. What do you suppose he expected all his future followers to do?

The next time we hear about Jesus is when he entered his public ministry. His life before it, with the exception of the birth narratives, appears almost to be irrelevant. But this is not an exception within the Jewish context and not even an exception within the Bible. It is human nature to be interested in a great man's life only after he appeared on the stage of history.

The next time we hear about Jesus is when he entered his public ministry. His life before it, with the exception of the birth narratives, appears almost to be irrelevant. But this is not an exception within the Jewish context and not even an exception within the Bible. It is human nature to be interested in a great man's life only after he appeared on the stage of history. A person must become well known first; otherwise, we really do not know he existed.

The Bible also, for the most part, is not interested in its heroes' lives prior to the time in which they begin to fulfill their calling. As in the case of Jesus, the Bible primarily deals with their birth and earlier years.

Both Moses and Samuel are perfect examples of this. In the Jewish world, there are plenty of examples as well. I suppose Rabbi Hillel, who we know as a contemporary of Jesus', is also a perfect example. We know nothing about all the years of development he spent in Babylon. Most of the information we find has to do with his life in Israel when he was actually taking on the role that God had planned for him.

In Hebrew, the word for obeying is the word SHMA, which literally means "to listen or to hear," but it is used idiomatically to mean "obey." In its meaning, it carries the connotation of "once you listen, you also have to do."

In discussing here the issue of subjection and submission, it is important to understand the meaning of these two words, which are synonyms to the word "obeying." Often, all three words are understood to mean the same thing, but this is not the case.

The words subject or submit mean "to subject oneself to someone or to something, such as a state. To become subordinate, to place under, to give way, to give another the first word, to surrender oneself to judgment, criticism, correction, advice and a treatment." Submission then is a voluntary yielding to someone else's will or wishes.

Obeying, on the other hand, means "to listen and to answer, or to listen and to do, it is an absolute submission"—no questions asked. Obedience is like a slave to a master—he has no rights!

In the New Testament, the Greek word for submitting or subjecting is the word HUPOTASSO, and there are different variations of it. In Hebrew, it is the word NICHNA, meaning "he surrendered"[2].

In Hebrew, the word for obeying is the word SHMA, which literally means "to listen or to hear," but it is used idiomatically to mean "obey." In its meaning, it carries the connotation of "once you listen, you also have to do."

In the Bible, this is the way it is used. A classic example is the words uttered by the children of Israel on Mount Sinai. Once they received the Torah, they responded with the words NA-ASE VE NISHMA—we will hear and we will do—meaning "we will obey" (Exodus 24:7).

In the New Testament, we find this word used in two main contexts:

With regard to obedience to God, it commanded those who followed Jesus to obey the master—no questions asked. The word is used in this sense in Matthew 8:27—the sea obeys God—and in Peter 1:2.

With regard to children obeying their parents—just as followers of Jesus are commanded to obey their Father in heaven, children are also commanded to obey their earthly parents. The word is used in this sense in Ephesians chapter 6 and in Colossians 3:20.

There is another Greek word that has been translated into English as "obeying," but it probably should have been translated as "submitting." This is the word PAITHO. It carries with it the particular meaning of submitting to someone in authority, usually a government or a ruler. It appears in Acts 5:29, where it says, "We ought to submit to God." But since Jesus' followers should obey God, the translation became "we ought to obey God."

However, obedience definitely implies submission. Unlike submission, however, it does not necessarily imply obedience. In this case, it does not matter, but elsewhere it does. It also appears in Hebrews 13:17, where it says, "Submit to one in authority." But again, it was translated in this text as "obey one in authority." At least it is consistent.

Part of the problem stems from people often not realizing the difference between obeying and submitting. This word is also used in Acts 27:2,1, where it was translated as "you ought to have followed my advice"—in modern language, "You should have listened to me." Paul did not expect obedience from them, but perhaps he did expect submission to his advice.

The Greek word that is mostly used for "submit" or "subject" in the New Testament is HUPOTASSO and variations. This is the word used here in our text and also in Romans 8:20, I Corinthians 15:28; 16:16, Hebrews 2:8 and I Peter 3:22.

In addition, the word is used in Ephesians 5:22, 24 and in Colossians 3:18 in regard to wives submitting to their husbands. In Romans 13:1 and I Peter 2:13, it is used with regard to the followers of Jesus submitting to the civil and political authorities. In Ephesians 5:21, it is used for their submission to one another.

To sum up, Jesus' followers were all told to obey God Almighty and children were commanded to obey their parents. In other words, an absolute and wholehearted submission to God, a complete trust that He knows what He is doing and wants the best for His people and they can only benefit from doing His will. This is what God is demanding of His people. So strong and powerful is this commandment that by not doing it, disobeying God leads to grievous consequences and a break in communication with Him.

The disciples were not told to obey the authorities, rather they were told to submit to them, to put themselves under their will voluntarily. Similarly, wives were not commanded to obey their husbands, but rather to submit to them. Thus as a general rule, wives are to listen to their husbands, unless the husband goes against the will of God or bears false witness to the truth. God must come first in all of our lives—Him we ought to obey; He takes priority.

Women, just like men, will one day have to appear before God Almighty and account for their actions. At that point, there would be no excuses. Saying, "but my husband made me do it Father" will not do. According to the New Testament, generally speaking, women ought to listen to their husbands as long as they are within the will of God. If they decide to go against their husband's will, they should have a very good reason for it because, by not submitting, they might also be called to account.

For example, if the husband decides that prostitution might be a good additional source of income for him, the wife is under no obligation to submit; she should not do it because it bears false witness to the truth and goes against the will of God. If her husband beats her up every other day, she does not have to submit to it; it goes against the will of God—and so on.

The same is true when it comes to submission to governments or rulers. As we have seen before, the disciples were not told to obey the authorities but rather to submit to them.

So if the government in any country goes against the will of God, modern disciples are not obligated to submit to it. If a government decides it is okay to kill babies, legalize euthanasia or oppress people, not only is it okay to go against it, but there is also an obligation to do so because that kind of a government goes against the will of God. Children of God are called to bear witness to the truth.

In Nazi Germany and in the countries it occupied, German soldiers were sent to knock on doors and find Jews hiding in houses. Many of those doors were the homes of Christians. And many of them turned Jews into the Nazis' hands, signing Jews' death certificates by their actions.

They justified their actions with the text from the New Testament, claiming that one should obey the authorities, and that the Bible commanded us not to lie. Although lying is not something a child of God ought to do, the Bible does not command us not to do it.

The disciples were not told to obey the authorities, rather they were told to submit to them, to put themselves under their will voluntarily. Similarly, wives were not commanded to obey their husbands, but rather to submit to them.

The commandment is found in Exodus 20:16, which say, "You shall not bear false witness against your neighbor." First and foremost, this has to do with bearing false witness against another in a court case or before a ruler who has the power to judge him. Also it has to do with not gossiping or jeopardizing someone else's good name.

In its basis is the understanding that this is a prohibition against bearing false witness in general. People bear true witness when they stand for the will of God. They bear false witness when they go against the will of God. It was not God's will for Jews to be murdered and persecuted in Germany.

Turning them over into the Nazis' hands constituted bearing false witness. It went against the will of God and everything He stands for.

On a personal level, it went against "You shall not murder." On a national level, it was an attempt to commit the genocide of the Jews and has continued against the state of Israel, something that went against and goes against the heart and will of God. Lying to the German authorities would have then constituted then bearing witness to the truth.

Regarding the issue of submitting to one another, it appears to be a bit confusing at times. Although the New Testament commanded the disciples to subject to one another, today most Christians ignore it because, in order to do so, they need to come up with some answers. When are they to submit to other Christians? Are they to submit to all Christians or only to certain Christians? Who should submit first to whom?

> People bear true witness when they stand for the will of God. They bear false witness when they go against the will of God.

This is where the confusion arises. There is no way that all can submit to all at the same time. It appears, though, that the New Testament does provide somewhat of an order for submission in the listing of spiritual gifts. According to this, each person has a spiritual gift that God has given to him or her in order to benefit the whole. These gifts are mentioned in Romans 12:6–8. Although this subject is outside the scope of this book, it is important to understand that each spiritual gift is given to meet the needs of others. Therefore, strength lies within each one of them. Each gift is given to teach others or to help others to do the things they do not know how to do.

Just like people can be trained, for the most part, for only one major profession, growing and developing once in it, so too God gave man one particular spiritual gift in which he is to continue growing and developing for the rest of his life.

In everyday life, we employ people who have different professions because we need their help and advice. We go to a lawyer in order to obtain legal advice. We go to a doctor in order to obtain medical advice, etc.... We usually pay quite a bit of money to obtain their advice, and once it is given to us, we accept it and act accordingly. For example, we submit ourselves to the doctor or the lawyer because we know they have expertise in that area. This is where their strength lies.

Spiritual gifts should be treated in similar manner. Seven are listed in the New Testament, and each one has a particular strength that others do not. The administrator can help people to be good stewards of time and to learn order. The doer can help people to be good servers and teach them how to help others. A person with the gift of mercy can teach others how to be merciful and kind toward others. The giver teaches people how to be a good steward of money. The exhorter teaches people how to comfort others. The teacher helps people to understand the Word of God better. And the prophet helps people understand the will of God for them.

And just as people submit to their doctor and lawyer, they also should submit to the people who have different gifts in their particular areas. The will of God is for people to develop in all these areas; therefore, they should submit to people in accordance with their gift. This is a good sensible way to be subjected to one another, without confusion and with clear guidelines as to when to submit and who to submit to. Always bearing in mind, however, that help is to be weighed and assessed.

CHAPTER 13 ENDNOTES

1. Mikraot Gedolot, Shmot (Exodus), Keli Yakar and Ramban on Exodus 20:12, Abraham, Yitzchak.
2. All Greek Vocabulary meanings were taken from *A Greek-English Lexicon to the NT and other early Christian literature* by: William F. Arndt & F. Wilbur.

JUDAH & ISRAEL
ILLUSTRATION OF THE
BOOKS OF KINGS & CHRONICLES
AND THE
CAPTIVITIES.
DATES OF CAPTIVITIES
Kenites
Rabbath Moab
Jericho
Merom
Wood of Ephraim
Hadrsh

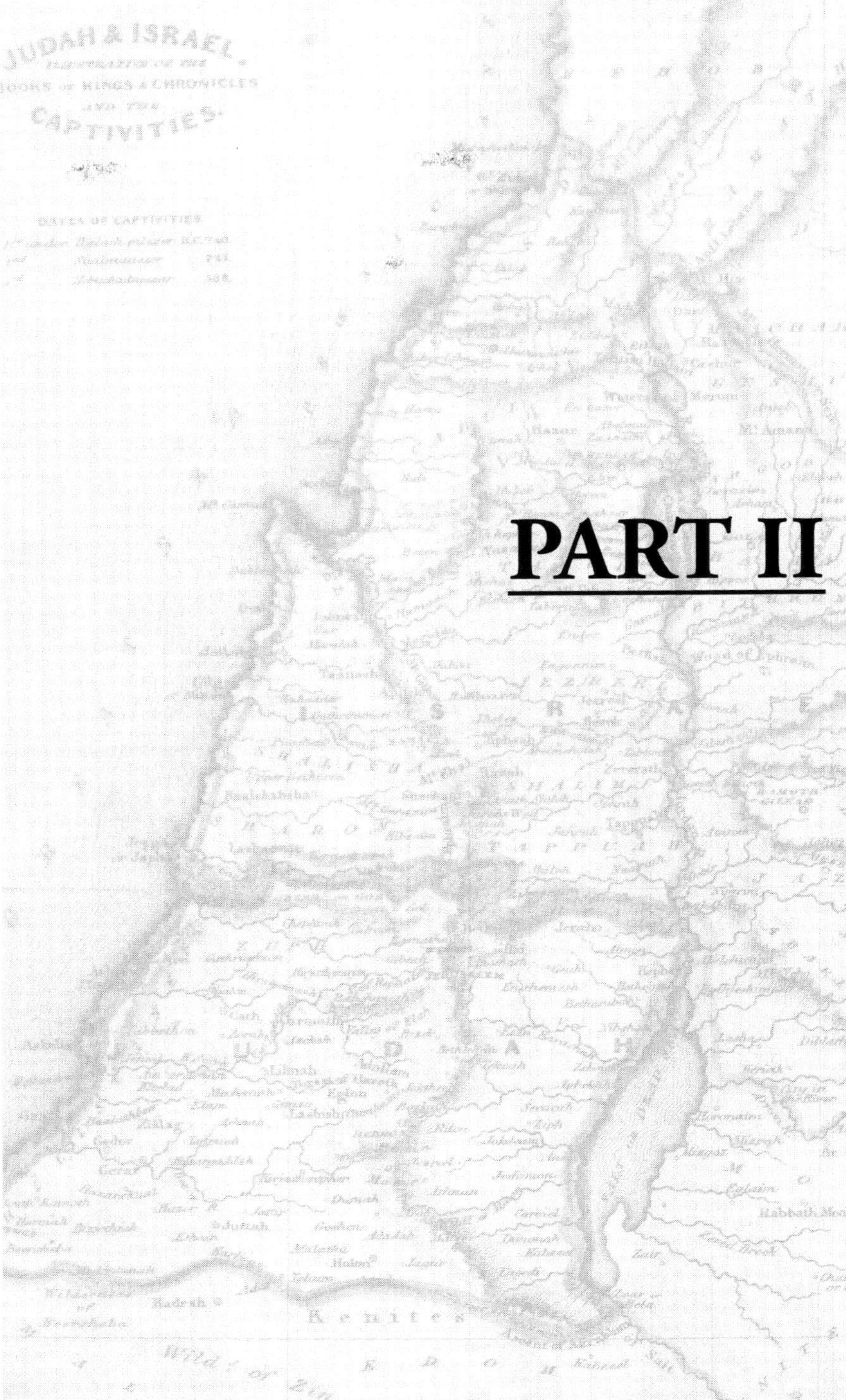

PART II

CHAPTER 14

INTRODUCTION TO YOCHANAN HA-MATBIL—JOHN THE BAPTIST

MATTHEW CHAPTER 3; MARK CHAPTER 1; LUKE CHAPTER 3

Just as in Jesus' case, so also in John's case, we have no information about his development years, but rather we have about thirty years of silence. We hear about him when he is ready to start his public ministry. According to Luke, he received a divine call to a prophetic vocation (Luke 3:2).

All the information we have about John comes from two sources. Most of it we derive from the New Testament, but Josephus also mentioned him. As I mentioned before, it is not clear at what point he went into the desert, or how many years he spent there. Neither do we know if it was a secluded desert. However, we do know that at the time, he received his call to ministry when was in the desert.

There is no doubt that the years he spent there prepared him for his ministry. Some believe that John, at some point, was a member of the Qumran community and that he left it because of the differences between his theological understanding and theirs[1]. However, there is no evidence supporting this, and there are actually some valid objections to this theory.

There is no doubt that some of John's teachings matched the Qumranian understanding. For example, the Qumranian understood Isaiah 40:3, which says, "Clear ye in the wilderness the way of The Lord"—literally. It appears that he did as well. His appearance confirmed the fact that he, more than likely, spent some time in seclusion. Although it may have been part of his preparation, he did not recommend seclusion to his followers.

Jesus described him in Matthew 11:18, saying, "John came neither eating nor drinking"—an indication of John's simple self-denying way of life. His appearance and his preaching, actually everything about him, recalled the prophet Elijah. He appeared from nowhere. He wore a garment of camel's hair, which must have been his outer garment.

We hear about John when he is ready to start his public ministry. According to Luke, he received a divine call to a prophetic vocation (Luke 3:2).

First-century people wore many garments. About five different garments were worn; the last was the outer garment. John also wore a leather belt around his waist. Curiously, Elijah was described as a hairy man bound with a girdle of leather about his loins in II Kings 1:8.

According to Zechariah 13:4, a hairy mantel was a sign of the prophetic office. The fact that John wore it was an indication of his understanding that his call was a prophetic one, and he must have been aware that the people would understand it accordingly.

He ate locusts and honey. Locusts seemingly used to be a popular food and were even considered to be suitable for a king[2]. Many different kinds of locusts used to exist, some of them were kosher others were not. Wild honey in Hebrew is DEVASH YA'AR, originally, it probably was YEA'ARAT DEVASH, meaning a honeycomb[3].

All of John's preaching reflected the Tanach, its imagery, content and style—and that is another similarity to Elijah. He was the voice announcing what

God is about to do. It seems it played an important role in the emergence of Jesus' ministry. According to the Gospels, he gave full approval to Jesus' ministry, and Jesus also approved of him and his work. Jesus held him in great esteem as Luke recorded him saying that "among those born of a woman, none is greater than John" (Luke 7:28), which is really curious since in Judaism, Moses is held above all the others. And as great as John was, he was not a match of Moses.

According to Zechariah 13:4, a hairy mantel was a sign of the prophetic office. The fact that John wore it was an indication of his understanding that his call was a prophetic one.

John had a tremendous movement of followers. Many of them continued following his teaching after his death, even years later after Jesus died. They continue to exist as a separate sect and at one point even progressed to believe that John was the priestly Messiah from the house of Aaron, in whose existence the Qumranians believed as well.

John, of course, was born to a priestly family of the house of Aaron; perhaps, that fact contributed to their beliefs.

Acts 18:24 and Ephesians 19:1–7 claim that the sect existed years after Jesus' death.

Here is what Josephus wrote about him:

> "But some of the Jews believed that Herod's army was destroyed by God, God punishing him very justly for Yochanan called the Baptist, whom Herod had put to death. For Yochanan was a pious man, and he was bidding the Jews who practiced virtue and exercised righteousness toward each other and piety toward God, to come together for baptism.
>
> "For thus, it seems to him, that baptismal ablution would be acceptable, if it were not used to beg off from sins committed; but for the purification of the body when they should have previously been cleansed by righteous conduct.

> "And when everybody turned to Yochanan—for they were profoundly stirred by what he said—Herod feared that Yochanan's extensive influence over the people might lead to an uprising—for the people seemed likely to do everything he might counsel. He thought it much better, under the circumstances, to get Yochanan out of the way in advance, before any insurrection might develop, than for himself to get into trouble and be sorry not to have acted, once an insurrection had begun.
>
> "So, because of Herod's suspicions, Yochanan was sent as a prisoner to Macherus, the fortress already mentioned, and there put to death. But the Jews believed that the distraction which overtook the army came as a punishment for Herod, God wishing to do him harm[4]."

As we can see, John was very popular among the Jewish people; many followed him. He was a righteous Jew—all of his teachings and instructions were within the framework of the Torah. His sect was just another Jewish movement within the pluralistic Judaism of the time.

CHAPTER 14 ENDNOTES

1. David Flusser, 1985, *Jerusalem, Judaism and the origins of Christianity*, The Magnes Press, The Hebrew University.
2. Midrash, Genesis Raba 67.2; Pliny, Natural History, VI. 35, VII. 2.
3. Klaussner, Jesus of Nazareth, *His Life, Time and Teaching*, 1946, N.Y. Macmillan, p. 243.
4. Josephus, Antiquities, XVII, v. 2.

CHAPTER 15

JOHN'S MESSAGE

MATTHEW 3:7–13, LUKE 3:7–18

John came offering what is known as "baptism," which is a reference to the Jewish practice of immersion in the Miqva (baptismal pool). He offered the service of immersion to the people who came to him for this purpose.

According to Matthew's account, these people were the Pharisees and the Sadducees, verse 7. According to Luke, it was the crowd, verse 7. In Hebrew, we have the term HAMON HA-AM, meaning "a crowd of the nation"—in other words, anyone and everyone from among the people of Israel.

We have here the first mention of the Pharisees and the Sadducees. We will not discuss these two groups in this context because they are discussed in the Appendices at the end of this book. According to Matthew, many of the Pharisees and the Sadducees were present, and they all came to be immersed. That by itself points to the fact that the Jewish leadership was not against John at this time. Otherwise, they would not have allowed him to officiate over their service of immersion.

John addressed them in verse 7, calling them a "brood of vipers." From this, many deduced there must have been some opposition from the Pharisees and the Sadducees already at this time. Otherwise, he would not have come out against them. However, it is not clear if John is actually criticizing the Pharisees or the Sadducees. More likely, he spoke to the crowd in general as is apparent from Luke's account when he referred to the crowd as the brood of vipers.

Even if this statement is to be considered as a criticism against these two groups, it is still important to remember that we have here the criticism of a Jew against his fellow Jew—in other words, an in-house argument.

Something considered a Jewish trend and clearly evidenced and demonstrated by historical records of the time, clashes between different sects were quite fashionable in the first century when all sects criticized one another.

Notice also he did not criticize anyone for being a Pharisee, but rather for being a viper. Vipers can be found among any group of people. The idea that all Pharisees were bad is wrong as well. Some of them probably were, but others, according to Jesus, "were not far from God's kingdom" (Mark 12:34).

In Hebrew, we have the term HAMON HA-AM, meaning "a crowd of the nation"—in other words, anyone and everyone from among the people of Israel.

Some Pharisees, while they remained loyal to their sect, also became followers of Jesus as is recorded in Acts 15:5. Paul, who identified himself as "a Pharisee son of a Pharisee" (Acts 23:6), should not be forgotten. This is an idiomatic expression, equivalent perhaps to the present day idea of "a Pharisee in his blood."

In Modern Hebrew, we speak about "a rabbi, son of a rabbi"—an indication there is no need to question it. Not only is the man a rabbi, but so was his father. It is in his blood; he is the real thing.

The same expression is also used in the negative form: "he is neither a rabbi nor a son of a rabbi." In other words, he is as far as possible from being a rabbi; he knows nothing about it. Paul, by calling himself "a Pharisee, son of a Pharisee," identified himself as a genuine Pharisee, not just someone who calls himself a Pharisee.

The expression "brood of vipers," which John used here, was also used by Jesus against the Pharisees in Matthew 12:34 and 23:33. The term "viper" also appears in the Bible in Isaiah 14:29 and Proverbs 23:33. It is usually assumed the expression means a "hypocrite," but this is not the case, although elsewhere Jesus did call some of the Pharisees hypocrites.

The word that is used here for viper is the word EXCHIDNA in Greek and TZIFONI in Hebrew. Both words refer to snakes from the viper family. Those are particularly poisonous snakes. Their sting is deadly. Isaiah 14:20 says, "Do not rejoice, o Philistia, all of you, because the rod that struck you is broken, for from the serpent's root a viper will come out…"

"Do not rejoice, o Philistia, all of you, because the rod that struck you is broken, for from the serpent's root a viper will come out…"

Because the poison of the viper is deadly, the term viper became, in Hebrew, an idiom for "evil"[1]. By calling the people "sons of vipers," John implied they were bad because they believed and probably communicated to others the notion that they could escape from the wrath of God.

By doing so, they spread deadly poison, just as a viper snake does. No one will escape the wrath of God, which is a reference to the Day of Judgment. John was obviously attacking a popular notion at the time that will be discussed shortly.

That the term refers to bad or evil is much more evident from another context in which Jesus used the same term. He said, "You brood of vipers, how can you, being evil, speak what is good? For the mouth speaks out that which fills the heart. The good man out of his good treasure brings forth what is good, and the evil man out of his evil treasure brings forth what is evil" (Matthew 12:34–35).

Since John addressed them as "children of vipers," some understood this to mean "seed of Satan," presumably the seed of the snake in reference to the Garden of Eden. But this is not the case either. As was stated before, the idiom developed relating to the deadly poison of the viper and not necessarily the snake itself. The word snake in Hebrew is NACHASH and not TZIFONI as used in this text.

In addition, the term "son of" or "child of" is another biblical Hebraic idiom. It is used to denote that someone is following a certain belief, or a certain teaching, or adopting a certain behavior. For instance, "children of Abraham" are those who follow Abraham's example of faith. They are his children in the sense that they have learned from him to believe in Almighty God. This topic will be further expounded in a future volume.

For the time being, all we need to realize is that there is no reference here to the seed of Satan. Such interpretations are not only incorrect, but also breathe anti-Semitic theologies and ideas, which are definitely an abomination to God.

Here, John was attacking the idea that people can escape the Day of Judgment. He asked them, "Who has taught you to flee from the wrath to come?.... and do not suppose that you can say to yourselves: 'we have Abraham for our father; for I say to you that God is able from these stones to raise up children to Abraham'" (Verse 9).

In the first century, there was a common belief in Jewish circles that the wrath of God would fall only upon the Gentile nations. One can find rabbinic statements such as "The night is only for the nations of the world, but the mornings are to Israel"[2], which demonstrate this idea. Behind this was the teaching that had already been developed by that time, the idea that "All Israel have a share in the world to come"[3].

This rabbinic teaching, incidentally, was quoted by Paul when he said, "all Israel will be saved" in Romans 11:26. The teaching that the wrath of God will fall upon the Gentile nations is pretty similar to the notion one can find in Christendom today, although we are discussing here two different kinds of the wrath of God.

In the case of Israel, 2,000 years ago, it related to Judgment Day when people will be judged according to their deeds while in this life. The Gentiles at that time still did not know God; therefore, people believed they would suffer the wrath of God unless a miracle took place. In addition, the Gentile nations often went against Israel, and God made sure that Israel knew He was going to punish them for it.

According to Christian end-time theology, there is a tribulation period coming and many Christians believe this tribulation period is against Israel. During that time, they say the wrath of God will come against the Jews and not upon the Church. Avoiding the issue of the end time, yet still dealing with this current trend, it is important to realize that God promised judgment also to the Gentiles. The Bible contains verses stating that God will judge the nations of the world "according to the way they treated my people Israel."

Isaiah 34:1–8 is an example:

> "Draw near o nations, to hear; and listen, o people! let the earth and all it contains hear, and the world and all that springs from it, for The Lord's indignation is against all the nations, and his wrath against all their armies; (verse 1)…..for The Lord has a day of vengeance, a year of recompense for the cause of Zion."

Isaiah 26:20–21 is another example:

> "Come my people, enter into your rooms, and close your doors behind you; hide for a little while, until indignation runs its course, for behold The Lord is about to come out of his place to punish the inhabitants of the earth for their iniquity."

Many other examples can be found. The Jewish belief that the wrath of God will come against the nations is based on the biblical text.

On the other hand, God promised restoration to Israel. Although there are plenty of instances where God pronounced judgment against Israel, He consistently also promised to restore her.

In Isaiah 62:1–4 God said:

> "For Zion's sake I will not keep silent, and for Jerusalem's sake I will not keep quiet, until her righteousness goes forth like brightness and her salvation like a torch that is burning. And the nations will see your righteousness and all kings your glory; and you will be called by a new name, which the mouth of The Lord will designate…you will be called 'my delight is in her, and your land married.' For The Lord delights in you and to him your land will be married."

The Church is not perfect! Some Christians believe it will escape the wrath of God because it is basically good and performs God's will. Whereas, Israel rejected the Messiah and is, therefore, bad and should be punished. Although there are those Christians who follow God faithfully, it might come as a shock to some to learn that the Church as a whole is far from perfection and steeped in grievous sin, no less than the sin one can find in the camp of Israel.

When the text is taken into consideration, we can clearly conceive how some in Israel, although misguided, could have reached the conclusion that the wrath of God would only come against the nations. The Church idea, on the other hand does not have this kind of scriptural support. Unlike His promises to Israel, God did not promise the Church that He would protect them during the wrath to come. Neither did He say anywhere in the Bible that He would punish only Israel for her iniquities.

Speaking about Israel, Paul reminded Jesus' followers in Rome that "the gifts and the callings of God are irrevocable" (Romans 11:29). God will never forsake His people Israel, nor will He break any of the covenants He made with them—for God is not a man that He should go back on His word. God has not given any promises to the Church outside the ones He gave to Israel. Neither did He make any covenants with the nations outside of the rainbow covenant that He made with mankind following the flood.

The term "son of" or "child of" is another biblical Hebraic idiom. It is used to denote that someone is following a certain belief, or a certain teaching, or adopting a certain behavior.

It is vitally important to understand that even the new covenant was to be made with "the house of Israel and the house of Judah" (Jeremiah 31:31). Therefore, statements communicating that Jesus delivered us from the wrath to come (I Thessalonians 1:10, 5:9) are evident—promises of the covenant that God made with Israel, and the Messiah who will deliver us is still a Jewish Messiah.

The Church's foundation for escaping God's wrath is Israel. For God's covenants, promises and gifts to Israel can only apply to them according to the New Testament by virtue of adoption (Romans 11:11–29; Ephesians 2:19–

20) since outside the nation of Israel there are no covenants, nor promises to be fulfilled.

John was speaking here against the Jewish concept of ZCHUT AVOT, which means "for the merit of the forefathers." He warned the people not to rely on this principle because no one will escape the Day of Judgment. The Day of Judgment will come to all.

According to the rabbis, merit is something a person can gain or lose depending on his or her actions. The following rabbinic passage demonstrate its usage quite well: "The rabbis say: Let a man ever regard himself as if he is half guilty and half deserving; then if he fulfills one command, he inclined the scale towards merit; If he commits one sin, woe to him, for he has inclined the scale towards guilt; as it is said: 'one sin (sinner) destroys much good' (Ecclesiastes 9:18). 'By the one sin that he committed, he caused himself to lose much good"[4].

Merit is something a person can gain or lose depending on his or her actions.

Zechut Avot is the idea that the merits of the forefathers can be counted towards their children. A common rabbinic saying states, "Everything comes to Israel on account of the merits of the fathers."[5] Abraham for instance was a righteous man; no doubt he gained much merit. The rabbis taught that merit could be stored; therefore, the merit of the patriarchs can help their descendants.

The following quote will illustrate this:

> "Rabbi Pinchas the priest said in reference to Proverbs 11:21: If you fulfill a command, do not seek its reward from God straight away, lest you be not quitted of sin, but be regarded as wicked, because you have not sought to cause your children to inherit anything, for if Abraham, Isaac and Jacob had sought the reward of the good deeds which they performed. How could the seed of these righteous men be delivered, and how could Moses say: Remember Abraham, Isaac and Jacob, so that God repented of the evil which He thought to do against His people (Exodus 32:13–14)?"[6]

It is important to understand that the Jewish concept of Zechut Avot is based on biblical verses such as were mentioned above and others. In the Bible, God often decided not to destroy, or decided to restore things because of His promises to Israel's forefathers. God keeps His word. This is another reason by which the issue of Zechut Avot is understood.

In addition, at times, the idea of the merit of the fathers was taught simply. It was explained that good discipline and teaching of the parents merited their children.

Furthermore, there is also the element of communal national interpretation of Zechut Avot, in which we all are guarantors for one another. This is the principle of the collective responsibility of Israel. The rabbis said:

> "'Ye stand this day, all of you before The Lord, all the men of Israel' (Deuteronomy 29:10). All of you are pledges one for the other: if there be but one righteous man among you, you exist all of you through his merit, and not you alone, but the whole world, as it says, 'And the righteous is the foundations of the world' (Proverbs 10:25). If one man sins, the whole generation suffers, as was the case with Achan (Joshua 22:20). How much more will the good done by an individual benefit his environment!"[7]

Although this teaching was common, the rabbis often discouraged people from relying upon it. They said that even if the right is there, a man should not count on it but rather gain his own merit.

And finally, Paul was also familiar with the concept of Zechut Avot and used it in his writings. He said, "As regards to elections, they are beloved for the sake of their forefathers" (Romans 11:28).

John came out against those whom he believed counted on Zechut Avot to protect them from the upcoming judgment. It helps to remember the timing of this event, which took place just before the Day of Atonement.

Rabbinic writings, the Dead Sea scrolls and the New Testament all teach that immersion without repentance has no value. One has to repent of his sin and ask forgiveness of God before he enters the water of purification.

Immersion in the Mikveh is considered to be a public declaration of that which already has taken place in the heart. So during the period of the Ten

Days of Awe that comes to conclusion on the Day of Atonement, Orthodox men, every year for over two thousand years, have gone into the Mikveh.

This is the only time of the year that the nation gets immersed for repentance. They first repent before God and then go to the Mikveh to show that their hearts are right before God, that they have opened a clean page with Him. If a person does not repent and yet goes into the Mikveh, it does not do him any good. And, of course, a person might be able to cheat his fellow men, but he definitely would not be able to fool God, Who knows our hearts. Understanding this fact makes it easier to understand the text that we are discussing here.

Consider the Jewish calendar for a minute. In the month of Tishray we have...

> On The 1st of the month Rosh Hashanah falls, which is the Biblical feast of trumpets.
>
> On the 10th of the month Yom Kippur falls, which is the Day of Atonement.
>
> On the 15th of the month the feast of Succot falls which is the feast of Tabernacles.

In between the first two feasts, we have the Ten Days of Awe.

Most Christian commentators agree that Jesus' public ministry lasted for three and a half years, and that he started his ministry during the time of the Feast of Tabernacles. This conclusion is drawn because it is believed that his ministry ended on the Feast of Passover. Counting three and a half years backward from Passover brings us to the time of the Feast of Tabernacles.

The Feast of Tabernacles is the Jewish messianic feast, where the Messiah is expected to come and set up his Kingdom upon the earth.

Just before Jesus appeared on the scene, a teaching was circulating in Israel on the subject of repentance. It was taught by every teacher and also by John, as can be seen here. The teaching encouraged people to repent, followed by immersion, and they went to be immersed in the Mikveh.

Just before the feast of Tabernacles we have the period of the Ten Days of Awe when a teaching of repentance takes place in Israel everywhere, today and throughout all the generations. As we have seen, once people repented, they went into the Mikveh to get immersed. John did not only call them to repent according to the time, but also to be immersed according to the custom.

People just flocked to him for this purpose because this was the time for them to do so. It was expected of them. It was a provision for them, and none of them questioned why he was doing it. John was not the only teacher who preached repentance during that time or who immersed people. Others did as well since this was the proper time to do so.

John's message that the Kingdom of God is at hand was also timely and typical for the period of the Ten Days of Awe as the kingship of God is also central to the Rosh Hashanah service. It is clear that judgment is just around the corner—Yom Kippur is coming; therefore, repentance should take place, and that should result in becoming an active member of the Kingdom of God.

Just before Jesus appeared on the scene, a teaching was circulating in Israel on the subject of repentance. It was taught by every teacher and also by John. The teaching encouraged people to repent, followed by immersion.

There are different aspects of the "Kingdom of God," which we will cover later as we progress in this study. However, it is important to understand at this point the concept of the Kingdom of God in Judaism, and that is "where and when God rules the kingdom of God is present." God is the King Who rules over His Kingdom. If God is the King of my life, then the Kingdom of God is present right here...and right now!

Some people assume that John was always teaching repentance and urging people to immerse, but there is no reason to believe that. John was a great teacher who taught many in Israel. From the Gospels, we learn that his teaching created a big movement. He had many followers, and later some of them became Jesus' followers. He probably taught many different subjects, but at this time of the year, just like every other teacher in Israel, he would have concentrated on the subject of repentance.

The people in our text came to be immersed and, therefore, should have repented according to the custom of the season. It appears that he must have known that some of their hearts were not right before God. They did not truly repent. Without repentance immersion had no value for them. John, who was officiating at the immersion ceremony, rebuked them for trusting Zechut Avot, rather than being engaged in repentance as the rest of Israel was at that time and as was proper for the season. He suggested they produce fruit worthy of repentance.

John also proceeded to tell them that God could raise sons of Abraham from stones. There is a play in words in the Hebrew text here. Sons in Hebrew are BANIM and stones in Hebrew are AVANIM. Although it appears differently in English, in Hebrew it is spelled almost the same. In other words, God can raise sons for Abraham from anything, from anyone.

According to Jewish teaching, repentance that is not matched by a change of behavior, and compensating the person who was hurt in some way to counterbalance the damage is not considered to be repentance.

Abraham is the first forefather of Israel, but he is also considered to be the father of the proselytes. Everyone who converts to Judaism is considered to be the son of Abraham, and is given his name. All converts, therefore, from all the nations become sons of Abraham[8]. John's audience must have known this practice as well.

The reference to the day of wrath is a reference to the Day of Judgment. The Day of Wrath used to be a common expression in Judaism during that period and afterward, at least up to 500 CE. Evidence for it can be found in many Jewish writings[9]. Enoch said, "The Lord shall come forth with wrath."[10] In Jubilees we find the statement, "No one shall be saved on the day of the wrath of Judgment."[11] In the New Testament, the expression appears also in Romans 2:5 and Revelation 6:17.

Both expressions "The Day of Wrath" and "the Day of Judgment" then are one and the same. John talked about it within the context of immersion. The Day of Atonement, which was just around the corner, is also considered to be a Day of Judgment and is definitely a reference to the Day of Judgment that is still to come.

The fact that John even brought up the idea of escaping the wrath to come also points out the time of the year in which this event takes place. They knew that judgment is coming and that Israel must repent in order to escape it.

Notice that although John expected them to repent, at no time did he furnish them with a definition of repentance. Such a definition was not provided to the people by Jesus or by Paul. All three had taken for granted the fact that their audience understood what it meant. There was no question in their mind that the masses were acquainted with the concept of repentance. Their knowledge came from teaching in the synagogues to which they were exposed from a young age.

After rebuking them, John suggested they bear fruit worthy of repentance. The kind of fruit that true repentance will lead to, and that will be expressed in good deeds.

According to Jewish teaching, repentance that is not matched by a change of behavior, and compensating the person who was hurt in some way to counterbalance the damage is not considered to be repentance. God is interested in our actions and not in cheap confessions. So a case in which someone had stolen five dollars from his friend, admitted his sin, and then gave him back the five dollars he had taken from him is not considered to be true repentance. One must admit his sin and give the person back a greater sum of money in order to show that he truly regrets the incident. It has to cost us something.

One also has to insist on being forgiven. We cannot come to a person, ask him to forgive us, face his refusal, and shake our shoulders and say, "Well, I tried. I have done my share." We cannot accept no in this case. One must bug the person, until he gets fed up with him and says, "Okay, I have already forgiven you."

In Judaism, this concept of repentance and forgiveness is important because if we have unforgiveness in our hearts, or sin against our brother, it jeopardizes our relationship with God. So we are always under the obligation of repenting and obtaining forgiveness from others.

The rabbis even considered cases in which one had sinned against his brother, was going to ask his forgiveness, but the brother died before he had the chance to do so. What happens then? Rabbinical solution dictated that the man go to his grave accompanied by 10 witnesses; there he should tell them about his sin against this man and the fact that he intended to ask his forgiveness but did not manage. Therefore, he should say, "You are my witnesses before God that I truly was going to do so, so he may forgive me for this sin." It has to be costly or painful in order to demonstrate the true intention and remorse of the heart.

The man who is repentant will surely do the will of God. He will love his brother as himself. He will do everything in his power to keep the word of God. He will gain a right of merit not because of his forefathers, but because of his own actions. Out of his love for God, he will treat his fellow man right.

The statement "You shall know them by their fruit" (Matthew 7:17–20) is definitely tied to this because those who are repentant lead a life of obedience to God and to His word. Jesus used this sentence to sum up a teaching about good and bad trees that is identical to John's teaching here.

John said if you are truly repentant, you should be concentrating on producing good fruit—a fruit worthy of repentance, rather than putting so much stock in the fact that you are Abraham's children. In particular, you should do it because "the axe is already laid at the root of the trees; every tree therefore that does not bear good fruit is cut down and thrown into the fire" (Verse 10).

Just as John's imagery of being a forerunner to Jesus was inspired by the Book of Malachi, it is quite possible that his imagery was also influenced by it. In Malachi, God said, "Behold the day cometh, burning like a furnace, and all the proud and they that do wickedly are stubble, and the day shall come, shall set them aflame, said The Lord of hosts, and shall not leave them root or branch" (Malachi 4:1).

In any case, good trees will always produce good fruit, and bad trees will produce bad fruit. Good fruit is obedience to God and to His word. Proverbs 11:30 says, "The fruit of the righteous is a tree of life, and he who is wise wins souls." The rabbis said that "the tree of life" is a reference to the Torah. Proverbs 3:18 defines it as "wisdom." In any case, it is the wisdom to do the will of God and walk according to His ways.

Deuteronomy 6:25 states, "And it will be righteousness for us if we are careful to observe all these commandments before The Lord our God, just as he commanded us."

Observing the Torah then produces righteousness or good fruit; the trees are used in this context as a metaphor for people. Rabbi Kook explained that the tree (a person) has to do everything in order to reach the goal, which is to produce fruit. The more it works on it, the more taste and meaning it will have. And the opposite is true as well. The more the tree turns its back on its ultimate goal, the more it becomes tasteless, superficial and empty.

Judaism, therefore, teaches us to sanctify our lives or to put the taste back into the tree. It should be our goal to attach all the practical everyday elements of our lives to spiritual goals that reflect the real meaning of life and the existence of Almighty God.

John said if you are truly repentant, you should be concentrating on producing good fruit—a fruit worthy of repentance, rather than putting so much stock in the fact that you are Abraham's children.

Although here John spoke on an individual level, emphasizing the personal need to repent, he must have also had in his mind the national element. Israel as a nation needed to repent because judgment was near. The axe was already laid to the root of the tree. Rome, a foreign and alienating force, was in control at the time, which could have brought destruction at any moment. Indeed the axe was laid to the tree, and was used in 70 CE when the city of Jerusalem was destroyed. The rabbis in the Talmud no doubt had seen it this way as they applied Isaiah 10:33–34 to the destruction of the city[12].

Luke recorded the response of the masses to John's rebuke:

> "And the multitude were questioning him saying, then what shall we do? And he would answer and say to them, let the man who has two tunics share with him that has none; and let him who has food do likewise. And some tax gatherers also came to be baptized and they said to him: teacher what shall we do? And he said to them, collect no more than what you have been ordered to. And some soldiers were questioning him saying, and what about us, what shall we do? And he said to them: do not take money from anyone by force, or accuse anyone falsely, and be content with your wages." (Luke 3:10–14)

In response to their questions, John continued to advise them to make fruit worthy of repentance. To treat their fellow man as they would like to be treated. John was faithful to the traditional view that repentance should be accompanied by good deeds like taking care of the poor and sharing with them food and clothes.

As for the soldiers and the tax collectors, John did not ask them to leave their professions. He instead asked them to lead a holy life appropriate to repented people. This fact by itself tells us that both groups here were comprised of Jews as John would not have expected the Gentiles to repent nor to lead a holy life at this point.

The people of Israel at that time suffered from a system that imposed on them very heavy taxation. They paid a poll tax, which was income tax and ground tax. All the property and income not covered by the ground tax was subjected to the poll tax. The poll tax included a per-head charge that was to be paid by everyone—women from the age of twelve and men from the age of fourteen up to the age of sixty-five.

John, being faithful to his calling, was only interested in the people's repentance and in leading them to a holy life. This was his message to all.

Crops were also taxed—all grain, wine and fruit, partly by produce and the rest was translated into money. In addition, all import and export was duty taxed. This was collected on public highways and at seaports. There were also bridge and road taxes and duty on everything that was bought and sold in the towns.

In addition, each Israelite had to pay a half-shekel tax to the Temple including tithes from his produce. What previously was given only to God was now also given to Caesar. This was one of the reasons for the resentment against Rome.

The system of collecting taxes protected the treasury of Rome and, therefore, was indirect. There were senators and ministers in Rome who created joint-stock companies that bought at public auction the revenue of a province at a fixed price for 5 years. These companies wanted to get their money back with revenue; they were the ones who hired the publicans to do their job and collect the taxes.

The publicans then hired slaves and others from the lower classes to do their job; they were the tax gatherers. All these people involved wanted to make a profit, so the cost of the tax collection was added to the amount due. Therefore, they often charged double the amount of the initial tax[13].

These tax gatherers were also in charge of the bridges, roads, and import and export taxes. They made the people unload everything off their animals, so they could examine their possessions. If anyone made a false declaration, then his merchandise would be confiscated.

People could not stand these tax gatherers. The fact that they applied for this job made them even more despised in the eyes of the people because they became rich by stealing from their own brothers. The rabbinic attitude towards them was fully justified. We will discuss them further in a future book in this series.

John advised these people to collect only the tax that was due. Bearing in mind the system, this was probably an impossible request. If they truly repented, then it would probably have meant leaving their position.

Soldiers also were entitled to confiscate the belongings of the people when they wanted. Thus it was also a fast way to become rich. Needless to say, John advised them to be satisfied with their wages. The people despised the soldiers as well.

John, being faithful to his calling, was only interested in the people's repentance and in leading them to a holy life. This was his message to all. They ought to know there is no way that they will escape the wrath of God, unless they repent and make fruit worthy of repentance. His message was geared to encourage everyone to repent and change his lifestyle. He was an accomplished preacher since the Gospels tell us that many followed him.

CHAPTER 15 ENDNOTES

1. Even Ben Shushan, *The New Dictionary* (Hebrew-Hebrew) Vol. 3. p. 1150.
2. Talmud Yerushalmi, Taanit 64a.
3. Talmud Bavli, Sanhedrin 10:1.
4. Talmud Bavli, Kidushim 40b.
5. Sifre on Deuteronomy 108b.
6. Exodus Raba, Ki Tetze XLIV, 3, 6, 9.
7. Tanchuma (Buber's edition) Deuteronomy, Nitzavim 25a.
8. Talmud Yerushalmi, Baba Kama 1:4, 64a.
9. Talmud Bavli, Baba Batra 10a; Avodah Zara 18b.
10. Enoch 91:7.
11. Jubilee 24:30.
12. Talmud Bavli Berachot 5:1.
13. Most of the information concerning the tax collecting systems in this passage is borrowed from Alfred Edersheim, *Sketches of Jewish social life in the days of Christ*, pp. 55–57.

CHAPTER 16

JOHN'S CALL FOR REPENTANCE

MATTHEW 3:1–6, LUKE 3:1–6, MARK 1:2–6

It is important to discuss immersion in Judaism before dealing with this text in order to understand how it was done and for what purposes.

The text starts with a quote from the prophet Isaiah:

> "Now, in those days, John the Baptist, came proclaiming in the wilderness of Judea, saying: repent for the kingdom of heaven has come near. For this is the one referred to by Isaiah the prophet, saying: 'the voice of one crying in the wilderness, make ready the way of The Lord, make his path straight!'" (Matthew 3:1–3)

According to this, John's location while preaching repentance was the wilderness of Judea. Mark 1:5 also recorded that he immersed people in the Jordan River. Luke provided more information and said that John actually preached in all the districts around the Jordan (Luke 3:3). Incidentally, this is the first time the same account appears in all three synoptic Gospels.

John's basic message was that of repentance. In Hebrew, the term is CHAZARA BETESHUVA, which literally means "to return with an answer." The returning, of course, means back to God and to His word. The origin of the concept of Chazara Beteshuva can be found in the Bible. The prophets called Israel to turn back to God and to the covenant they had broken, using the terms LASHUV, meaning "to return" or SHUVU, which is a command "to return," which comes from the same root as the word TESHUVA[1]. The same term is also found in the Dead Sea Scrolls, in which the community was made of "those who turned from iniquity," and the covenant was "a covenant of repentance."[2] The need for repentance became a central theme in rabbinic theology.

Repentance, of course, is from our sins. And although we do not often stop to define sin, it is important to realize that sin constitutes a violation of the Torah. This is also the teaching of the New Testament. "Whosoever commits sin transgresses against the Torah, for sin is transgression of the Torah" (I John 3:4)[3].

John's basic message was that of repentance. In Hebrew, the term is CHAZARA BETESHUVA, which literally means "to return with an answer."

The term Torah is translated consistently as "law" in the different English versions of the Bible. The term "lawlessness," which is understood to be "without law" or "against the law" should be understood literally as "without the Torah" or "against the Torah." Therefore, the man of lawlessness of II Thessalonians 2:3, which is usually refers to the Antichrist, appears in the Greek text literally as the anti-Torah. But this is a totally foreign concept to the Church.

Sin is a transgression against God's Law. Christians often do not realize this is the biblical concept of sin, as the Torah, unfortunately, is rarely considered to be valid by the Church. It is presented as something belonging to the past, which Christians should not concern themselves with. Yet, in reality, the Torah was extremely important to Jesus. He quoted it all the time. It was part of his Bible as the TANACH—the Hebrew Scriptures—was the only Bible that existed at the time. This no doubt points to the fact that he did not wish his followers to violate it, but rather as he often stressed, he taught it and hoped they would keep it.

John did not only call people to repent, but also encouraged them to be immersed and to confess their sins. Both are elements of repentance within Judaism. As was mentioned before, immersion of repentance took place in Judaism only once a year, during the Ten Days of Awe between Rosh Hashanah—the start of the Jewish year and the biblical feast of Trumpets—and Yom Kippur—The Day of Atonement.

Immersion is a natural follow up to the act of repentance. It is known in Judaism as "repentance of purification." According to Jewish teachings, one can achieve different levels of repentance. One can ask forgiveness from God and achieve KAPPARA, meaning "atonement," and yet not go as far as achieving a higher level of self-purification known as TAHARAH.

This is a reference to the ritual immersion in water during that time. Rabbi Solovetchik said, "Immersion in water represents the analytical plunge into the sea of knowledge which is done through intense self-contemplation and profound soul-searching."[4]

Immersion of repentance then is a symbol of what had already taken place in the heart. It is a statement that people did not just repent because of a fear of God, or His coming judgment, or because they wanted to receive a benefit, or to enjoy His future promises. It is instead a deep recognition that comes as a result of serious heart and soul searching of our truly pitiful existence in comparison to God. It is facing our failures, our state of despair and our spiritual bankruptcy.

This is the kind of repentance John preached to all the people of Israel[5] and wanted them to achieve. He wanted them to turn away from sin and turn to God. Judaism teaches that man is always standing before God, regardless of where he is and what he is doing. Once he committed a sin, he removed himself from the presence of Almighty God. As it is written: "Your iniquities have separated between you and your God" (Isaiah 59:2).

Therefore, within the concept of repentance, there is the idea of longing and yearning to enjoy once again the presence of God. Repentance, in light of all this, is considered to be necessary, serious and important. The people who heard John understood perfectly since so many of them came to him in order to be immersed.

In addition, Judaism teaches that every person has an obligation to repent, and it is the love of God that enables us to do so. God is the one who had created the whole concept of repentance and He is the one who provided it for mankind. He is also the one who brings us back to Him, as it is stated in the Bible: "Turn us unto you, o Lord, and we will be turned. Renew our days as of old" (Lamentations 5:21).

John also urged them to confess their sins. The rabbis, based on Numbers 5:6–7, encouraged confession of sin. It became recognized as part of the process of repentance. There is no evidence that a formula of confession existed that people had to follow. Probably each person had to make up his own confession.

Confession to God for sins made against Him could have been uttered in silence. Confession to a fellow man for sins committed against him could have been done either in silence or in public. The exception was the sin of gossip, in which confession had to be done in public in order to clear the reputation and good name of the person involved.

Confession is considered to be a necessity in Judaism. Rabbi Solovetchik said, "Repentance contemplated, and not verbalized is valueless."[6] This is because our feelings, emotions, thoughts and ideas become clear to us only after we express them in logical sentences. As long as they remain repressed and are not out in the open, they appear to be distant and foreign to us. Emotions and thoughts take clearer shape and form when we express them. Because of this, confession completes the process of repentance.

Confession should be a clear expression of the truth within us. This is something we are unwilling to do most of the time. We cultivated, after the sin of Adam and Eve, a defense mechanism that enables us to reject unpleasant facts about us and flee from reality. Only when we are in a state of torment are we willing to admit the true facts. Therefore, confession is understood to be a sacrifice, a breaking of our will that involves both remorse and shame.

Confessions have been composed throughout the generations by various rabbis to help people to confess, although each person is encouraged to compile his or her own. Most of these confessions are intended to be said on Yom Kippur, when all of Israel has to approach God individually and collectively in repentance.

Rabbi Hamemuna composed an example of a typical individual confession for Yom Kippur:

> "O God, before I was created I was worthless, and now that I have been formed, I am as if I was not formed. I am dust in my life, how much more in my death. Behold, I am before thee as a vessel filled with shame and reproach. Now may it be thy will before Thee that I sin no more, and that, which I have sinned, cast out in thy mercy but not through painful troubles."[7]

The three elements of repentance, immersion and confession of sins were encouraged and preached in Israel each year during the Ten Days of Awe that come before Yom Kippur; all three are part of the requirements for this day. All three were also preached by John during this period as is the custom within Judaism.

It is important to realize here that all of John's actions were within the framework of Judaism. John did not call Israel to abandon its customs or to change its religion and adopt a new one, although this is the understanding of many Christian commentators.

Christianity did not yet exist, nor did the Gospels. He did not call on them to repent and believe, instead he called on them to "repent and to be immersed"! Immersion, as mentioned before, is a Jewish custom that was adopted by Christianity.

Within Judaism, there is also an immersion of converts. It is also possible that from immersion of repentance developed the concept of "immersion of proselytes," since the proselyte needed to repent, and repentance involved immersion.

John did not only call people to repent, but also encouraged them to be immersed and to confess their sins. Both are elements of repentance within Judaism.

However, according to the rabbis, a proselyte had to do three things in order to enter into God's presence. He had to be circumcised, had to offer a sacrifice and had to be immersed. The main results of his actions were that he entered into the covenants of Israel by his conversion[8].

The two concepts of immersion—immersion as an essential part of repentance and immersion as a must do before entering into a covenant—are more likely the origins of Christian baptism.

John preached immersion because it was the requirement of the time. According to Mathew, John preached it because "the Kingdom of Heaven was within reach." Jesus preached the same message as well[9]. The theme of repentance as preceding restoration is extremely common in Jewish literature[10]; both in relation to the restoration of the individual and in relation to the restoration of the nation as a result of collective national repentance.

Regarding the term "Kingdom of Heaven," one can often find the phrase OL MALCHUT SHAMAIM, which means "The yoke of the Kingdom of Heaven." The Kingdom of Heaven is recognized as the rule of God in people's lives. The yoke of the Kingdom is the Torah.

This concept is not only expressed in the Bible, but also in Jewish literature. We find statements that if Israel will turn back to God, then Jerusalem will be rebuilt (Isaiah 59:2). It is clear that the redemption of Israel from Gentile captivity will be preceded by their returning to The Lord[11] and that the restoration of the dispersed of Israel will follow repentance[12]. The rabbis continued with this understanding and said that "great is repentance, which brings near redemption"[13]. In order to get into the Kingdom of God, one has to repent of sin. This is true with regard to eternal life but also with regard to a personal relationship with Almighty God right here on Earth.

John not only discussed the fact that the kingdom is within their reach, but he also discussed, later on, the coming of the Day of Judgment. In reality, then, he gave them two reasons for repentance:

1. The kingdom is within their reach.
2. The Day of Judgment is coming.

His message concerning it is a continuation of the admonitions of the prophets, which understood the day of The Lord to be a day of punishment to all the nations[14].

The term "Kingdom of Heaven" used here by Matthew is a substitute for the term "Kingdom of God," which was used by Luke. The word "God" was changed to "Heaven" in order to protect the sanctity of the name of God.

Luke did not use the substitute since his Greek audience, more likely, would have not understood his message, nor were they concerned to sanctify God's name.

In Judaism, many other substitutes for the name of God developed. For instance, we refer to God as "The Holy One" or as HAMAKOM, meaning "The Omnipresent." The sacred name of God is not pronounced and instead we refer to God as HASHEM, which literally means "The Name." The word ELOHIM, which literally means God(s), is pronounced by some Orthodox Jews as Elokim for the same reason.

Regarding the term "Kingdom of Heaven," one can often find the phrase OL MALCHUT SHAMAIM, which means "The yoke of the Kingdom of Heaven." In rabbinic theology, accepting the yoke of the Kingdom of Heaven means accepting God as the king of our lives and accepting His Torah as guidance for living. The Kingdom of Heaven is recognized as the rule of God in people's lives. The yoke of the Kingdom is the Torah.

And indeed we learn from early rabbinic writings that the two phrases "The Yoke of the Kingdom" and "The Yoke of the Law" are synonymous. For instance, the rabbis said that Israel has taken upon itself the yoke of the Kingdom of Heaven on Mount Sinai. Or Israel, in a state of unbelief, was said to be rejecting the Kingdom of Heaven, the Kingdom of the House of David and the rebuilding of the Temple[15]. Repeating the Shema[16] twice a day was considered to be taking upon oneself the yoke of the Kingdom of Heaven[17] and so on.

In the Gospels, the term "Kingdom of Heaven" has the same meaning. It is important to know that this term is not referring to the visible or invisible Church as is often interpreted. The Kingdom of Heaven or the kingdom of God is a reference to the rule of God in peoples' lives and not to the church.

The quote we have here is taken from Isaiah 40:3 and is interpreted as a fulfillment of Malachi 4:5–6 (in the Hebrew text Malachi 3:23–34). It is found in Matthew 3:3: "The voice of one crying in the wilderness, make ready the way of The Lord, make his paths straight!"

The Hebrew text of Isaiah 40:3 says, "A voice is calling, clear the way for The Lord in the wilderness, make smooth in the desert a highway for our God."

The Hebrew text does not state that "A voice is crying in the wilderness," but instead that a voice is crying to make a way for God in the wilderness. The emphasis is not on where the voice is crying since the text provides us with no clue concerning the location of the voice. Instead, the emphasis is on the location of the way made for The Lord.

We have here one of the common Hebraic biblical doublets. In other words, we have here two sentences that communicate the same thing using different words. "Clear the way for The Lord" is parallel to "make smooth a highway for our God." And "in the wilderness" is parallel to "in the desert." The verse says the same thing twice for emphasis. And in both cases, it states that a way is to be cleared for God in the wilderness.

Since God is going to appear in the desert, it is, in fact, a calling for Israel to come and hear God in the wilderness. The prophet relates to God here as he would have related to a human king. One makes a way before a human king; how much more than before The King of the universe Himself. The rabbis taught that when Israel was exiled, so was God. When Israel will be restored, God will return with them. Just as at the days of the exodus from Egypt, God went at the head of the camp in the desert, so also it will be when God will restore the Kingdom back to Israel[18].

The desert has been an important location for Israel since many things happened there, so it is not surprising that this is also the location God had chosen for the future. It was in the wilderness that God revealed himself for the first time to the nation of Israel when he gave it the Torah (Exodus 19:1–5).

This is also where Moses and Aaron received their calling (Exodus 4:27). In the wilderness, God had provided an escape for the nation (Exodus13:18) and will provide an escape in the future as well. In the desert, God made a major provision for the people for 40 years. He was also with David and Elijah in the desert when they needed him (I Samuel 23:14, I Kings 19:4–5).

That the wilderness occupies an important place in Judaism is clear and evident from rabbinic writings as well. In the Midrash, we find that "Israel's elevation is from the wilderness; her decline is from the wilderness; her death is from the wilderness… The Torah came from the wilderness, the priesthood from the wilderness, the service of the Levites from the wilderness, royalty from the wilderness… and all the excellent gifts that God bestowed on Israel came from the wilderness. Rabbi Shimon Bar Yochai said, 'In the wilderness they were invested (with their ornaments) and in the desert they were divested of them. Prophecy was from the wilderness; thus Israel's elevation was from the wilderness'"[19].

Only Luke provided the timing of the event. As always, he is concerned to give us historical details, and here he provided for us a time reference for both Jewish and Roman chronology. The 15-year reign of Tiberius probably corresponds to August–September 26–27 CE. Luke mentioned here Herod Antipas who ruled over Galilee from 4–39 CE, and also Philip who ruled from 4 BCE–34 CE.

Abilene was a well-known area located Northwest of Damascus, near the town of Abila. Luke also mentioned a person named Lysanias, about whom we hardly have any information. Josephus also mentioned him several times, but did not provide us with further details. He basically talked about "Abila which belonged to Lysanias"[20].

"A voice is calling, clear the way for The Lord in the wilderness, make smooth in the desert a highway for our God."

Both Matthew (3:5) and Mark (1:5) mentioned that people from Jerusalem and Judah went out to John.

Although Jerusalem is a part of the territory of Judah, the city is mentioned most probably because of its importance as a separate political entity. This distinction is something that has continued from earlier times. This can be seen in Ezra's genealogies of those who returned from exile when he listed those of Jerusalem separately from those of Judah[21].

Luke also provided us with the Jewish timeframe for John's activity. He wrote, "In the days of the high priests Annas and Caiaphas, the word of God came to John the son of Zechariah, in the wilderness" (3:2).

Examining this text carefully appears to show that Luke is claiming that when these events took place, there were two high priests serving in the Temple at the time. However, by Jewish law, having two high priests at the same time is impossible. At any given time, the Jewish authorities appointed only one high priest. He could not be discharged of his position because it was given to him for life. So what is the story here then?

According to the Mishna[22], when the authorities appointed the high priest, they also appointed a person to the office of the SEGAN. The Segan was not equal to the high priest, but was very close to him in rank. He was the second in command to the high priest, much like one who is heir to a throne or has the position of the vice president. The Segan then was just below in position to the high priest and above all the other priests.

In the Bible, the Segan is described as a "second priest." Examples are II Kings 23:4, in which the term appears in the plural form, "second priests," and from which we, therefore, learn there could be more than one second priest at the same time. It also can be found in II Kings 25:18, which talks about Tzefanaia, the second priest or the Segan. They used to appoint a Segan to ensure that at any given time, there would be a substitute available for the high priest in case he came into contact with some uncleanliness and, therefore, was considered to be defiled and thus could not enter the Temple.

The Torah came from the wilderness, the priesthood from the wilderness, the service of the Levites from the wilderness, royalty from the wilderness... and all the excellent gifts that God bestowed on Israel came from the wilderness.

As a result that the office of the Segan existed, some commentators, when interpreting this verse, came to the conclusion that one of the two mentioned here was the priest and the other was the Segan. But Luke seems to have been concerned with historical accuracy and would have indicated if this were the case, He would probably have used the term Segan or second priest instead of the ambiguous plural form for a priest.

And indeed, Luke here is not referring to a high priest and a Segan. He is instead speaking of an awkward reality in which Israel, despite being against Jewish Law, had two high priests at the same time. The Romans, who ruled over Israel at the time, took the liberty of appointing high priests in Israel.

According to Jewish Law, no outsider had the authority or the inside knowledge one needed to enable him to appoint the high priest. But the Romans did not have much regard for Jewish Law, and the Jews, being subjected to a foreign ruler, could not do much about it. The Roman procurators had absolute power in the small territories of which they were in charge.

Caiaphas was known as Kifa in Hebrew and was also mentioned in the Talmud. He was appointed to the high priesthood by Valerius Gratus in 18 CE and served for 18 years in his office until 36–37 CE. From the history of that time, we know that during the period from the beginning of Herod's rule to the fall of Jerusalem, there were twenty-eight high priests appointed.

The office was frequently sold to the one who paid the most to the Romans in charge of the high priestly garments from 6–36 CE[23]. Rabbi Judah Ben Illai said that "Because one gives money for the high priesthood, they change every twelve months"[24]. The occupancy of the high priesthood changed four times before Caiaphas was found to be a submissive instrument at the hands of Rome. Caiaphas was a puppet of the Roman regime, a political favorite of the Roman authorities.

The character of the high priesthood during these years is described in very negative terms, both in the Talmud[25] and by Josephus[26].

Annas—CHANAN in Hebrew, meaning "he pardoned"—was the legitimate high priest at the time. In spite of Jewish Law, the Romans replaced him with Caiaphas.

Although Annas was deprived of his position, the Jewish people continued to consider him as their high priest. He continued to preside over the Sanhedrin. In Acts 4:6, he was mentioned as the actual high priest, whereas Caiaphas is merely mentioned as one of them.

CHAPTER 16 ENDNOTES

1. Ezekiel 33:7–20.
2. DSS, CD 19:16.
3. The translation was changed in order to fit the original.
4. Solovetchik on repentance, Pinchas H. Peli, p. 63.
5. Acts 13:24.
6. Solovetchik on repentance, Pinchas H. Peli, p. 92.
7. Talmud Bavli, Yoma 87.
8. Encyclopedia Judaica, Vol. 13, p. 1183.
9. Matthew 4:17, Mark 1:15.
10. Tovit 13:5.
11. Jubilees 1:15. Solovetchik on repentance, Pinchas H. Peli, p. 63.
12. Philo, De Pramiis 52–5.
13. Talmud Bavli, Yoma 86b.
14. Amos 5:18.
15. The Midrash on I Samuel 8:7.
16. The Shema is the key statement of faith in Judaism. It is found in Deuteronomy 6:4: "Hear o Israel, The Lord our God, is one God."
17. Talmud Bavli, Ber. 13b, 14b.
18. Rabbi Cook commentary on Isaiah 40:3.
19. Midrash, Song of Solomon, Raba 3:7.
20. Josephus, Antiquities XIX 5:1, XX 7:1.
21. Ezra 10:7; Nehemiah 7:6.
22. Mishna, Yuchasin (Rambam) 57:1.
23. Josephus, Antique. XV 11:4, XVIII 4:3, XX 1:1.
24. Talmud Bavli, Yoma 8b.
25. Ibid. Psachim 57, Yoma 35b.
26. Josephus, Antiquities XX 8:8.

CHAPTER 17

THE RESPONSE TO JOHN'S PREACHING

MATTHEW 3:11–13, LUKE 3:15–18, MARK 1:7–8, JOHN 1:26–27

As discussed previously, John's line of preaching had been very effective. As a result, he had many followers. A Messianic movement had now been formed that appeared to have the potential of posing a political threat.

According to John's Gospel's account, it looked like a group of Pharisees came to question John concerning his actions. They demanded some answers in order to form a report for those who had sent them. This group must have been sent by the Sanhedrin to investigate John because of the influence he had on the people.

The Sanhedrin was the Jewish Supreme Court; therefore, all the judicial and theological arguments were submitted to it for a final decision. In this particular case, they had to decide who John was. Since he was the head of a movement, they had to reach a conclusion determining whether he was posing a danger to the nation or not.

According to John 1:19–22, they were the ones who were questioning his identity. It says, "And this is the witness of John when the Jews sent to him priests and Levites from Jerusalem to ask him, 'who are you?' and he confessed and did not deny, and he confessed 'I am not the Messiah.' And they asked him, 'what then? Are you Elijah?' And he said, 'I am not. Are you the prophet?' and he answered 'no.' They said then to him, 'who are you, so that we may give an answer to those who sent us? What do you say about yourself?'"

The Sanhedrin was the Jewish Supreme Court; therefore, all the judicial and theological arguments were submitted to it for a final decision.

Luke, in addition, recorded that some people thought John was the Messiah (Luke 3:15). It is clear that John was quite popular among the people. Many wondered who exactly he was, and others believed him to be the Messiah. Many followed him. Since Messianic expectations as a result of Israel being ruled and suffering under a foreign power were up in the air at the turn of the first century, the public response to John was not surprising at all.

John, of course, went against this idea by telling them three statements:

1. I am not the Messiah.
2. The Messiah will be much greater then I am.
3. He will perform different kinds of immersions.

Examining these three statements, it becomes apparent that John made sure his followers and the authorities would understand that not only was he not the Messiah, but also he was not claiming to be Elijah either. Furthermore, he was not even seeing himself as a prophet. No doubt, he was quite humble. He saw himself only as "the voice calling in order to make a way for God in the wilderness."

John knew that in order for God to rule over Israel once again, the nation must repent; therefore, he did all he could to bring it to repentance. All of his actions pointed out to his perfect identification with the nation of Israel and its future.

The Messiah will be greater than I am—Luke 3:16 says, "As for me, I immerse you with water; but one is coming who is mightier then I, and I am not fit to untie the thong of his sandals…" An ancient rabbinic saying states that "all manner of service that a slave performs for his master, a disciple must render to his teacher, except the loosing of his sandal thong"[1].

The untying of the shoe was considered to be such a low chore that a disciple was not obligated to do it for his rabbi. In the Roman world, the carrying of the shoes to the bath was the job of the slave; therefore, it became a symbol of servility. John was telling them that he is not even worthy to do the most menial of duties for the Messiah.

John is not even worthy to be the Messiah's slave. In other words, no comparison can be made between him and the Messiah, and they should not even consider him as a possibility. Note again that John—although he was considered to be great by many people as well as by Jesus himself—was an extremely humble person.

The Messiah will perform different kinds of immersions. When John compared his and the Messiah's immersions, he said in Matthew 3:11–12:

> "As for me, I immerse you with water for repentance, but he who is coming after me is mightier then I, and I am not fit to remove his sandals; he will immerse you with the Holy Spirit and fire. And his winnowing fork is in his hand, and he will thoroughly cleanse his threshing floor; and he will gather his wheat into the barn, but he will burn up the chaff with unquenchable fire."

John spoke here about two kinds of baptisms or immersions, which the Messiah was going to perform. The Messiah, he said, would immerse some people with the Holy Spirit. Those people he compared to the wheat. The wheat he said will be gathered into the barn. This is a metaphor for God's Kingdom in this case. Others the Messiah will immerse with fire. Those people he compared to the chaff, and they are going to be burned with unquenchable fire. Unquenchable fire can be found according to the New Testament in the lake of fire.

What is unquenchable fire? It is a fire that cannot be put out, but which goes out when it has turned everything to ashes. Jeremiah 17:27 states that Jerusalem is to be destroyed with unquenchable fire. In II Chronicles 36:19–21, the Bible says this fire burned the city "to fulfill the word of The Lord by the mouth of Jeremiah" and left it desolated. And we know that this fire went out after it destroyed the city.

To quench means to extinguish or put out. No one will be able to put out the fire that clearly is a fire of God. No one will be able to escape from it by extinguishing it. Isaiah said of that fire, "Behold, they shall be as stubble; the fire shall burn them; they shall not deliver themselves from the power of the flame: there shall not be a coal to warm at, nor a fire to sit before it" (Isaiah 47:14).

After it has accomplished its work of destruction, that fire will go out. No one can deliver himself from its flame by putting it out, but finally not a coal will be left.

John, therefore, told them that the Messiah was going to immerse everyone. Some will be immersed with the Holy Spirit, those who were the people among them who repented and who followed God and obeyed him. These people will be gathered into His Kingdom. Others will be immersed with fire, and those will eventually be burned with unquenchable fire. And although John does not specify here where this will take place, the usual assumption is that it will happen in the lake of fire. Incidentally, the term "lake of fire" is a concept that belongs only with the New Testament. The Tanach does not mention it at all.

Indeed, John more likely, was referring to unquenchable fire right here on Earth—more precisely, in the city of Jerusalem as he had predicted its destruction. The New Testament did not exist at the time. Therefore, John was not familiar with its concept of the lack of fire since it was not part of his Bible, nor was it part of his tradition.

Furthermore, both John and his audience were familiar with the concept of unquenchable fire from a place known as Geh Ben Hinnom—which literally means the valley of the son of Hinnom, located in the city of Jerusalem. The word "Gehenna" developed from it and literally means "Valley of Hinnom," referring to a valley just outside Jerusalem.

The "Valley of the son of Hinnom" is located south of Jerusalem (Joshua 15:8, II Kings 23:10; Jeremiah 2:23; 7:31–32; 19:6, 13–14) and used to be the place where children were sacrificed to the god Moloch (II Chronicles 33:6). For this reason, the valley was deemed to be accursed. "Gehenna," therefore, it soon became a figurative equivalent to "hell."

It was a place that—from the time of King Ahaz of Judah—was known as the seat of the worship of Moloch, a god worshiped by the Ammonites, who came to be worshiped by Israel as well (Leviticus 18:21; I Kings 11:3,5,7; II Kings 23:10; Amos 5:26; Acts 7:43).

King Ahaz sacrificed his sons there according to II Chronicles 28:3. Since his legitimate son—by the daughter of the High Priest Hezekiah—succeeded him as king, this must be referring to children he had by unrecorded pagan wives or concubines. The same thing is recorded of Ahaz's grandson, King Manasseh, in II Chronicles 33:6.

The valley was known as a place of fiery torture and sacrifices to honor pagan gods. When King Josiah burned down the pagan altars, the location remained a site for burning pagan artifacts as the country was purged of idolatry. As time went by and there were no more idols to burn, some historical records suggest that the people of Jerusalem began dumping and burning their trash there.

The meaning of Gehenna must be established from facts furnished by the Scriptures, not by falsehoods that come from human or pagan tradition. To the Hebrew who reads the Tanach, Gehenna can not only mean a verdict that condemns a man to death, but also ordains after death that his body should be cast into the Valley of Hinnom. Since this is the sense of Gehenna in the Hebrew Scriptures, we can be sure this is the sense in which Jesus used it as well.

Often this text is understood to be saying that the Messiah will immerse all who believe in Him with both the Holy Spirit and fire. Baptism of fire is conceived at times to be a real baptism, as a modern movement in Christendom recently claimed. At other times, it is understood to be a reference to the sanctification process. Regardless of the interpretation concerning its nature, we need to understand that such ideas are based on the assumption that John was addressing people who believed in Jesus. But in reality, he was not.

The Messiah would immerse some people with the Holy Spirit. Those people he compared to the wheat. The wheat he said will be gathered into the barn. Others the Messiah will immerse with fire. Those people he compared to the chaff, and they are going to be burned with unquenchable fire

John was speaking at the time to the congregation of Israel, in general, and to the Pharisees and Sadducees who questioned him, in particular. At all times, he must have had his goal in mind; he needed to bring these people to repentance. They should consider the judgment that is coming; they should know, therefore, that with the Messiah they are longing for will come both reward and punishment. Some will be benefiting from the presence of God in their lives, but others will be condemned. Therefore, it is important to repent.

Some people believe that immersion of fire is a reference to the process of sanctification.

Although, some people believe that immersion of fire is a reference to the process of sanctification. And although some of the rabbis also referred to this process as an immersion of fire, nevertheless, the context favors an interpretation of judgment rather than sanctification.

Considering the issue of sanctification, one also needs to remember that God did not say that in order to purify us; He will pass us through the fire. We human beings are not capable of going through fire. He said that He would purify us just as gold and silver are purified through the fire. Metals such as gold and silver, after passed through fire, come out totally pure. Nothing is left but pure gold. God is saying that by the time He will finish purifying us, we will be as pure as gold and silver become after the fire. No impurity will be left in us.

According to John's account, the day after this discussion took place, Jesus came to him to be immersed (John 1:29). In the same account, John also claimed that he did not know Jesus, but that he had received a revelation from God concerning Him.

Verse 33 states:

> "And I did not recognize him, but he who sent me to immerse in water said to me, he upon whom you see the Spirit descending and remaining upon him, this is the one who immerses in the Holy Spirit."

It appears that despite John and Jesus belonging to the same family—they were second-generation cousins—they really did not know each other. This is a bit strange to us Israelis, as Israel is small, and at that time had half of the Jewish population we find today. The Jewish calendar is saturated with holidays that provide many opportunities for families to gather together. And that is what they do, according to custom. Second-generation cousins should definitely expect to know one another.

As the information about the years of development of Jesus and John is extremely limited, we are left with no way of determining why it was they did not know each other. Some attribute it to the geographical distance between Judea and Galilee, although it is probably safe to assume that Joseph and Mary attended the Temple in Jerusalem yearly during God's feasts as He commanded. Surely their boys older than the age of thirteen accompanied them regularly on visits that provided them with the opportunity to get together with other family members. Perhaps some other unknown factors had contributed to this.

John insisted on emphasizing this fact; he mentioned it twice in this text. Clearly, he deemed it important to assure those present that in not knowing Jesus, he could not possibly favor him. Jesus was a stranger, and as such he did not exalt him. The whole thing was God's idea.

Although the general understanding is that Jesus did not need to be immersed in an immersion of repentance according to the New Testament, he was sinless. Nevertheless, according to this text, Jesus came to be immersed in an immersion of repentance and insisted on being immersed.

To John's objections, Jesus replied, "It was proper to do this in order to fulfill all righteousness." More likely, Jesus referred here to the Jewish requirement to be immersed after repentance during the Ten days of Awe since Yom Kippur was approaching.

But the question that is often asked is was it okay for Him to do so? Yes! Jewish men during this season went to the Mikveh after they were engaged in prayers for repentance for a period of thirty days. It is still the custom of Orthodox Jews today to visit the Mikveh before the holidays.

The Mikveh existed to complete the process physically of what had already transpired spiritually. The only time the immersion of repentance had value is when the person had repented. Without repentance there was no point in getting immersed. It was only an outward declaration that he was indeed pure now because he had opened a new page with God. At the point, when he entered the Mikveh, his heart was already right before God. Surely Jesus' heart was right before God; therefore, there was no reason for him not to be immersed.

It is important to notice here that Jesus' immersion took place before and with the people of Israel (Luke 3:21). In this we have a full and complete identification of Jesus with the people of Israel and with their customs. John's practice of immersion was definitely a Jewish custom. Incidentally, this is the only recorded time in the Gospels that John and Jesus were together.

According to all the Gospel accounts immediately following Jesus' immersion, three things happened:

1. The heavens opened up.
2. The Holy Spirit came down in a form of a dove and rested upon him.
3. A voice came out of heaven declaring, "This is my son, my beloved, in whom I am well pleased."

According to Luke, all this happened while Jesus was praying (Luke 3:21). According to John's account, John testified that he saw the Spirit coming down and resting on Jesus (John 1:32).

The Heavens Opened Up

This term reminds us of Ezekiel 1:1: "Now it came about in the thirtieth year, on the fifth day of the fourth month, while I was by the river Chebar among the exiles, the heavens were opened and I saw visions of God."

This Jewish expression can be found in the Hebrew Bible as we have just seen. It is also used in the New Testament in Acts 7:5–6, in connection to Stephen's speech and in Acts 10:11, in connection to Peter's vision. Examples of it can be found also in other literature of the time, for instance, in the Testimony of Levy. Here we have mentioned two of the things that are involved in Jesus' immersion:

> "The heavens shall be opened and from the Temple of glory shall come upon him with sanctification with her Father's voice (Bat Kol) from Abraham to Isaac."[2]

This term is used always in a context that brings about God's message and/or His presence. In Ezekiel, the vision is given to him while he is in exile, after Nebuchadnezzar had already conquered Jerusalem. The people of Israel who were taken into exile believed that God had forsaken the land and forsaken them. But the appearance of the divine presence in a vision that was given to Ezekiel in the heavens over Babylon showed them that God was with them even in exile.

The whole idea of the Heavens being opened up stems from the understanding that the Heavens contain the throne of God; therefore, any revelation that comes from there comes directly from His throne.

The Holy Spirit Came Down in a Form of a Dove

Often, scholars claim the dove was not really used as a symbol for the Holy Spirit, although it does appear in this way in some Jewish writings. The reason behind this doubt is the fact that elsewhere in the Bible the dove symbolizes other things. Hosea likened the dove to the people of Israel, saying the exiled dove was going to come home (Hosea 7:11, 11:11). Isaiah the prophet also did so in Isaiah 60:8. In the Song of Solomon, the dove symbolizes beauty, innocence and purity (Song of Solomon 1:15, 4:1, and 5:2).

In rabbinic writings, we find the Holy Spirit often compared to a dove. The following are a couple of examples:

Rabbi Simon B. Zoma said:

> "I have been contemplating the creation (and came to the conclusion) that between the upper and the nether waters there is but two or three fingers breaths … For it is not written here 'and the Spirit of God blew', but hovered, like a dove flying and flapping with its wings, its wings (barely touching the nest)."[3]
>
> "And the Spirit of God hovered over the water (Genesis 1:2) as a dove which hovers over her young without touching them."[4]

In addition to the dove, in rabbinic writings the Holy Spirit is also compared to other birds: "The Holy Spirit hovered over the waters as an eagle hovers over its young in the nest"[5].

Although the dove symbolizes different things within Judaism, we should ask ourselves what possible understanding did Jesus and John derive from the descending and landing of the dove following his immersion. Or what did it mean to the people who stood around? Even so, it is not clear whether or not they have seen it or heard it. It is logical that they might have, just as John did. According to this text, John actually was told by God that the dove symbolized the descent of the Holy Spirit. This was not a foreign concept to him, nor was it to Jesus or to the Jewish people at that time.

The Voice from Heaven—The Bat Kol

"The voice from Heaven" was not a strange phenomenon to the Jewish people of the first century CE. In fact, the opposite is true. It was a common experience to most of the people who had been immersed by John, since they were all Jewish. It used to be called THE BAT KOL, meaning literally "daughter of the voice." It is defined as "A heavenly or divine voice, which revealed God's will, choice or judgment to man"[6].

"The voice from Heaven" was not a strange phenomenon to the Jewish people of the first century CE. It was a common experience to most of the people who had been immersed by John.

The Bat Kol was very well known during this time. The rabbis spoke of it as an echo voice; they said it reminded them of the sound of a chirping bird or the cooing of a dove[7].

They also described it by saying that "when a voice came out of heaven, another voice came out of it"—hence the idea of the echo voice.

It probably was believed to be an echo of God's voice; it was uttered in Heaven and heard on Earth. It was definitely understood to be a "divine communication"[8].

Most of the references to the Bat Kol are referring to an external voice that was heard out loud by the people who received the message. But we also have references to people who claimed that the Bat Kol appeared to them in their dreams[9].

Historically, we know that after The Holy Spirit left Israel, the last prophet died and the canon was closed. They then started to use the Bat Kol—Voice from Heaven—for guidance. They decided that "with the cessation of prophecy, the Bat Kol remained the sole communication between God and man."[10]

Some of the rabbis claimed that the Bat Kol was heard already during biblical times. They said, for instance, that the Bat Kol proclaimed Tamar's innocence, and that it communicated that the prophet Samuel did not benefit materially from his position, and that it validated Solomon's judgment in giving the child to the right mother[11]. These claims are not supported by biblical text.

They also said that a Bat Kol was often heard at the death of martyrs, and that Channa and her seven sons, who had been brutally executed by the Greek dictator Antiochus Epiphanies in 165 BCE, are examples. They claimed that at the time of her death, a voice came out proclaiming, "A joyful mother of children."

After Rabbi Akiva's execution by the Romans, they said a heavenly voice declared, "Happy are thou Rabbi Akiva that thou are destined for the life of the world to come"[12].

According to the rabbis, It was also by the authority of the Bat Kol that Halacha—Jewish Law—was determined. It solved the controversy between Beit Hillel and Beit Shamai—the house of Rabbi Hillel and the house of Rabbi Shamai—by stating that "The words of both are the words of the living God, but the Halacha is in agreement with the rulings of Beit Hillel"[13]. The result was that the teaching of Beit Shamai was declared null and void. Today's Judaism, therefore, is the continuation of Beit Hillel.

There are many other stories that can be quoted in order to show the wide usage that was made of the Bat Kol in the early period of Judaism. There is no doubt that, just like anything else, this was also misused by people at the time. Some of the records we have definitely are accounts of fables, superstitions and even wishful thinking. Because of its abuse by the populace and by the rabbis, some scholars[14] refused to see a reference to it here in Jesus' immersion.

Nevertheless, it is clear that the Bat Kol was used as a guiding force and that many decisions have been determined by it. And like it was just mentioned, it also has been abused. However we cannot determine its validity by the negative misuse of it. If we are willing to allow for this kind of judgment, we should treat the Holy Spirit in the same way. Unfortunately, today in Christendom, many fables and wishful stories are attributed to it. In the same manner, we will also need to treat the name of God, which sadly is misused regularly, as well.

The term that appears here in the Gospel referring to a heavenly voice is definitely corresponding to what we know as Bat Kol. A similar reference to a heavenly voice was also recorded in the account of the transfiguration (Luke 9:35).

According to the record, immediately following Jesus' immersion, a Heavenly voice—Bat Kol—came out declaring, "This is my son, my beloved, in whom I am well pleased." This appears to be a combination quotation from Psalm 2:7 and Isaiah 42:1. Psalm 2:7 says, "I will surely tell of the decree of The Lord: he said to me, 'thou art my son, today I have begotten thee.'"

Isaiah 42:1 says, "Behold, my servant, whom I uphold; my chosen one in whom my soul delights. I have put my spirit upon him; he will bring forth justice to the nations." The phrase "This is my son" corresponds to "Thou art my son, today I have begotten thee." The phrase "My beloved in whom I am well pleased" corresponds to "My chosen one in whom my soul delights."

The words "my chosen" in Hebrew are BECHIRI, which literally means "my chosen." Some believe it means "my firstborn," which in Hebrew is BECHORI. There is no linguistic relationship between these two words, and they do not come from the same root, although they sound alike. Bechiri—my chosen—is written with the letter chet, which is the eighth letter in the Hebrew alphabet—בְּחִירִי.

Bechori—my first born—is written with the letter chaf, which is the eleventh letter—בְּכוֹרִי. The term "firstborn" is not at all in the text, and cannot be read into it.

In Jewish thinking, Psalm 2 refers to the "anointed one," which in Hebrew is MASHIACH, and it is translated into English as "the Messiah." Initially, it was understood that the anointed one was a reference to the King of Israel.

The kings of Israel had to be anointed with oil for their office (Exodus 30:25), and they were considered to be "God's representatives on Earth," who might bring freedom to the people. By the first century CE, this was changed, and "The son" of Psalm 2 was now understood to be a reference to the future Messiah.

Probably, this was in lieu of the fact that, by that time, Israel was no longer a kingdom; therefore, there were no more kings appointed to it. King Messiah was also going to be God's representative upon the earth, and he was going to save them and re-establish the Kingdom of Israel.

Taking a look at Psalm 2 provides insight to how this is interpreted within Judaism. The rabbis understood the statement "You are my son, today I have brought you forth" as God saying to His King, "This is how I relate to you, as a Father relates to his son. Today is the day in which you will assume your responsibility, and I have brought you forth, and today I have made you."

The Targum—which comes to us from the end of the first century CE and provides us with a fairly good understanding of how the Bible was interpreted at the time—translated Psalm 2:7 as "Beloved as a son to his father, art thou to me."

Referring, of course, to King David is verse 12: "Not only did I make you but from this day on I will consider you to be my son, I will also give all authority to you, you will rule over all the nations, and the earth will be your possession. The people of Israel will have to obey you and to take refuge in you."

> According to the record, immediately following Jesus' immersion, a Heavenly voice—Bat Kol—came out declaring, "This is my son, my beloved, in whom I am well pleased."

The term that was translated in verse 12 as "do homage to the son," in the Hebrew Masoretic text, it appears as "kiss the son." A kiss was a sign of showing that one was accepting the authority of another upon him. A disciple that was kissing his rabbi was making a statement that he is receiving the rabbi as his master. God in this Psalm was instructing the people to accept the King's authority upon them, to obey him.

Jesus' immersion was the last act of his private life and the first act of his public one. At his immersion, Jesus was said to be presented to his people and to be empowered by the Holy Spirit. There had to be something tangible for the people to see in order for them, or even for John to know that indeed The Spirit of God rested upon him. And in this case, it was the dove that rested upon him and which could be seen by them all.

The empowerment is for service. It is interesting that the rabbis associated the empowering of the Spirit with the coming of the Messiah. They claimed that the anointed one would receive power to accomplish his mission. To have arrived at this concept, they must have interpreted both Psalm 2 and Isaiah 42. But they came to this conclusion considering other verses as well. For instance, they said the statement "The spirit of God hovered" in Genesis 1 is alluding to the Spirit of Messiah because it is written as "And the spirit of The Lord shall rest upon him" (Isaiah 11:12).

In Jesus' immersion then, we also have his call to ministry. His calling was accompanied by the Holy Spirit and was confirmed by the Bat Kol. During Jesus' ministry, according to the Gospels accounts, God spoke three times audibly.

CHAPTER 17 ENDNOTES

1. Talmud Bavli, Ketuvot 96a; Eruvin 27b; Midrash, Exodus Raba 21:2.
2. The testimony of Levi 18.
3. The Midrash, Genesis Rabbah 2:4.
4. Talmud Bavli, Chagiga 15a.
5. Ibid, Chagiga 2:5; Talmud Yerushalmi, Chagiga 2:1.
6. Tosefta, Talmud Bavli, Sanhedrin 11:1—here it is presented as an echo of the voice of God.
7. Talmud Bavli, Megilah 32a; Midrash, Genesis Rabbah 37:7.
8. Ibid, Chagiga 14b.
9. Ibid, Yoma 9b.
10. Ibid, Makot 23b.
11. Ibid.
12. Talmud Bavli, Berachot 61b.
13. Ibid, Eruvin 13b.
14. Alfred Edersheim, *The Life and Time of Yeshua the Messiah*, Vol. 2, p. 286

CHAPTER 18

JOHN'S TESTIMONY

JOHN 1:29–34

> "The next day he saw Jesus coming to him, and said, 'behold, the lamb of God who takes away the sin of the world! This is he on behalf of whom I said, 'after me comes a man who has a higher rank then I, for he existed before me.' And I did not recognize him, but in order that he be manifested to Israel, I came baptizing in water.' And John bore witness saying, 'I have beheld the spirit descending as a dove out of heaven, and he remained upon him. And I did not recognize him, but he who sent me to baptize in water said to me,' he upon whom you see the Spirit descending and remaining upon him, this is the one who baptizes in the Holy Spirit. And I have seen, and have borne witness that this is the son of God."

In this section, we have the first proclamation by John of Jesus' greatness; he called Jesus "The Lamb of God." This was not just a descriptive statement, but it was instead an exclamation, Look! Here is the Lamb of God! John must have thought the people would know what he was talking about. But this term does not appear anywhere in the Tanach. And even in the New Testament, it only appears twice—and both instances are in John's Gospel.

Since the phrase "the Lamb of God" was not one of the names or Messianic titles given to the Messiah, people around him could not possibly have understood that his words referred to the Messiah.

At best, they perhaps could have deduced that the "The Lamb of God" might be a reference to a sacrifice of some sort. And John, in this text, actually alluded to it by saying he takes away the sin of the world. But since human sacrifice was forbidden by God, and is a totally foreign concept to Judaism, it is difficult to understand how John came up with this idea. It is even harder to understand how he expected his audience to be able to relate to it.

According to the Tanach, Deuteronomy 12:30–31 states:

> "Beware that you are not ensnared to follow them, after they are destroyed before you, and that you do not enquire after their gods, saying, 'how do these nations serve their gods, that I also may do likewise?' You shall not behave thus toward The Lord your God, for every abominable act which The Lord hates they have done for their gods; for they also burn their sons and daughters in the fire to their gods."

Other similar references express God's feeling about this, but we are not dealing with this right now. So back to our text. This statement appears in the Gospels only here. John declared that Jesus was the one of whom he had previously spoken to the leadership when they questioned him regarding his own identity (John 1:26–27).

> The term "Lamb of God" does not appear anywhere in the Tanach. And even in the New Testament, it only appears twice—and both instances are in John's Gospel.

Many scholars feel that it is not quite clear what John the writer meant here by the phrase "the next day." Since most scholars believe that Jesus was taken to the desert immediately following his immersion, this text seems to create a problem. After all, Jesus was in the desert 40 days. Obviously, this could not be taken literally as the next day. They suggested, therefore, that he referred here to the day after Jesus returned from the desert. But that kind of interpretation presents a problem. John did not record or even mention the temptations. Why then would he make such an obscure reference to the event? And how would his readers guess what event he is alluding to?

But Jesus was not taken to the desert immediately after the immersion as we have seen before. Jesus was expected by God and everyone else to be in town for the Feast of Tabernacles in accordance with God's commandment. He was more likely around until the feast was over and only then was taken by the spirit to the desert. Therefore, there is no reason to doubt that John indeed saw him the day after his immersion. That is the day after he was questioned by the Sanhedrin concerning his actions. Understanding when the immersion took place helps us to see that there is no conflict here in the text.

When John saw Jesus he announced, "Behold the Lamb of God which takes away the sin of the world. This is he of whom I said, after me comes a man who is preferred before me" (John 1:32).

Looking at this account, we clearly see the similarities between John and Jesus' relationship to Samuel and Saul's relationship. Here are some examples:

Samuel recognized Saul a day after God announced his coming. John recognized Jesus a day after he announced his coming (John 1:19).

When Samuel saw Saul, God said, "Behold, the man of whom I spoke to you! This one shall rule over my people." When John saw Jesus he announced, "Behold the Lamb of God which takes away the sin of the world. This is he of whom I said, after me comes a man who is preferred before me" (John 1:32).

Just before Saul's coronation—before he started his ministry—we are told that the Spirit of God entered him and he became a new man (I Samuel 10:6). And also during Jesus' immersion, we are told that the Spirit anointed Him, just before he started his ministry (John 1:33).

To become a new man in Judaism means to be reborn. So Saul here was reborn. There are seven ways in which a man can be born again in Judaism, which we will discuss in a future book in this series. One way is by becoming a king, which is exactly what happened here to Saul. Not everyone has the opportunity to go down this route; most of us do not become kings.

In any case, within Judaism, becoming a king was also associated with becoming "a son of God." This was based on the following Scriptures:

Psalm 89:26–27—God, speaking about King David, said, "He will cry to me, 'thou art my father, my God, and the rock of my salvation.' I also shall make him my first born, the highest of the kings of the earth."

II Samuel 7:13–14—God, speaking about King Solomon, said, "He shall build a house for my name, and I will establish the throne of his kingdom forever. I will be a father to him and he will be a son to me…" The same is also stated in I Chronicles 17:13.

John also testified, "And I have seen and born witness that this is the son of God" (John 1:34).

So these are the similarities to this account that we find in the story concerning the coronation of Saul. Here are some other points to consider:

John said, "Behold the Lamb of God, who takes away the sin of the world!" The phrase "takes away" is a translation of the Greek word AIRO, which basically means "to raise, to pick up, to take, to lift, to elevate." The same word is used in John 8:59, where we are told, "some of the leadership picked up stones in order to stone Jesus." Therefore, a better translation here would probably have been "The Lamb of God that lifts up the sin of the world." In other words, "gets rid of the yoke of sin."

Paul had this understanding in mind when he spoke about "being a slave to sin" in Romans 6:7 and in other places. Slavery to sin brings about a disruption in a personal relationship with God. But people who have in them the divine spark, the Spirit of God, are able to live a life free of sin, a life of service to God. A person can have either the yoke of sin or the yoke of God—i.e., a person can live either according to the law of the flesh, according to his/her carnal desires, and be a slave to sin, or a person can live according to the Law of God, which is the Torah, and be a servant of God.

Many commentators dealing with Romans chapters 6 and 7 talked about freedom from the Law. In reality, Paul was speaking about freedom from sin, not from the Law.

The Torah is not the problem, sin is. Paul taught the followers of Jesus that they should die to their flesh. They should die to their sinning nature, not to the Torah. So the freedom is from sin, not from the Torah. Paul spoke to Jews, and the Jewish people signed an eternal, irrevocable covenant with God. Therefore, they are never to be free from the Torah.

While we are alive on this earth, there are two forces claiming us—our physical desires and God Almighty. Once we die physically, we become free from this influence. Then we have only one force claiming out attention and that is God. Throughout our life, we have to struggle against the negative physical desires and live a life of obedience to God.

While we are alive on this earth, there are two forces claiming us—our physical desires and God Almighty. Once we die physically, we become free from this influence. Then we have only one force claiming out attention and that is God.

John said twice in this text, “And I did not recognize Him.” It is not clear what exactly he meant here. After all, they were relatives, cousins. Although they lived in two different locations, one in Galilee and the other in Judea, they had plenty of opportunities to meet. Over the years, Jesus’ family must have made many trips to the Temple. John could have meant, “I did not recognize him, although we are related.” This is the second time that John here emphasized this curious point.

John, the writer of the Gospel of John, seems to be taking for granted here that his readers are familiar with the Synoptic Gospels. John said, “I beheld the spirit…” recalling the event of the immersion, without previously recording it, or explaining to his audience what exactly he is talking about. That presents a problem because at the time this Gospel was written, the synoptic Gospels did not yet exist in the form of a Gospel.

The word lamb is the translation of the Hebraic word KEVESH and the Greek word AMNOS. In the Bible, “Lamb” refers to the following:

1. It is a sacrificial animal.
2. It is the principal animal for Israel’s offering. It was offered twice daily, in the morning and the evening (Exodus 29:38–42).
3. It was the sacrifice for the following special days and events:

For a new month—Numbers 28:11
For Passover—Numbers 28:16–19
For Shavuot (Pentecost)—Numbers 28:26
For Rosh Hashanah—Numbers 29:1–2
For Yom Kippur—Numbers 29:7–8
For Succot—Numbers 29:12–16

4. For the cleansing of a woman after giving birth—Leviticus 12:6
5. For the healing of a leper—Leviticus 14:10–18
6. For the Sabbath, when two lambs were sacrificed—Numbers 28:9

It is a reference to Jesus in the New Testament in John's Gospel. In addition, it also refers to:

1. Israel—the lamb represented God's compassion, and the prophets portrayed God as a shepherd (Psalm 23).

2. The prophet Jeremiah compared himself to a lamb led to the slaughter—Jeremiah 11:19.

3. In the New Testament, the term lamb also symbolized Jesus' disciples. It says that seventy of his disciples were sent as "Lambs in the midst of wolves" (Luke 10:3). In addition, Jesus told Peter to "Feed his lambs."

4. In the Book of Revelation, the term lamb appears 28 times as a reference to a triumphant Messiah. It is interesting to note that John, who wrote the Gospel of John, also wrote the Book of Revelation, according to tradition.

5. The futuristic age is described as a time when "Lambs will dwell with wolves"—Isaiah 65:25, 11:16.

6. In rabbinic writings, Israel is called "the Lamb." For instance, "Hadrian said to Rabbi Joshua: 'Great indeed must be the lamb, Israel that can exist among seventy wolves'. He replied: 'Great is the shepherd who rescues and protects her'"[1].

What was John thinking about when he called Jesus "The lamb of God"? Here are several possibilities, which he may have had in mind:

1. **The "Tamid" sacrifice—Numbers 28:4.** Tamid means "perpetual." The daily sacrifice, a sin offering that was offered on behalf of the people of Israel. Two lambs, one was offered in the morning and the other was offered in the evening. According to the Mishna, "The Tamid offering was slaughtered at eight and a half hours and was offered at nine and a half hours"[2]. This is according to the Hebraic counting, in which the hours of the day start at 6:00 a.m. Eight and a half hours later corresponds to 2:30 p.m., and nine and a half corresponds to 3:30 p.m. This time of the day was considered to be "twilight time," or as it is described in Hebrew, BEN HA ARBAYIM, meaning "between the two evenings." The rabbinic definition of BEN HA-ARBAIM is "From the time that the sun commences to decline in the west"[3].

2. **The binding of Isaac—Genesis Chapter 22.** The binding of Isaac was a trial for Abraham, which he passed with flying colors. God started speaking to him with the words "Go forth," in Hebrew LECH-LECHA.

   God used the same expression when He commanded him to leave his country and his father's house. This was a trial as well, but probably not as difficult as this one. In the first trial, he was asked to give up his past. In this trial, he was asked to give up his future as it was through Isaac's seed that God was going to fulfill his promises. He was the son of the promise.

   Even so, Abraham went about this without delay. He rose early in the morning, saddled his donkey by himself, although he had plenty of servants. The donkey, incidentally, is unimportant and did not have to be mentioned in the text, but yet it was. God emphasized all the details in Abraham's behavior in order to stress how great Abraham's obedience to Him was. The donkey is associated with kings in the Bible and also, of course, with King Messiah, who will ride a donkey into the city of Jerusalem in the future. Jesus also rode a donkey into the city of Jerusalem as we know from the Gospels.

   He took his son and two of his servants since a man in his position was not expected to be traveling alone. He embarked on a journey to where he gave them no information. On the third day, he saw Mount Moriah. It was on that day that he tied Isaac to the altar. The third day is also associated with Jesus' death.

Abraham left the servants and the donkey behind. He told the servants that they would come back, which at the time could have constituted a lie, but really it pointed out to the depths of his faith in God. He put the wood for the fire on Isaac's shoulders and continued his journey to Moriah. The rabbis said, "Isaac was carrying the wood on his shoulder as one carrying his own cross."

At this point, Isaac started to suspect the real nature of the journey. So he asked his father, "Where is the lamb for the offering?" Isaac, who started to realize the truth, perhaps tried to invoke compassion for himself.

Abraham's answer was, "God will see a lamb for himself, my son." Communicated here was his great hope and his faith in God that He would come through, despite the circumstances. His words were prophetic for two occasions:

A. In his immediate circumstance—God provided a ram.

B. In Egypt—God provided lambs for the people.

As a result of Abraham's words, the name of the place became "God will see," HASHEM YIREH. This literally means, "God will provide." Within Christendom, the name of the place was assigned as one of the names of God, although in the Bible, it is a description of one of God's attributes—He is our provider. However, it is not pronounced the same.

The word lamb is the translation of the Hebraic word KEVESH and the Greek word AMNOS.

In English, it became God Jirah, which is definitely not one of God's names. This word is offensive to the Hebraic mind because it brings a terrible association with it. The closer word familiar to Israelis is the word Jorah, which means "sewer." Therefore, people should refrain from using it in this manner. In this context, it meant that "God will see and will remember this place forever," and indeed this was the case as it later became the site of the Temple.

When they arrived, he tied Isaac to the altar and was going to proceed when the angel of God stopped him. The Bible does not record Isaac complaining. Isaac must have resigned himself to his fate. He was 37 years old at the time. Here also we find a similarity to Jesus, who was about the same age at the time that he started his ministry[4]. Abraham could not have forced him to cooperate. He must have laid down his life voluntarily. In this, we see that he trusted God no less than his father. He was no less great than Abraham.

God provided a ram, and the ram was a substitute for Isaac. According to Jewish tradition, "during this event he experienced: a supernatural birth, a prophetic event and a Messianic message." His sacrifice was also ordained by God. Tradition tells us that upon the altar, he received a vision and was filled with the Holy Spirit. At that time, he was informed that a sacrifice would be necessary to guarantee the compensation of the sin of the whole nation.

According to the same tradition, Isaac died but God resurrected him, similar to the Gospel accounts concerning Jesus. Isaac's blood pouring over the woods, they claim, had the same effect as the Passover lamb that was slaughtered in Egypt many years later.

Furthermore, tradition tells us that during the event, the Holy Spirit descended over Abraham, and he said, "Behold, my son, in whom I am well pleased." These are almost the identical words that were recorded by Matthew as a statement that God made during Jesus' immersion.

God substituted a ram for Isaac. The sages speak of Isaac's ashes, even though he was not sacrificed. The ram died instead of Isaac, and it fully represented him. It was as if Isaac remained upon the altar and indeed died on it[5]. Correct are the rabbis, therefore, who claim that he died. Because Isaac ascended from the altar to a higher world and a higher spiritual position, his willingness to become that sacrifice must have never departed from God's memory. The spiritual effect of his willingness remained for eternity[6].

The Isaac who walked away from the binding was not the same one who went there. Afterward, Isaac was considered to be a living sacrifice, sanctified and spiritual. For this reason, he was forbidden to leave the land of Israel. Abraham was able to come and go as he wished, as did Eliezer, the servant who was sent to find him a wife. But Isaac, as a holy offering, had to remain on holy soil.

But despite this tradition, we cannot assume that those who were present and heard John's announcement realized what he was talking about. They were probably not very familiar with the same traditions because these rabbinical traditions were not submitted in writing at that time.

3. **The Passover Lamb.** The blood of the Passover lamb in Egypt was a substitute for the first-born sons who had death coming to them that night.

The Passover lamb was offered just before the evening of Passover commenced, in the afternoon. On that day, the evening Tamid sacrifice, which was offered daily, was delayed a couple of hours because, according to the Torah, it was forbidden to bring any other sacrifice after the Tamid was offered. Still they made consensus in the case of the Passover sacrifice because it was impossible for all of Israel to bring the sacrifice in two hours. Therefore, they started to slaughter the offering after midday and offered them about one hour later. This took place from about 12:00 p.m. to 5:00 p.m. Otherwise, it would have been slaughtered like the Tamid at 2:30 p.m. and offered at 3:30. p.m. The Passover sacrifice constituted an act of provocation in Egyptian culture.

The blood of the Passover lamb in Egypt was a substitute for the first-born sons who had death coming to them that night.

The Passover sacrifice was a lamb, and a lamb was sacred to the Egyptians who worshipped it as one of their main gods. The act was public and confrontational since God commanded the Israelites to take the lamb four days before it was sacrificed. They had to keep it somewhere outside their homes, for everyone to see.

The offering of a lamb, therefore, was a statement of identification with the God of Israel and a break from all that represented Egypt, a pagan society. According to the rabbis, Israel also worshipped the lamb in Egypt, so this was vital for them to do. It is no wonder that when they rebelled shortly afterward when Moses was on top of Mount Sinai, they reverted to their old ways and created the Golden Calf, their old god from Egypt (Exodus 32:4).

The way the Pascal sacrifice was to be offered also pointed to the purpose of doing away with the pagan gods of Egypt. Not one bone was to be broken, and it was to be roasted almost whole (Exodus 12:46, Numbers 9:12). So it was always recognizable for what it was. This clearly was an annulment of the idol.

According to the rabbis, God, of course, could have spared the Israelites from having to deal with this whole issue of putting the blood of the lamb on doorposts as a covering for themselves, but He did not because they were not worthy of redemption. By having to put the blood on, they recognized that they should have been punished, but God chose to forgive them after all.

4. **The suffering servant—Isaiah 53.** This Scripture speaks of the anointed one as the suffering lamb. According to Judaism, the suffering servant of Isaiah 53 could not possibly have been in John's mind when he declared, "Behold the lamb of God" because Judaism always understood Isaiah 53 to be a reference to Israel and not the Messiah as it still does today. Others say that it is true today, but it was not true in the past.

   Here are several ways in which some in Israel interpreted this chapter, supporting the idea that the suffering servant refers to the Messiah.

   Targum Jonathan, which developed during the Second Temple period, has in Isaiah 52:13—which starts the description we find in chapter 53—the words, "Behold my servant the anointed one shall prosper." Right at the start, it claims that this whole section refers to some future king and not to the nation of Israel or anyone else.

   In the Talmud, which was developed during the 3rd to the 5th centuries CE, we read, "His name is the leper scholar as it is written, surely he has borne our grief, and carried our sorrows; yet we did esteem him a leper, smitten of God and afflicted" (Isaiah 53:4)[7].

   The Midrash says, "And eat of the bread" refers to the bread of royalty, "and dip thy morsel in the vinegar" refers to his sufferings as it is said, "But he was wounded because of our transgressions (Isaiah 53:5)"[8].

   The Karaite Yefeth Ben Ali who lived in the 10th century wrote:

"As for myself, I am inclined to regard it alluding to the Messiah, and as opening with a description of his conditioning in exile, from the time of his birth to his ascension to the throne. For the prophet begins by speaking of him as being seated in a position of honor and then goes back to relate all that will happen to him during the captivity. He thus gives us to understand two things: In the first instance that the Messiah will only reach his highest degree of honor after long and severe trials; and secondly, that these trials will be sent upon him as a kind of a sign, so that, if he finds himself under the yoke of misfortunes while remaining pure in his actions, he may know that he is the desired one."[9]

Another old Midrash, Mysteries of Rabbi Shimon Ben Yochai (of uncertain date) states:

"And Armilaus will join battle with the Messiah, the son of Ephraim, in the East Gate… and Messiah, the son of Ephraim, will die there, and Israel will mourn for him. And afterward the holy one will reveal to them Messiah, the son of David, whom Israel will desire to stone, saying, 'thou speaks falsely; already is the Messiah slain, and there is no other messiah to stand up (after him); and so they will despise him, as it is written' (Despised and forlorn of man) but he will turn and hide himself from them, according to the words, 'like one hiding his face from us.'"[10]

Judaism always understood Isaiah 53 to be a reference to Israel and not the Messiah as it still does today.

Another Midrash, Lekach Tov from the 11th century, says, "And let his (Israel's) kingdom be exalted, in the days of the Messiah of whom it is said, 'Behold my servant shall prosper; he will be high and exalted, and lofty exceedingly.'"[11]

Rabbi Alshich in the 16th century said, "Our rabbis with one voice accepted and affirmed the opinion that the prophet is speaking of the King Messiah." Many other examples can be cited.[12]

Even in works from a later time period, we read from Herz Homberg (18th–19th Century):

"The fact is that it refers to the King Messiah, who will come in the latter days, when it will be the Lord's good pleasure to redeem Israel from among the different nations of the earth... Whatever they underwent was in consequence of their own transgressions, The Lord having chosen him to be a trespass offering, like the scapegoat which bore all the iniquities of the house of Israel."

So when did it change from being understood as a reference to the Messiah to being understood as a reference to Israel? Rashi, Rabbi Solomon Yitzchak, who lived between 1040–1105, also initially applied Isaiah 53 to the Messiah, but later he changed his view and claimed it was talking about Israel.[13]

Beforehand, it was accepted by some of the Jewish authorities. However, Rashi influenced the opinion of other well-respected commentators like Kimchy and Even Ezra. But Maimonides, who is known as a great rabbi in Judaism, rejected Rashi's opinion as being unsatisfactory. He said of those who—for controversial reasons—applied this prophecy to Israel, that by doing so "The doors of the literal interpretation of the parasha were shut in their face and that they wearied themselves to find the entrance, having forsaken the knowledge of our teachers and inclined after the stubbornness of their own hearts and of their own opinions."

Furthermore, he said that "The interpretation adapted by Rashi distorts the passage from its natural meaning and that it was given by God as a description of the Messiah, whereby, when any should claim to be the Messiah, to judge by the resemblance or non-resemblance to it, [to see] whether they were the Messiah or not."

Rashi was the first to apply this interpretation to Israel at a later period. He first wrote a commentary on the Talmud, in which he said Isaiah 53 refers to the Messiah. Later he wrote a commentary on the Tanach, and he said that Isaiah 53 refers to Israel. In between writing the two commentaries, the first crusade took place.

When he saw what people did in the name of Christ, he said, "People who commit such atrocities cannot possibly have the right interpretation of the Scriptures. Since they also believe that Isaiah 53 refers to the Messiah, this interpretation must be wrong and needs to be changed."

So he changed his view that Isaiah 53 refers to Israel, and it eventually became the accepted view within Judaism.

From the Sidur, for the High Holidays, the additional service for the Day of Atonement, Philips (20th Century) reads:

"Our righteous anointed is departed from us: horror has seized us, and we have none to justify us. He hath born the yoke of our iniquities, and our transgressions, and is wounded because of our transgression. He beareth our sins on his shoulder, that he may find pardon for our iniquities. We shall be healed by his wounds, at the time that the Eternal Will created him (the Messiah) as a new creature. O bring him up from the circle of the earth. Raise him up from Seir, to assemble us the second time on Mount Lebanon, by the hand of Yinnon"[14].

In Christendom, of course, Isaiah 53 was always identified with Jesus. In Acts 8:32, Philip used Isaiah 53:7 to proclaim Jesus. The early Church Fathers also understood Isaiah 53 as a description of the suffering servant, which they believed to be Jesus[15]. Some recent scholars have observed that the Greek phrase "Lamb of God" was a translation of the Aramaic term TALYE DE LAHA, which could be understood as both "Lamb of God" and "Servant of God."

Some recent scholars have observed that the Greek phrase "Lamb of God" was a translation of the Aramaic term TALYE DE LAHA, which could be understood as both "Lamb of God" and "Servant of God."

Professor Joachim Jeremias, a very well known Christian scholar, pointed out the double meaning in the way the passage was used by the writer of the fourth Gospel. He also pointed out that the Greek word PAIS, meaning "son," is used in the LXX instead of the word DOULOS, meaning "servant" or "slave," in reference to the suffering servant. He concluded that PAIS, therefore, could mean a son or a servant. References to this word are in Acts 3:15, 26, 4:27, 30, Matthew 12:18, Isaiah 42:1[16].

But in all fairness, the idea that Isaiah 53 refers to Israel is indeed biblical. Isaiah himself in his book defined the phrase "servant of God" to be Israel, and that biblical testimony cannot be ignored.

The following are some biblical examples:

Isaiah 41:8–9 says: "But **you, Israel, my servant**, Jacob whom I have chosen, descendant of Abraham my friend. You whom I have taken from the ends of the earth, and called from its remotest parts, and said to you, 'you are my servant; I have chosen you and not rejected you."

Isaiah 43:10–12: "You are my witnesses," declares The Lord, "**and my servant whom I have chosen**, in order that you may know and believe me, and understand that I am He. Before me there was no God formed, and there will be none after me. I, even I, am The Lord; and there is no savior besides me. It is I who have declared and saved and proclaimed, and there was no strange God among you; so you are my witnesses," declares The Lord, "and I am God."

The idea that Isaiah 53 refers to Israel is indeed biblical. Isaiah himself in his book defined the phrase "servant of God" to be Israel, and that biblical testimony cannot be ignored.

Isaiah 44:1–2: "But now listen, **o Jacob, my servant**; and Israel, whom I have chosen: thus says The Lord who made you and formed you from the womb, who will help you, 'do not fear, **o Jacob my servant**; and you Jeshurun whom I have chosen.'"

Isaiah 45:4: "For the sake of **Jacob my servant**, and Israel my chosen *one*, I have also called you by your name; I have given you a title of honor though you have not known me."

Isaiah 48:20: "Go forth from Babylon! Flee from the Chaldeans! Declare with the sound of joyful shouting, proclaim this, and send it out to the end of the earth; say, 'The Lord has redeemed his servant Jacob.'"

Isaiah 49:3: "**You are my servant, Israel**, in whom I will show my glory."

Throughout the Book of Isaiah, Israel is identified as God's servant. Often, people ask how it can be that the servant in Isaiah 53 is Israel when Isaiah speaks about him in the singular form. Isaiah refers to the servant in a singular form no less than sixty-seven times in his book, and mostly, it is a reference to the nation of Israel.

So it is very difficult to determine what John was thinking about when he spoke about the Lamb of God. It is also difficult to grasp what his immediate audience understood by the concept and how they were able to relate to it.

CHAPTER 18 ENDNOTES

1. Taanit, Toldot # 8, 45a Fin–46b init.
2. Mishna, Psachim 5, Mishna 1.
3. Talmud, Psachim 58a.
4. The idea of Jesus death taking place when he was about 40 years of age was discussed above, in the chapter dealing with the time of his birth.
5. Michtav Me Eliyahu, Dessler, Rabbi Eliyahu E.
6. Rabbi Brachya.
7. Talmud Bavli, Sanhedrin 98b.
8. Midrash on Ruth 5:6 (Soncino, Vol. 8. Page 64).
9. S.R. Driver and A. Neubauer, editors, The fifty-third chapter of Isaiah according to Jewish interpreters (2 volumes, N.Y.; Ktav 1969) pp. 19–20. The English translations used here are taken from volume 2. The original texts are in volume 1. Cf. Soloff, pp. 107–09.
10. Ibid. Page 32, citing the edition of Jellinek, Beth ha Midrash (1855), part iii, p. 80.
11. Ibid, p. 36.
12. Maimonides, letter to Yemen (12th C.); Zohar II, 212a (medieval); Nachmanides (R. Moshe Ben Nachman–13th C.); Yalkut II; 571 (13th C.) Yalkut II 620 (13th C.) in regard to Psalm 2:6; R. Moshe Cohen Iben Crispin (14th C.); R. Elijah de Vidas (16th C.); Rabbi Moshe Alshech of Tzfat (16th C).
13. Ibid, PP. 400–401.
14. A. TH. Philips, Machzor Leyom Kippur/Prayer book for the Day of Atonement with English translation; revised and enlarged edition (N.Y. Hebrew Publishing company 1931), p. 239.
15. I Clement 16:7.
16. J. Jeremiahs—servant of God.

APPENDIX 1: THE SADDUCEES—(TZADOKIM)

THE SECT OF THE SADDUCEES WAS FORMED, MORE LIKELY, in the second half of the second century BCE. It appears that prior to the success of the Maccabees war against the Greeks, most of the groups in Israel were united and supportive of their traditional Jewish religion in their struggle against Hellenism. After their victory, different disagreements between different groups slowly started to be expressed. And so, shortly after the Maccabees war was over, three main groups had evolved: the Sadducees, the Pharisees and the Essenes.

The Sadducees operated during the Second Temple period in Israel, from the time of their formation to the time in which the Temple was destroyed in 70 CE. We are not sure from where their name came, although many believe it was derived from Tzadok, the high priest at the time of King David (II Samuel 8:17, 15:24), and during the time of King Solomon (I Kings. 1:34, I Chronicles 12:29). The main reasons behind this idea are:

1. High priests who lived before the time of the Maccabees (165 BCE) referred their ancestry to Tzadok (Hagai 1:1).

2. The prophet Ezekiel had legitimized Tzadok's descendants as worthy of being entrusted control over the Temple (Ezekiel 40:46, 43:19, 44:10–16).

There is no confirmation, however, that the Sadducees indeed traced their priestly succession to Tzadok, although they probably did since the Bible indicates they should have authority over Temple affairs, and the Sadducees went by the Scriptures.

According to rabbinic tradition, both the Sadducees and the Boethiusians, another priestly group that belonged to a particular priestly family and that existed in the first century BCE, are named after two disciples of a scholar known as Antigonos of Soko[1]. The disciples' names were Tzadok and Boethius. It is said that both of them did not understand or agree with their teacher.

They denied the afterlife and the resurrection, and they formed two sects named after them.

The Talmud, at times, uses Boethiusians and Sadducees as interchangeable terms, and some scholars believe that the Boethiusians were a branch of the Sadducees. Modern scholars, however, believe this is a legend. They trace the existence of the Boethiusians to a high priest named Simon Ben Boethius, who was appointed by Herod the Great in the year 24 BCE[2].

Although, at times, the theology of the Boethiusians resembles the Sadducees theology, there were also differences between them; they were not the same group. For instance, they were not as aristocratic as the Sadducees. The Sadducees used to support the Hasmonean dynasty; the Boethiusians were loyal Herodians. It is possible they are referred to in the New Testament as Herodians in Mark 12:13, although that statement could be also a references to people who actually worked in Herod's service.

The New Testament and Josephus both refer to the Sadducees as "a party." In the Mishna they are seen as a different school of biblical interpretation[3]. And indeed the Sadducees were a priestly political party. And although they were in the minority in Israel, in comparison to the other two main parties, they were the ruling party at times.

The Sadducees were comprised of the wealthier elements of society: The priest, merchant and aristocrat. They were referred to as "The Judean Aristocracy." They were very active in the political and economical life in Israel. They dominated the Temple worship and were in charge of Temple affairs. The high priest was almost always a Sadducee. Many of them were Sanhedrin members, and in the first century CE they constituted the majority of Sanhedrin members.

Although the Sadducees were the aristocrats at the time, it is important to understand that not all aristocrats were Sadducees. Josephus said, "The Sadducees doctrine was made known only to a few males, but they were foremost in worthiness,"[4] pointing to the exclusive nature of their party. They were influenced by Hellenism and were in good standing with the Romans.

The Sadducees had very high regard for Temple services and its sacrifices. Just like the Pharisees, they also gave priority to the Word of God. But they stood as an opposition to the various Pharisaic schools, including the time leading up to the destruction of the Temple.

The main difference between them and the Pharisees was their understanding of the Oral Law—the Mishna. The Pharisees accepted the Mishna as a binding force, a correct system, and a guide—according to which one should fulfill God's commandments, which are found in the Torah. The Sadducees, on the other hand, refused to accept the oral Torah as binding, unless it was based directly on the Torah.

The two groups had two different concepts of God. The Sadducees aimed at bringing God down to man. They worshipped him like one would pay homage to a human king. In relationship to this, Josephus Said:

> "As for the Sadducees, they take away fate and say there is no such thing, and that the events of human affairs are not at His disposal. But they suppose that all of our actions are in our own power, so that we ourselves are the cause of what is good and receive what is evil from our own folly"[5].

The Pharisees, on the other hand, aimed at raising man to divine heights. They wanted to bring man closer to God, who is spiritual.

By believing that God is not involved in human affairs, it seems they also rejected God's presence upon Earth. In addition, the Sadducees believed that God does not see evil or do evil. Perhaps they based this idea on Habakkuk 1:13. The idea was that God is completely good.

Ben Sirach, who lived in the middle of the second century BCE, also believed we are quite capable of sin and should be responsible for it. He said:

> "Say not, from God is my transgression, for that which He hate made He is not... God created man from the beginning and placed him in the hands of his inclination. If thou so desire, thou can keep the commandment, and (it is) wisdom to do His will"[6].

This idea has not been rescinded from the Bible necessarily. Ben Sira did not believe that God had abandoned His involvement with human affairs, nor did he believe that God did not create evil. The idea that God is removed from the sight of evil has its source in Platonic teachings that claimed that no cause of any evil can be ascribed to God, and that it is not in the Bible.

The Bible state differently. In Isaiah 45:5 God is speaking and He said, "I form the light and create darkness; I make peace and create evil; I am the Lord, who has made all this things."

And indeed all things were created by God, including the tree of knowledge of good and evil that He placed in the Garden of Eden, which made it possible for humans to exercise their neutral potential for evil. And that potential was unleashed for the first time when Cain killed Able. God created Satan, but God also created light and darkness; light will increasingly overcome darkness one day.

God is the source of everything that exists, and if He did not create evil, then do we conclude that He is not the source of all?

To put it in the language of Yeshua Ben Sirach:

> "Good is the opposite of evil and life the opposite of death; so the sinner is the opposite of the Godly. Look upon all the works of The Most High; they likewise are in pairs, one the opposite of the other"[7].

Thomas Aquinas, the Catholic theologian, had summed it well when he stated, "There is no possible source of evil, except good"[8].

The Sadducees' denial minimized God's part in human destiny and stressed human free will and responsibility. They probably understood God's system of reward and punishment as the enjoyment or suffering we experience in our earthly life.

The Sadducees rejected Pharisaic supernatural beliefs on the ground that their beliefs had no basis in the Torah. They denied the doctrine of the Resurrection (Matthew 22:23, Mark 12:18, Luke 20:27, Acts 23:8). They denied the immortality of the Soul[9]. They rejected the Pharisaic doctrine of the existence of angels and ministering spirits (Acts 23:8). They believed that each individual must make good his transgressions during his earthly life since there was no soul to survive or return after death.

The Pharisees who supported the afterlife, later argued that it is found in the Torah[10] and, therefore, it is based on it. In the New Testament, Jesus communicated to the Sadducees that there is a resurrection by quoting Exodus 3:6, in which God had said to Moses, "...I am the God of your forefathers, the God of Abraham, the God of Isaac, and the God of Jacob..."[11].

The Mosaic principle communicated in Exodus 21:24—"eye for an eye and tooth for a tooth..."—was interpreted by them literally instead as monetary compensation, the way the Pharisees understood it.

In addition, they opposed the Pharisaic practice of Eruv, in which the Pharisees had joined house to house in order to permit carrying things on the Shabbat. The Eruv is an imaginary line created in order to link an area of several blocks together. The Pharisees believed, based on a text in the book of Nehemiah, we should not carry anything on the Sabbath out of our homes, but we are permitted to carry things in our homes.

There was a need to create a situation in which people were able to carry things outside of their homes on the Sabbath, things like a stroller or a diaper bag. They needed to be able to carry them to the synagogue, for instance. So they came up with the idea of creating a border around a neighborhood that would turn it into a larger home, and therefore everything found within it was considered to be part of that one home[12]. This custom is still practiced today.

The conflict between the Sadducees and the Pharisees was to some degree a renewal of the conflict between the prophets and the priests of the pre-exilic time. The Sadducees were opposed to change. They did not favor a religious service that consisted of study and prayer alone, like the Pharisees did, because it would have weakened the importance of the Temple and its sacrifices.

They were less lenient than the Pharisees. Josephus claimed, "they were harsh in judgment and rather boorish in their behavior, being rude even to their peers"[13]. The New Testament paints a similar picture. In Acts 4:1-6 and 5:17, the Sadducees appear to be the main opponents of the early followers of Jesus. While Rabbi Gamliel, the Pharisee, argued for leniency (Acts 5:34–39).

In spite of it all, we should try to see the Sadducees in a more objective light. We need to realize that although they went against the Oral Law and the traditions of the Pharisees, there were some traditions they accepted. They could not avoid tradition altogether because the Bible is often silent concerning the "how" when it comes to man fulfilling God's commandments. For instance, we know they had accepted the traditional Jewish calendar. They could have accepted the Qumran community calendar, which was different, but they did not. The calendar is traditional.

When the Bible is silent concerning how a punishment should be executed, they accepted the mode of punishment prescribed by tradition. It appears they had rejected non-biblical traditions of which they did not approve, particularly when those traditions had originated with the other two groups: the Pharisees and the Essenes.

They must have, at one point or another, researched the Bible for themselves and created their own rulings on different issues. That a Sadducees book of rules did exist, we know from different writings of the period. However, none of their writings survived.

The Pharisees claimed authority on the basis of personal piety and learning, whereas the Sadducees claimed authority based on genealogy and their position in the priesthood. In the first century, there were many disputes between them and the Pharisees and between the Sadducees and other sects like the Nazarenes as is evident from the New Testament.

The Sadducees were concerned with their own well being; therefore, they were not popular with the people. After 70 CE when the Temple in Jerusalem was destroyed, aristocracy declined, and the Sadducees dropped out of sight; they ceased to exist as a sect.

APPENDIX I ENDNOTES

1. Avot, R. Nathan 5.
2. Josephus, Antiquities, 15:320.
3. Mishna Yadaim 4:6.
4. Josephus, Antiquities 18:16.
5. Josephus Antiquities 13:173.
6. Ben Sira 15:11–20.
7. Apocrypha book of Ecclesiasticus, 33:14–15.
8. Summa Theologica I, q. 49, a. 1.
9. Josephus War, 6:162 Antiquities 18:16.
10. Sanhedrin 10:1.
11. Matthew 22:32.
12. Eruvin 6:2.
13. Josephus, war, 2:166; Antiquities 20:199.

APPENDIX II: THE PHARISEES—(PERUSHIM)

THE PHARISEES WERE A JEWISH POLITICAL GROUP THAT existed during the Second Temple period. And just like the other two main groups at the time, the Sadducees and the Essenes, the Pharisees also immerged as a sect after the Hasmonean revolt that took place in 160–165 BCE. They were more likely the successors of an ancient group of Hassidim (meaning the pious ones). Hasidism promoted the observance and the study of the Torah and so did the Pharisees after them. The Pharisees are first mentioned by Josephus at the time of Jonathan the high priest who served during the years 161–143 BCE[1].

The Pharisees started as a small group but by the time of the first century CE, they represented the beliefs and practices of most of the Jewish people in Israel. According to Josephus, they delivered to the people a great many observances handed down from their ancestors not written in the Torah. Most of them came from middle-class families who were zealous to the Torah.

They saw themselves as the true followers of Ezra, whom they considered to be only second to Moses among the people of Israel and one of the founders of Judaism. Although not all the Pharisees were scribes, the majority of scribes were Pharisees. The Pharisees were led by the distinguished sages of the day, such as Rabban Gamliel the elder, Rabban Shimon (his son), and Rabban Yochanan Ben Zakkai.

The meaning of the name "Pharisee" is uncertain. But it was probably derived from the Hebrew word PRISHA, meaning "separation." So they were called "The separated ones."[2] Many understand this term to mean that they avoided contact with others for reasons of ritual purity, or that they separated themselves from the heathens.

That they have separated themselves from the Gentiles for particular reasons, there is no doubt. Peter demonstrated this clearly in Galatians 2:12. But even their separation from the Gentiles was not complete since they proselytized and, therefore, had much contact with them. With the help of the Pharisees, proselytism became widespread. So perhaps the separation from the Gentiles was mostly with regard to food and Temple worship.

As for the separation from others, I found no justification for this claim either since they were very involved with the people. We do know, however, that the Pharisees did separate themselves from those who were publicans and sinners. They definitely disapproved of Jesus' contact with them[3]. This separation was probably for two reasons:

1. They separated themselves in order to avoid associating with evil as the Bible teaches.
2. In order to bring the sinners to repentance faster.

Their separation, therefore, must be understood in terms of their attempt to lead a holy life, sanctified to God, and in this sense be separated from the customs of the world.

Although their name was first given to them as a derogatory name by their opponents, the Pharisees liked it and so they decided to keep it. But according to its alternative Hebraic meaning "the exponents"—or PERUSHIM, literally meaning "interpretations"—of the Torah. And indeed, Josephus described the Pharisees as being "exact exponents of the Torah."

The Pharisees tried to help the masses to gain a spirit of holiness by spreading traditional religious teachings. In order for the Kingdom of God to come, Israel had to be faithful and obedient to God. Therefore, they remained nearby to the common people. They worked alongside them as humble tailors, shoemakers, tent makers, carpenters, butchers and other professions.

They educated the children of the masses and provided schooling for them, and they erected synagogues in all the cities and villages so that people would be able to worship and study the Torah and Jewish traditions.

Under their leadership, the synagogue network flourished, and the synagogue became a focus of Jewish social and religious interaction. They devoted much of their time to education. After 70 CE, they were the only ones who continued to promote Judaism via the synagogues and their schools. They operated as a highly sophisticated assembly of men and believed that their work was very important.

They created the synagogue system and exercised full control over it. Some of the ceremonies that had taken place in the Temple had now been moved into homes. And men who were not from priestly descent began to play an important role in national religious affairs.

Since their religious values were much higher than their political values, they were willing to submit to foreign rule as long as it did not interfere with their way of life and the Word of God. And that was in spite of the fact that they were nationalistic in nature and waited for the day in which the Messiah will come and overthrow the Romans, and Israel will be a free nation once again.

Evidence indicates that most of the Pharisees had believed in an attitude of "live and let live," not only amongst themselves but also with regard to all other sects that appeared in Judea during that time. This understanding did not prevent them from arguing theological issues or presenting their interpretation of the text. Instead it meant they would not resort to violence against any group holding different opinions nor would they seek to inflict capital punishment on religious dissidents.

Just like the Temple was the power base of the Sadducees in Israel in the first century, the synagogue was the power base of the Pharisees during that time.

In the Talmud we read about seven different kinds of Pharisees:

1. The Shchemite Pharisee – He who keeps the Torah for profit can gain from it. Just like Schem submitted to circumcision in order to obtain Dina (Genesis 34:19).

2. The Tumbling Pharisee – He who in order to appear humble, hangs down his head and is in danger of falling down.

3. The Bleeding Pharisee – He who is often wounded because he walks around with his eyes closed in order not to see a woman.

4. The Mortar Pharisee – He who wears a cap shaped like a mortar in order to cover his eyes, so he would not to see impurities or indecencies.

5. The "What am I yet to do" Pharisee – He who does not know much about the Torah and because of it he says, "Tell me what my duty is now, and I will do it."

6. The Pharisee from fear – He who keeps the Torah because he is afraid of future judgment.

7. The Pharisee from Love – He who obeys the Lord because he loves Him with all of his heart.

The Pharisees rising to power is a story of raw courage, daring heroics and deep dedication to God. It took time, but it happened in spite of many assassinations, mass murder and political plotting against them. The Pharisees sect first attempted to gain power during the struggle to remove control over the Temple and religion from the hands of the Sadducees leadership who had sole control over it.

The persecution against them started before the Maccabean Revolt, during the reign of Antiochus Epiphanies in 168 BCE. Under the rule of John Hyrcanus, during the years 134–104 BCE, the problems continued because the Pharisees did not approve of his kingship. Although, according to Josephus, John Hyrcanus was originally a disciple and a supporter of the Pharisees.

All this changed in one of the public occasions organized by Hyrcanus when he asked for the opinion of the people concerning his government. In public, a Pharisee named Elazar suggested to him to resign. He went on to explain that Hyrcanus, more likely, was not a descendant of Levi, but probably a son of a Greek soldier because his mother was captured and violated by them. Therefore, John Hyrcanus had no right to serve as a high priest. When Hyrcanus proved this story was a lie, a Pharisaic court recommended lenient punishment of lashes for the slanderer.

Hyrcanus came to believe this was the opinion of all Pharisees. He resented them as a result of this and developed a close relationship with the Sadducees[4]. He quit the Pharisees party and became a Sadducee. During this time, the Pharisees were expelled from membership in the Sanhedrin. It was also during this time that they were given their name. By the time of the Hasmonean Civil War, it was obvious that the Pharisaic theological doctrines were providing hope to the oppressed masses and affecting their entire life.

Things got much worse for the Pharisees during the reign of Hyrcanus' son Alexander Jannaeus (103-76 BCE). During the ceremony of water of one of the feasts of Tabernacles, Alexander poured water over his feet instead of on the altar as required by Pharisaic decree. As a result the religious Jews in the Temple showered him with Etrogim, a citrus fruit that looks like a lemon.

Alexander, outraged at this attack, commanded the soldiers to slay six thousand of the offenders. This incident brought about a civil war that lasted for six years and cost fifty thousand Jewish lives.

When the war was over, Josephus tells us that Alexander transported some of his Jewish prisoners, more likely Pharisees, to Jerusalem. There, while he was feasting with his concubines, in front of the entire city, he ordered about eight hundred of the prisoners to be crucified. And while they were still alive, he ordered the throats of their children and wives to be cut before their eyes[5].

The Sadducees had much influence in Israel until Alexander's death in 76 BCE. On his deathbed, Alexander encouraged his wife, Salome, to make peace with the Pharisees.

During the reign of Queen Salome Alexandra in 76–67 BCE, the Sadducees lost much of their power, and the Pharisees experienced a much better time and managed to flourish. She supported them openly, so they were able to develop into a political party. In reality they became the actual power behind the throne.

Herod the Great ruled between 37–4 BCE. One of Herod's political goals was to reduce the power of the Pharisees. The Pharisees objected to the fact that he was an Idumæan, a half-Jew. They also objected to his friendship with Rome. Herod punished those who opposed him and rewarded those who took his side.

Josephus tells us about two Pharisees who encouraged the Jews to accept Herod because they interpreted the fact that Israel had a foreigner for a ruler as a divine judgment. Those two were Pollio and Sameas, who generally are identified with Shamai and Hillel. Because of this, Herod had a good relationship with the Pharisees. He avoided conflict with them throughout most of his reign.

By the time of the first century, approximately six thousand Pharisees lived in Jerusalem and about four hundred and eighty synagogues spanned throughout the countryside.

The Pharisees were concerned with two things above all: 1) the study of the Torah. 2) The practice of the Torah. The Pharisees saw the Oral Torah as binding upon the Jews. This was the practical guide through which one should live out God's commandments. The Torah was at the center of their teachings, and they believed it was sufficient for all man at all times. They believed the Scriptures to be the inspired Word of God. They also believed that everything was ordained by God but that man still had the power to choose between good and evil. They would declare, "Everything is in the hands of God, but the fear of God"[6]. And "Although everything is foreseen, yet freedom of choice is given"[7]. They also asserted that everything is accomplished by Faith[8].

They believed in the resurrection of the dead and in rewards for mankind in the next life for actions taken by him in this life. According to their understanding, man's existence was not confined to this world alone. They taught "that only the souls of the righteous pass into another body, while those of the wicked are punished"[9].

They conceived God to be the omnipotent spiritual being, all wise, all knowing, all just and all merciful. They taught that God loves all of His creatures and expects man to walk in His ways, to act justly and to love kindness. In contrast to the Sadducees who believed that God took very little interest in human affairs, the Pharisees believed that God, though infinite, was also a personal God and very much interested in the affairs of man.

They said that God could not be described in human terms nor could the totality of his being be expressed in one name. So they used several names to describe Him. They spoke of him as "The Creator"—BORE OLAM; as "The Place"—HA MAKOM[10], and as "The Divine Presence"—The Shekinah. They believed in the existence of angels and demons, in the pre-existence of God, and in the Messiah.

The great opponents of the Pharisees used to be the Sadducees. There was a great conflict between these two sects over the interpretation of the Torah—in other words, over Mishnaic issues. They argued over decisions that were required to be made over everyday issues of life that were brought constantly before the Sanhedrin. The antagonism between the two groups extended to many political issues and to other non-religious issues.

The Pharisees, of course, are the most infamous group within Christendom. Often, when hearing people speaking against them, I am tempted to ask, "Who are you talking about? Which Pharisees?" Questions to which they don't have any answers, since the Pharisees are usually linked together in one lump.

But in the first century, there were different kinds of Pharisees who held different kinds of theological ideas. It is definitely wrong to blame a group for things they did not do or did not believe. It is even worse when people claim that a certain group did things they actually fought and stood against. This is done daily as a result of sheer ignorance. If one is going to criticize them, then the least one ought to do is to get familiar with them, so he might be able to provide somewhat of an intelligent criticism.

The Pharisees, as mentioned before, constituted different small groups in the first century. We cannot possibly discuss all of them; however, we can make a comparison between the main two groups that existed at the time, two schools of thought: Beit Hillel (the school of Hillel) and Beit Shamai (the school of Shamai).

Both of these were Pharisaic schools. Both of them accepted all of the commandments contained in the Torah. They also had accepted the authority of the Mishna, but there were great debates and disagreement between the two schools concerning issues presented in the Oral Law.

The Mishna was forming at the time. It was not yet completed and so different that rabbis still presented their understanding as to how the commandments of the Torah should be practiced in reality. The Oral Law was the cause for many arguments and fights among the different groups that existed at the time; we learn this from rabbinic writings, but we also see it in the New Testament. During the first century, Beit Hillel and Beit Shamai clashed more than 350 times on Mishnaic issues.

The School of Shamai came upon the scene two decades before Jesus was born. They flourished for a hundred years in Israel. After the destruction of Jerusalem in 70 CE, the Sanhedrin was moved to Yavneh, and the authority of Beit Hillel over interpretation of the Scriptures was established.

According to the Talmud, this was the result of a heavenly voice—THE BAT KOL—declaring that the interpretation of the Torah should be accepted according to the understanding of Beit Hillel. As a result of this prophecy, towards the end of the first century, the Jewish people declared the teaching of Beit Shamai to be null and void.

Something drastic must have happened for them to take the value of 100 years of teaching and declare it no good. It is good they did not destroy it because today we still have a record of the teachings of Beit Shamai, which help us understand the makeup of first-century Judaism. Orthodox Judaism today is the continuation of Beit Hillel.

According to Rabbi Meir[11], the first two controversies between the schools were over the "18 measures"[12] prayer (also known as the AMIDAH prayer) and the bringing of the Feast burnt offering sacrifice on the first day of the holiday[13].

Around the year 20 BCE, an attempt was made to keep peace between the two schools. As a result, they started to meet at the house of Hananiah Ben Hezekiah, who was a member of one of the leading zealot's families at the time. His father was actually executed by Herod, but he himself was not really interested in fighting the foreign elements ruling Israel because he was much more interested in the Torah.

In one of the meetings that took place at his home, a vote was taken in order to settle the debate over the 18 measures. The Talmud[14] tells us that members of Beit Shamai killed many members of Beit Hillel in the course of the debate.

There are two different records of this event, and both are communicated by eyewitnesses. Though, it seems that the zealots actually committed the act and not members of Beit Shamai. We know that Beit Shamai was associated with them and that they were present in the house that day because the Talmud recorded that swords were present in the house of study on that unfortunate day and that the house itself belonged to a zealot family.

Israel mourned the day heavily; it was compared by the rabbis to the day Moses came down from Mount Sinai and discovered the golden calf. It is important to realize that the disagreement between these two schools were major and, therefore, should not be taken lightly nor should the two schools be lumped together.

By the time the second debate took place, Beit Shamai was already in full control in Israel and so the sacrifice was not offered on the first day of the feast[15].

The two schools differ also concerning the issue of polygamy. There are records of Beit Shamai practicing Polygamy; Beit Hillel, on the other hand, was totally against it. Rabbi Hillel believed that marrying two wives constituted an act of fornication[16].

In the Damascus covenant scroll of the Qumranians, there is a criticism of the Pharisees for marrying multiple wives. The scroll does not make clear which Pharisees did it. Why? Well, there was really no need because everyone knew that Beit Shamai practiced polygamy, and so the criticism was against them. But today we don't know it without research, and so it is easy to assume that all Pharisees practiced polygamy, but it is an incorrect assumption. Unfortunately, we come to similar wrong conclusions about the Pharisees from reading criticisms against them in the New Testament.

According to the Talmud[17], Beit Shamai constituted the majority of the Pharisees in Israel at the time of Bava Ben Buta, who lived during the Herod administration. It was about the same period of time that the decision concerning the eighteen measures passed. Actually, Beit Shamai was in control during most of the first century CE[18]. Only after the fall of Jerusalem did Beit Hillel manage to gain control[19].

The opposition between Beit Hillel and Beit Shamai took place from 30 BCE to 70 CE. The two rabbis who instituted the school, though, died much earlier. Rabbi Hillel died in 10 CE and Rabbi Shamai In 30 CE. Rabbi Hillel was a descendant of King David[20]. Initially, he came to Israel from Babylon because he was hungry for knowledge and, eventually, he became the greatest sage of his generation. Rabbi Shamai was the AV BEIT DIN,—the head of the Sanhedrin—and Rabbi Hillel served in the position of NASI—President—the political leader of the nation.

Rabbi Shamai was strict when it came to the application of the Torah while Rabbi Hillel was lenient. The Talmud states, "A person should always be humble, such as Hillel, and not strict, such as Shamai"[21]. Incidentally, Shamai is the only rabbi described by the Talmud as KAPDAN—strict.

The differences between these two men can also be seen through the statements they made. Hillel made his famous statement: "To love peace, pursue peace, love all creatures, and bring them closer to Torah." This was his advice and his concern. His ultimate goal was achieving harmony among the people of Israel.

Shamai also made a statement:

> "Make your Torah a set thing, sat a little and do a lot, and receive every man with a cheerful face." While the two statements at first glance look similar, there are differences between them. Shamai was concerned with the Torah above all, while Hillel was concerned with the Torah as well, he also appeared to be a man of the people and therefore the peruse of peace was very important to him[22].

The two schools also differed in their understanding concerning the salvation of the Gentiles. It is important to realize that as the first century came along, people in Israel had a sense that the end of time was just around the corner. People believed that the conqueror Messiah would come soon and deliver them from foreign Roman rule. With the coming of the Messiah, the door would be open for the Gentiles to join Israel in worshipping almighty God and to become a part of the Jewish faith.

Therefore, a very important issue had to be dealt with, and that was the issue of the salvation of the Gentiles. My Goodness! The Gentiles are now going to flock into Israel's faith, what are we going to do with them? On what basis should we accept them? Should we tell them to do everything that we do? After all, what is the difference? Why should they not do what we do? Or should we just accept them without any obligations? Or perhaps we should tell them to follow some of the commandments? And if so, which ones?

It was not a simple issue to deal with. Every important rabbi who had any following had to take a stand and provide it for his followers. So was the case with Rabbi Hillel and Rabbi Shamai at the beginning of the century. Later, according to the Gospels, Jesus' disciples struggled with the same issue with his followers.

There is a famous story about three different Gentiles who wanted to convert to Judaism and came to Rabbi Shamai who rejected all three of them. One of them said to the rabbi that he would like to convert to Judaism, studying the Torah while standing on one foot. Needless to say, Shamai was outraged over such disrespect to the Torah! This he did not encounter every day. He threw the guy out of his office. But the man did not give up.

The guy then went to Rabbi Hillel and posed to him the same question. Hillel answered, "What is hateful unto thee, do not do unto thy neighbor, this is the entire Torah, the rest is but a commentary, go and study it." This became known in Judaism as the golden rule; it is derived from the commandment to "love your brother as thyself."[23] Two decades later, Jesus utilized the golden rule, but he communicated it in the positive; Rabbi Hillel had communicated it in the negative. Both statements communicate the same thing.

In ancient times, two types of converts existed in Israel: GER TZEDEK, a righteous convert, and GER TOSHAV, a resident convert. Ger Tzedek accepted all 613 commandments and after circumcision and immersion in the Mikvah, he was considered to be a newborn baby into the Jewish family. Today this is the only kind of conversion to Judaism that is available. Ger Toshav obligated only to keep the Noachite laws and by doing so he was permitted to settle in the Land of Israel[24].

According to Rabbi Shamai, the Gentiles had to be totally converted to Judaism, thus they had to abide by the whole Torah before being considered a part of Israel and, therefore, having a share in the world to come. Rabbi Hillel, on the other hand, said no! There is no need to put upon the Gentiles all the requirements of the Torah at the point of their entry. They should take upon themselves the Noachite laws. Rabbi Shamai was reluctant to accept converts to Judaism. He denied the understanding that those who took upon themselves the Noachite laws had a share in the world to come.

What were the Noachite laws? The rabbis believed that everything that was applicable at the time of Noah, in other words, before the Torah was given to mankind, was applicable to all of man. The earliest format of the Noachite laws consisted of four laws only. In time they developed to seven, up to thirty at one point, but then back to seven. Today we speak about the seven Noachite laws. During the first century, however, the Noachite laws were recognized as four laws only.

The seven Noachite laws are against idolatry, blasphemy, killing, stealing, sexual sins, eating the limb of a living animal (cruelty to animals), and the need to establish courts of justice.

According to the Talmud and the Tosefta, Gentiles who observe the Noachite laws are considered to be the Hassidim (the righteous) of the nations and will have a share in the world to come. They were highly respected. The rabbis said that "one should honor a Gentile who zealously observes the Noachite commandments, more than a Jew who does not occupy himself with the Torah"[25]. They also said that "a Gentile who studied the Noachite laws is considered to be equal of a high priest."

The earliest format of the four Noachite laws are found in the Talmud[26]. The same exact format can be found also in Acts chapter 15. The council of Jerusalem headed by Jacob—or James, as he became to be known—had to decide exactly the same thing. Now that the Gentiles were going to join the ranks of the followers of Jesus, they had to know exactly on what basis they are to accept them.

The council of Jerusalem decided to accept them according to the ruling of Rabbi Hillel, so they put upon the Gentiles the obligation to keep the Noachite laws. Not that the church live by it, but nevertheless this is what the New Testament obligates the followers of Jesus to keep.

In the New Testament, we often find references to the Pharisees. Most of the time, they are understood in a negative light and as a reference to all of the Pharisees like in Matthew 3:7 and Luke 18:19. Those references are general and do not apply to all of the Pharisees. Most of Jesus' criticism against the Pharisees was against Beit Shamai who was in control at the time. It is interesting that the Pharisees themselves were quite aware of those among them who were insincere; they described them as "sore spots" or as "plagues of the pharisaic party"[27].

The Pharisees are often compared to one or other groups that exist today. People say, "These are the modern Pharisees." In reality, there is no group today that can be compared to them. The reason this happens is because people tend to think about them as Hypocrites, and that is all that they know. I hope that by now, people have gained better understanding.

Jesus debated with the Pharisees. the Sadducees and some others. But it seems that his debates with the Pharisees had to do with disputes that took place between the Pharisees and the Sadducees. Those disputes are recorded for us in the Talmud.

Most of the time, it seems that Jesus supported the views of Beit Hillel.

Paul was a Pharisee and a son of a Pharisee and was proud to be one. He was taught by one of the greatest rabbis of the Pharisaic sect, Rabbi Gamliel the elder, the grandson of Rabbi Hillel. Paul's insistence on admitting Gentiles to the faith was in accordance with Beit Hillel's position.

Rabbi Emden, who lived in 1697–1776 and was a great rabbi in his day, said that Jesus and Paul acted entirely within the Halacha in creating a religion for the Gentiles based upon the Noachite laws[28].

Although it may come as a surprise, Christianity has much more in common with the Pharisees than with any other sect operating in Israel in the first century. It was Pharisaism that actually prepared the ground for Christianity to be accepted and developed. The Pharisees paved the way with their theological concepts like Messiah, monotheism, end time, eternal life, resurrection and the existance of angels.

The Pharisees appeared to consider Jesus as an equal to them. In the Gospel of Luke in particular, we see them inviting him to their meal and addressing him with the respectful title of Rabbi. There is no doubt in my mind that Jesus was a Pharisee; his theology and all of his teachings are in line with the Pharisaic theology, mostly with the teachings of Beit Hillel.

APPENDIX II ENDNOTES

1. Josephus Antiquities 13:171.
2. The Mishna, Kidushin 66a Imply this meaning.
3. Mark 2:14-17; Matthew 9:9-13; Luke 5:27-32.
4. Josephus, Antiquities, 13:288-98.
5. Ibid 13:14, sec.2.
6. Talmud Bavli, Berachot 33b.
7. Mishnah, Pirkay Avot 3:16.
8. Josephus, Antiquities, XVIII, 1,3.
9. Josephus, Wars of the Jews, II, 8, 14.
10. "Why is God called Makom? Because He is the place of the world and the world is not His place. (Yalkut Shimoni Vayetzeh Remez 117).
11. Talmud Bavli, Sanhedrin 59a.
12. Ibid, Shabbat 13b-17a.
13. Ibid, Beitza 19a-20b.
14. Talmud Yerushalmi, Shabbat 1:4.
15. Ibid, Beitza 2:4.
16. Talmud Bavli, Ketuvot 62b.
17. Ibid, Beitza 20a.
18. Mishna, Sukka 37b.
19. George Foot More, Judaism in the first centuries of the Christian era, 1:81.
20. Talmud Bavli, Ketuvot 62b; Talmud Yerushalmi, Taanit 4:2.
21. Ibid. Shabbat 31a.
22. Mishna, Avot, 1:12-15.
23. Leviticus 19:18.
24. Leviticus 23:35; Talmud Bavli, Avodah Zara 64b, Avodat Kochavim 10:6.
25. Sefer Hassidim # 358.
26. Tosefta, Avodah Zara 9:4.
27. Talmud Bavli, Sota 3:4, 22b.
28. Seder Olam Rabbah Vezuta.

ABOUT THE AUTHOR

Rivi Litvin is a third-generation Israeli scholar, author and lecturer who is widely regarded worldwide as an authority on the time period dating from 400 BCE to 400 CE.

Over the course of her career, Riv has spoken in front of thousands at universities, various religious and theological institutions and national gatherings. She has lectured in 15 countries, and her work has been translated into several languages including German and Spanish. Her teachings have been distributed internationally in nearly 30 countries.

Rivi was born in Bat-Yam, Israel, and was educated in the Orthodox Jewish tradition. She served in the Israeli Defense Forces (IDF) during the Six-Day War in 1967 and was part of the reserves in the 1973 Yom Kippur War.

Impacted deeply by her time in the IDF, Rivi developed an interest in other religions and left Israel to study abroad. While spending several months at the Dr. Francis Schaeffer Center L'Abri in the Swiss Alps, Rivi developed a great interest in the Gospels, realizing the intricate connection to the Jewish tradition.

In 1980, Rivi moved to the United States to study theology, and together with her late husband, Daniel Litvin, opened the educational outfit H.I.M.

H.I.M. reached thousands of people worldwide as Rivi and Danny researched and taught Judaism, the Gospels, and the Hebrew Scriptures together.

In 1986, Danny passed away from a sudden heart attack at the age of 30, leaving Rivi to raise their three daughters and to continue the work of H.I.M on her own.

Rivi returned to Israel in the '90s where she founded and operated an educational center nestled in the hills of Galilee for a decade. The center welcomed hundreds of visitors who came to Israel to study from all over of the globe.

Rivi now resides in Southern California where she continues to teach and is working on the final volumes of her book series: Jesus, the Son of Israel—a Jewish Commentary on the Gospels.

To contact Rivi please visit RiviLitvin.com or Facebook.com/RiviLitvin.

BIBLIOGRAPHY

Arndt, William F. & Wilbur, F. "A Greek-English Lexicon to the NT and other early Christian literature", University of Chicago Press, Chicago, 1952

Rabbi Bahya Ben Asher, "Commentary on the Torah", Translated by Eliyahu Munk

Avot de Rabbi Nathan, Talmud Bavli, Seder Nezikin, Vol. XVI, Schechter, Vilna, 1887

Bazes, Moshe, "Jesus the Jew—The historical Jesus, The true story of Jesus", self-published, Jerusalem, Israel, 1976

Ben Nachman Gerondi, Moses Rabbi, Nachmanides (The Ramban), "Commentary on the Torah", the Artscroll, Mesorah Publications Ltd, New York, 2008

Bromiley, G.W, "The International Standard Bible Encyclopedia", William B, Erdman's Publishing Company, Grand Rapids, Michigan, 1979

Brown, Raymond E., "The birth of the Messiah", Doubleday & Company, Inc., Garden City, New York, 1977

Burrows, Millar, "The Dead Sea Scrolls", The Viking Press, New York, 1957

Cicero: De senectute De amicitia, De divination, Harvard University Press, Cambridge, Massachusetts, 1966

Clement of Rome, "The First Epistle of Clement to the Corinthians", New Testament Apocrypha, translated into English by Robert Lubbock Bensly, 1899, The St. Pachomius Orthodox Library, St. Photius, 2004, http://www.voskrese.info/spl/

Cohen, Abraham, "Everyman's Talmud"—The major teachings of the rabbinic sages, Schocken Books Inc., New York, 1975

Dessler, Rabbi Eliyahu E., Michtav Me Eliyahu (unknown binding) 1985

Driver, S.R. and Neubauer, A. (eds.), "The fifty third chapter of Isaiah according to Jewish interpreters", various volumes, Ktav Publishers, New York, 1969

Edersheim, Alfred, "The life and times of Jesus the Messiah", William B. Erdman's Publishing Company, Grand Rapids, Michigan, 1971

Edersheim, Alfred, "Sketches of Jewish social life in the days of Christ", William B. Erdman's Publishing Company, Grand Rapids, Michigan, 1984

Ehrman, Bart D., "Misquoting Jesus", Harper San Francisco Publishers, A division of HarperCollins Publishers, New York, 2005

Eisenmenger, M. J.A. Entdecktes Judenthum, Vol. 1, Konigsberg, Derlag Von Dtto Brandner, Dresben, 1893

Encyclopedia Judaica, Keter Publishing House, Jerusalem, Israel, 1972

Eusebius, Pamphilus, "Early Christian history, ecclesiastical history", Book III, Baker Book House, Grand Rapids, Michigan, 1981

Even Shushan, Abraham, Hamilon HaChadash, "The new dictionary" (Hebrew-Hebrew), Kiryat Sefer Ltd., Jerusalem, Israel, 1993

Finegan, Jack, "Light from the ancient past: The archaeological background of the Hebrew-Christian religion", Volume II, Princeton University Press, Princeton, 1969

Flavius Josephus, Complete Works, Kregel Publications, Grand Rapids, Michigan, 1972

Flusser, David, "Jewish sources in early Christianity", Adama Books, New York, 1987

Flusser, David, "Judaism and the origins of Christianity", The Magnes Press, The Hebrew University, Jerusalem, Israel, 1985

Friedman, M. (ed.), Pesikta Rabbati, Jellinek in "Bet ha-Midrash", Vienna, 1880

Halkin, A.S. (ed.), Moshe Ben Maimon Maimonides (The Rambam), "Epistle to Yemen", New York, 1952, https://en.wikisource.org/wiki/Epistle_to_Yemen/Complete

Herodotus, Histories, with an English translation by A. D. Godley, Harvard University Press, Cambridge 1920

Rabbi Ibn Crispin, Moshe, "Moshe Ibn Crispin on Isaiah 53", Cordova, Spain, 14th century

Irenaeus, "Adversus Haereses (against heresies)", Gaul, France, CE 180

Jeremias, Joachim, "Neuestamentliche Theologie", Vol. I, Gütersloher Verlagshaus G. Mohn, 1971

Karo, Yosef, "Shulchan Aruch, The code of Jewish Law", Venice, 1565

Kasher, Aryeh, Witztum Eliezer, "King Herod: A persecuted persecutor: a case study in psychohistory and psychobiography", The Deutsche Nationa Bibliothek, Berlin, Germany, 2007

Klaussner, "Jesus of Nazareth, his life, time and teaching", Macmillan Publishing, New York, 1946

Ktav Publishers, Jerusalem, Israel. It was first published in Naples 1492

Lachs, Samuel Tobias, "A rabbinic commentary on the New Testament", Ktav Publishing House, Hoboken, New Jersey, 1987

Leon, H.J., "The Jews of ancient Rome", JPS, Philadelphia, 1960

Lightfoot, John, "A commentary on the New Testament from the Talmud and Hebraica", Baker Book House, Grand Rapids, Michigan, 1979

Lindsey, Robert Lisle, "Jesus Rabbi and Lord", Cornerstone Publishing, Oak Greek, Wisconsin, 1990

Mahari Kara, Rabbi Yosef Ben Shimon, "Commentary on the prophets", Bar-Ilan University Press, Haketer Project, Ramat-Gan, Israel, 2010

Matt, Daniel C., "The Zohar", Pritzker Edition, Volume 2, Stanford University Press, Stanford, 2003

McNamara, M., "The NT and the Palestinian Targum to the Pentateuch", Analecta Biblica 27: Rome, Pontifical Biblical Institute, Rome, Italy, 1966

Midrash Rabbah, The Soncino Press, London, England, 1983

Midrash Tanchuma, Eshkol Publishers, Jerusalem, 1972

Mikraot Gedolot (Hebrew), Abraham Isaac Friedman Publisher, New York, 1971

Moore, George Foot, "Judaism", Volume 1, Harvard University Press, Cambridge, 1932

Neusner, Jacob, "The Tosefta", Hendrickson Publishers, Peabody, Massachusetts, 2002

Origen, Luc. Hom, (Commentary on Matthew), preparatory addition, Coptic Theological College, Sydney, Australia, 1995

Peli, Pinchas H. "Solovetchik on repentance", Paulist Press, Ramsey, New York, 1984

Pirkay, Avot, "The Ethics of the Fathers", Schocken Books Inc., New York, 1978

Philips, A. TH, "Machzor Leyom Kippur/Prayer book for the Day of Atonement", with English translation; revised and enlarged edition, Hebrew Publishing Company, New York, 1931

Philo, De Legume Allegoria, Harvard University Press, Cambridge, Massachusetts, 1971

Philo, De Legibus Specialibus lll, Harvard University Press, Cambridge, Massachusetts, 1971

Philo, De Mutatione Nominum, Harvard University Press, Cambridge, Massachusetts, 1971

Philo, De Pramiis, Harvard University Press, Cambridge, Massachusetts, 1971

Pirkay De Rabbi Eliezer, Eshkol Publishers, Jerusalem, Israel, 1983

Rabinowitz, Zvi Meir, Introduction to Midrash Hagadol (Book of Numbers), "Sifri Zuta", (4th printing–Hebrew), Mossad Harav Kook, Jerusalem 1983

Sifrei on Deuteronomy, unknown binding, Israel, 1978

Talmud Bavli, (Babylonian Talmud), Traditional Press, New York, New York, 1983

Targum pseudo-Jonathan, Michael Glazier Inc., Wilmington, Delaware, 1935

The Fathers of the Church, Jerome—"Epistle to Paulinus", ed. Philip Schaff, William B. Erdman's Publishing, 2001

The Fathers of the Church, Jerome—"Lives of illustrious men", ed. Philip Schaff, William B. Erdman's Publishing, 2001

The Fathers of the Church, Origen—"Contra Celsum", ed. Philip Schaff, William B. Erdman's Publishing, reprint 2001

The Jerusalem Talmud, the Israel Institute for Talmudic Publications, Jerusalem, Israel, 1987

The Gospel of Pseudo-Matthew, Anonymous, Christian Apocrypha, 600 CE https://www.biblicaltraining.org/library/gospel-pseudo-matthew

The Jerusalem Institute of Rav Cook Commentaries (Hebrew), Hamakor Press Ltd., Jerusalem, Israel, 1991

The Mishna (Hebrew), Keter Publishing House, Jerusalem, Israel, 1977

The Old Testament Pseudepigrapha, James Charlesworth, (ed.), Vol. II, "Enoch", Doubleday & Company Inc., Garden City, New York, 1983

The Old Testament Pseudepigrapha, James Charlesworth, Ed., Vol. II, "Jubilees", Doubleday & Company Inc., Garden City, New York, 1983

The Old Testament Pseudepigrapha, James Charlesworth, (ed.), Vol. II, "The testaments of the twelve patriarchs, Levi", Doubleday & Company Inc., Garden City, New York, 1983

The Old Testament Pseudepigrapha, James Charlesworth, (ed.), Vol. II, "The testaments of the twelve patriarchs, Simon", Doubleday & Company Inc., Garden City, New York, 1983

The Old Testament Pseudepigrapha, James Charlesworth, (ed.), Vol. II, "Psalms of Solomon", Doubleday & Company Inc., Garden City, New York, 1983

The Oxford Annotated Apocrypha, "I Maccabees", Oxford University Press, New York, 1977

The Oxford Annotated Apocrypha, "Judith", Oxford University Press, New York, 1977

The Oxford Annotated Apocrypha, "Tovit", Oxford University Press, New York, 1977

The Oxford Annotated Apocrypha, "The wisdom of Solomon", Oxford University Press, New York, 1977

Vermes, Geza, "Jesus the Jew, a historian's reading of the Gospels", Fortress Press, Philadelphia, 1981

Yalkut Shimoni, Frankfurt, 13th century

Zimmerli Walther & Jeremias Joachim, "The servant of God", CSM Press, Eugene, 1965

INDEX OF LITERATURE

The Tanach - Old Testament

JEREMIAH

EZEKIEL

The Apocrypha

The Pseudepigrapha

The Dead Sea Scrolls

INDEX OF SUBJECTS AND NAMES